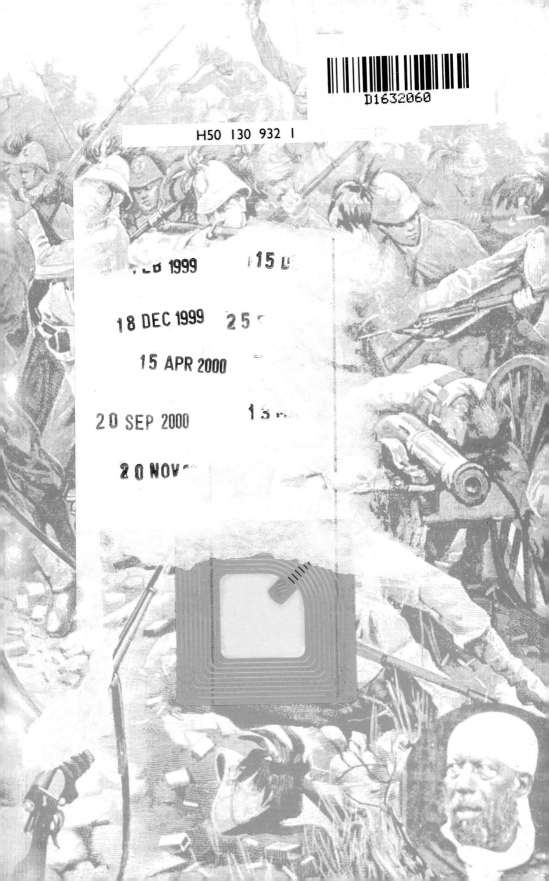

MASSACRE AND RETRIBUTION

FORGOTTEN WARS OF THE NINETEENTH CENTURY

IAN HERNON

FOREWORD BY
SIR ROBERT RHODES JAMES

SUTTON PUBLISHING

First published in 1998 by
Sutton Publishing Limited · Phoenix Mill
Thrupp · Stroud · Gloucestershire · GL5 2BU

British Library Cataloguing in Publication Data
A catalogue record for this book is available from the British Library.

ISBN 0-7509-1846-2

TM   ALAN SUTTON™ and SUTTON™ are the
trade marks of Sutton Publishing Limited

Typeset in 10/12 pt Plantin.
Typesetting and origination by
Sutton Publishing Limited.
Printed in Great Britain by
WBC Ltd, Bridgend.

CONTENTS

For my family

Foreword

by

Sir Robert Rhodes James

There is a strange mythology that there was a golden age of peace between the ending of the Napoleonic wars in 1815 and the subsequent Congress of Vienna, where, as Duff Cooper eulogised, the participants danced and enjoyed themselves and 'created a hundred years of peace', and the opening of the Great War in 1914.

A century that included the Crimean War, the Indian Mutiny, the American Civil War, the Franco-Prussian War, the series of conflicts in Southern Africa, culminating in the 1899–1903 South African War, the Indian Wars in Northern America, the British conquest of Upper Burma, Egypt and the Sudan, almost incessant conflicts on the North-West Frontier of India, the gradual and bloody dismemberment of the Ottoman Empire and a succession of Balkan Wars, and the Russo-Japanese war, can hardly be described as notably pacific. Nor were Ceylon or New Zealand brought under the British Crown without bloodshed and hardship.

Ian Hernon's selection of some of the 'forgotten wars' of the nineteenth century adds further strength to the destruction of this mythology. What Kipling called 'the savage wars of peace' were often very savage indeed, including the brutal suppression of the Jamaica uprising by the British Governor Eyre, the Maori and Kandy wars, the extraordinary Magdala campaign in Ethiopia, the Riel rebellion in North-West Canada, the 1900 Ashanti campaign, and the terrible Modoc Indian War in the United States.

What is so sobering is that this list could have been much longer. As he states, 'there was not one month in which British forces were not engaged somewhere across the world', and not only British ones, either. It was a century of almost incessant conflict, culminating in the greatest one of all.

He describes these individually, with insight and shrewdness, and one of his most remarkable achievements is to bring them, and the people concerned, back to vivid life. I had certainly never heard of 'Shacknasty Jim', nor of many others who play varying roles, some honourable, many tragic, and others loathsome and deplorable. And he never loses sight of the fact that these were people; indeed, one of the great qualities of his accounts of these long-ago and too often bloody conflicts is the pervasive humanity with which he describes the sufferings of those involved, and of the guilty as well as the innocent.

There is in reality no such thing as 'a small war' for those involved. Whether the contestants are numbered in hundreds, thousands, or tens of thousands, the same grim rules apply. For some there may be glory, promotion, honours and fame; for the majority the end was an unknown grave far from home. Most died of disease rather than on the battlefield, but the result was the same.

These forgotten sagas have been sadly neglected by professional historians. I hope that Ian Hernon will continue to explore and relate others. There is, unhappily, no shortage of them.

Acknowledgements

The purpose of this book is not to ape, much less rival, the far more erudite and scholarly volumes already published about the military adventures which helped to create and sustain the british Empire. Rather it is to tell, I hope in the straightforward tone of a reporter, some of the astonishing stories largely forgotten outside academic, specialist and military circles.

How natives, converted to Christianity, were only defeated when they observed the Sabbath and assumed their British opponents would do likewise; how a mad King was beaten in his seemingly unassailable fortress after taking hostages; the barbaric revenge taken by 'civilized' soldiers against former slaves; and the massacre of redcoats in paradise. Throughout I have used, whenever possible, the words of the participants themselves: semi-literate or beautifully scripted, bewildered or boastful, they are the authentic voices of their age.

The bulk of this book concerns British forces and their opponents. I could not resist, however, including one American colonial conflict. It shares many of the characteristics of the Empire wars, not least the unwillingness of the native defenders to act as expected. More importantly, it is a terrific if tragic story – and that has been the main criteria for choosing the sample of forgotten wars included here.

Many people have given me advice, practical help and encouragement, and I thank them all. In particular: Sir Robert Rhodes James, without whom the road to publication would have been much rockier; my agent Mike Shaw of Curtis Brown; Jonathan Falconer, commissioning editor at Sutton Publishing; and editor Sarah Fowle.

I must also thank my wife Pauline and my daughters Joanna and Kim, not least for putting up with a lifetime partially spent trampling among 'piles of old bricks'.

Introduction

For Britain the nineteenth century began, in military terms, with the global upheavals of the Napoleonic Wars and ended with a 'modern' conflict in which machine-guns and a scorched-earth policy were deployed against the Boers. In between there was a supposed peace, marred only by glorious, if tragic, enterprises in the Crimea, Africa and Afghanistan, against the Zulus, the Boers, the Mahdi and Indian mutineers, providing the battles whose names remain proudly emblazoned on regimental banners: Balaclava, Sevastopol, Alma, Lucknow, Kabul, Khartoum, Omdurman. These are the campaigns, it seems, that forged an Empire unparalleled in size before or since, and built the careers of such military leaders as Garnet Wolseley and Lord Kitchener. They were the source of many *Boy's Own* stories and novels, as well as romantic cinema epics full of dramatic cavalry charges with sabres drawn against hordes of painted savages.

The long periods between such dashing conflicts have been dubbed the *Pax Britannica*, a time when the grip of the Empire was so strong and so benign that the simple presence of a few red tunics was enough to cow the natives. Yet this is misleading. In fact there was not one month in which British forces were not engaged somewhere across the world. Queen Victoria herself said that if Britain was to be truly 'Great' the nation had to be prepared for wars 'somewhere or other' at all times. They were what Rudyard Kipling called the 'savage wars of peace'. Some involved a handful of British officers and native levies, others were major expeditions, the Victorian equivalent of the Falklands campaign of 1982. Most are now forgotten outside regimental museums.

These small wars often came about by accident, or as a result of misunderstandings, incomprehension between races, an insult real or imagined. They were blatantly about race, trade, religion and, above all, land, the root causes of all wars since recorded history began. All were the inevitable result of Britain's 'Forward Policy' which saw more and more of the world map coloured pink. Existing frontiers could be better protected by extending them. Trade routes and influence had to be safeguarded. British citizens had to be guaranteed safety and privilege wherever they were. And, as historian Byron Farwell wrote, 'Vigorous, self-confident, prideful, determined and opinionated people . . . will always provide themselves with armies and the temptation to use them to enforce national desires is seemingly irresistible.'

It is not the intention of this book to consider the rights and wrongs of colonial expansionism, but rather to celebrate the heroism, stamina and determination (and in some cases condemn the stupidity, cruelty and cowardice) of the participants in these forgotten wars. They came from all walks of life: gentlemen officers, foot soldiers from the Scottish Highlands, sappers from the Belfast docks, troopers from Northamptonshire estates, and brawny sergeant-majors born into the Army. Sent across the globe, they suffered dysentery, cholera, barbed arrows, gunshot, starvation, intense heat, freezing winds and the lash, all for a pittance during their service and, too often, the workhouse thereafter. They faced numerous adversaries: Maori warriors who swiftly overcame the terror of cannon and rocket attacks, the Riel rebels who fought for freedom and died on the gallows, the Ethiopian labourers who shifted mountains for their mad king.

The major wars of the era have remained in the collective folk memory. Most people know of Rorke's Drift, but not of another incident when five members of the same regiment won Victoria Crosses on the same day. The fate of General Gordon at Khartoum is remembered, but not another massive expedition to rescue European hostages from a remote African mountain-top. The Indian Mutiny is still taught in schools but not the massacre of a British column in the Highlands of Ceylon. Such amazing stories have been largely erased from the national conscience, partly because they often involved inglorious defeats, partly because their adversaries did not fit the domestic stereotype of howling, unsophisticated 'fuzzy-wuzzy' savages, slaughtered or cowed by British discipline and moral superiority. They were wars in which modern armies aimed to subdue the supposedly ignorant, wars in which well-disciplined and well-armed white men were meant to crush poorly equipped and ill-led heathens. It did not always go to plan.

*   *   *

The British Army saw superficial changes during that stormy century, such as the final transition from scarlet to khaki, but its regimental system remained essentially the same. It was based on class and caste distinctions. The staff officers were drawn from the aristocracy and squirearchy, the ruling classes and professions, from public schools and family estates. Farwell wrote: 'An army – that least democratic of social institutions – is dominated by its officers: it is they who establish its moral and social codes, the standard of discipline, and the degree of inhumanity to be tolerated; they determine its organisation, its tactics and strategies, its weapons and clothes, and, most importantly, its attitudes and opinions. As has often been proved, armies can be constructed from the most unpromising of human materials and be successful on the field of battle if they are provided with excellent officers, from subalterns to generals, who have time to mould their men.'

For much of the century commissions were bought and officers were too often drawn from a small pool of families whose sons might have been born on a different planet to the men who served under them. Such class distinctions were actively encouraged by the very idea of the 'officer-

Dragoons and Hussars, 1867 (Print by G.H. Thomas)

gentleman', the hostility of the generals towards any reform, the traditions of Wellington, the self-interest of the officers themselves, and the bureaucracy by which Army affairs were divided between the War Office, the Colonial Office, the Home Office, the Treasury, the Horse Guards and Royal Ordnance.

Even the abolition of purchased commissions did little to change the balance. Poor pay, which did not even cover the cost of lavish uniforms, never mind mess bills, meant that a private income was vital for any officer. Most came from public schools which did not teach military subjects, although half were subsequently trained at Sandhurst or Woolwich. The ordinary soldier came from a despised underclass – thieves, beggars, vagrants, drunkards, convicts, the destitute unemployed and starving – whom Lord Palmerston's biographer Jasper Ridley said joined the army 'to escape from the village constable or the irate father of a pregnant girl'.

The Army could never get enough men under the system of voluntary enlistment. Among the labouring classes the Army, with its poor pay, unsavoury conditions, long service requirements and traditions of suppressing domestic revolt, was simply not considered an honourable or worthwhile alternative to poverty at home. During the 1840s the natural wastage among infantrymen who served twenty-one years and cavalrymen who served twenty-four required 12,000 new recruits a year.

As a result recruitment depended on conning recruits with drink and fraudulent promises of pay, booty and women, at least until the late 1860s when attitudes changed and the Empire became inextricably linked with patriotism. The military authorities, who held their men in contempt, urged their recruiters to pursue 'the foolish, the drunken, the ungodly and the despairing'. The only requirements were a very basic physical fitness and a constantly fluctuating minimum height.

Such men were famously described by Wellington: 'The scum of the earth – the mere scum of the earth. It is only wonderful that we should be able to make so much of them afterwards. The English soldiers are fellows who have all enlisted for drink – that is the plain fact.' He continued: 'People talk of their enlisting from their fine military feeling – all stuff – no such thing. Some of our men enlist from having got bastard children – some for minor offences . . . you can hardly conceive such a set brought together.' Yet he could also say of them with justifiable pride: 'There are no men in Europe who can fight like my infantry . . . my army and I know one another exactly.' On an earlier occasion he said: 'Bravery is the characteristic of the British Army in all quarters of the world.' And those who have served in India 'cannot be ordered upon any Service, however dangerous or arduous, that they will not effect, not only with bravery, but with a degree of skill not often witnessed in persons of their description in other parts of the world.'

Such men, drawn from stinking gutters and gin houses, from gaols and poorhouses, from pit villages and dockyards, from behind ploughs and lowly desks, forged an Empire through their grit, endurance and courage. Why? An escape from poverty or prison at home was one factor, certainly. So, too, was the lure of booty and a chance to exercise naked aggression. But the overriding reason lay with the nature of the regimental system itself. The Regiment was home, family, provider, past and future all wrapped in one. To let down your comrades, and through them your regiment, was unthinkable – more serious even than letting down Queen and Country. It was a narrow form of patriotism, and one that in its fully developed form saw men march slowly towards the guns across the bloody fields of Flanders and the Somme. The love of regiment united officers and men. Sons followed fathers into the same regiment, whatever their rank. Identity with regiment was strengthened by its original regional roots. Highland regiments are said to take Scotland with them wherever they go. They did not get on with the Welsh regiments. Regimental pride was strengthened with the roll of battle honours, and the nicknames they accrued. The Middlesex Regiment became known as the 'Diehards' because of the valour they displayed at Albuera in 1811; the men of the Northamptonshire Regiment, however, were known as the 'Steelbacks' as they never flinched at a flogging.

Throughout the century the pattern of recruitment shifted away from rural areas and towards the new, rootless and increasingly destitute unemployed in the mushrooming cities. In 1830 more than 42 per cent of NCOs and men were Irish, most of them Roman Catholics; a decade later that figure was 24.5 per cent. Even the famous Scottish regiments relied more and more on attracting men from the slums of Manchester, London, Leeds and Cardiff.

Soldiers and NCOs hardly ever moved from their company, much less their regiment, during their entire service careers. In *The Mask of Command* John Keegan wrote: 'The effect was to produce a high degree of what today is called "Small unit cohesion". The men knew each other well, their strengths and weaknesses were known by their leaders and vice versa, and all strove to avoid the taint of cowardice that would attach instantly to shirkers in such intimate societies. Motivation was reinforced by drill. Both infantry and cavalry fought in close order . . . under strict supervision and to the rhythm of endlessly rehearsed commands.' James Morris wrote: 'The Army lived ritualistically. Flags, guns and traditions were holy to it, and loyalty to one's regiment was the emotional keynote of the service.'

Such men would wade through malarial swamps, hack through jungles, clamber over mountain crags, to get at the enemy for the sake of their regiment. They would also beef and grumble and dodge duties, and drink and steal and pick fist-fights; they would abuse natives and women, they would loot and occasionally slaughter the defenceless. But the savage little wars of the nineteenth century bear witness to their courage. Without them no Empire would have been won, whatever the genius of generals and strategists, whatever the ambitions of monarchs and politicians.

'But for this a price must be paid,' wrote Sir Arthur Conan Doyle, 'and the price is a grievous one. As the beast of old must have one young human life as a tribute every year, so to our Empire we throw from day to day the pick and flower of our youth. The engine is worldwide and strong, but the only fuel that will drive it is the lives of British men. Thus it is that in the gray old cathedrals, as we look upon the brasses on the walls, we see strange names, such names as those who reared those walls had never heard, for it is in Peshawar, and Umballah, and Korti, and Fort Pearson that the youngsters die, leaving only a precedent and a brass behind them. But if every man had his obelisk, even where he lay, then no frontier line need be drawn, for a cordon of British graves would ever show how high the Anglo-Saxon tide had lapped.'

General Sir Garnet Wolseley, in his general orders for the 1873 Ashanti expedition wrote: 'English soldiers and sailors are accustomed to fight against immense odds in all parts of the world; it is scarcely necessary to remind them that when in our battles across the Pra (River) they find themselves surrounded on all sides by hordes of howling enemies, they must rely on their own British courage and discipline, and upon the courage of their comrades.'

The men themselves were rather more laconic, in an era which prided modesty, when describing their own acts. Sergeant Luke O'Connor of the Welch Fusiliers described a charge at the Russian guns at Alma: 'Getting near the Redoubt, about 30 yards, Lieutenant Anstruther was shot dead and I was badly wounded in the breast with two ribs broken. I jumped up and

Major-General Sir Garnet
Wolseley, hero and self-
publicist (National Army
Museum)

took the Colour from Corporal Luby, rushed to the Redoubt and planted it
there.' O'Connor was awarded one of the first Victoria Crosses. Another old
soldier, G. Bell, recorded the storming of the French defences at Badajoz:
'Hundreds fell, dropping at every discharge which maddened the living; the
cheer was ever on, on, with screams of vengeance and a fury determined to
win the town; the rear pushed the foremost into the sword-blades to make a
bridge of their bodies rather than be frustrated. Slaughter, tumult and
disorder continued; no command could be heard, the wounded struggling to
free themselves from under the bleeding bodies of their dead comrades; the
enemy's guns within a few yards at every fire opening a bloody lane amongst
our people, who closed up and, with shouts of terror as the lava burned
them up, pressed on to destruction. . . .'

    By 1814 the British Army had been trained and tested against the might
of Napoleon. Its men were hardened, disciplined and experienced in warfare
anywhere from hot arid plains to steaming jungles. They were its muscle,
sinews and blood. Its NCOs, risen from the ranks, were, in Kipling's words,
its backbone. The officers had been blooded too and were beginning to
display the talents of a professional elite; men who, as Wellington put it,

A Maori 'equipped for fighting' (*Illustrated London News*)

'have something more at stake than a reputation for military smartness'. At last, after years of bought commissions and talentless amateurism, they were beginning to provide some brains.

General Sir John Moore's reforms of the Light Brigade had an impact throughout the Army. There was less emphasis on ceremony and drill and more on training which reflected actual battle and campaign conditions. Riflemen were taught to support each other as they moved into the best positions to slay the enemy. As Arthur Bryant wrote: 'At the back of every rifleman's mind Moore instilled the principle that the enemy were always at hand ready to strike. Whether on reconnaissance or protective duty, he was taught to be wary and on guard . . . It was the pride of the light infantryman never to be caught napping . . . each one an alert and intelligent individual acting in close but invisible concert with his comrades.'

The ordinary soldier's firepower, however, was inadequate in an age of quickly changing technology. Too often British forces, as in the Maori Wars, found themselves facing 'savages' armed with more modern weapons than they carried themselves. From Waterloo until the 1850s the standard infantry weapon was the flintlock musket which weighed 10.5 lb and was accurate to 80 yards. It was cumbersome and slow to load. Lieutenant John Mitchell wrote: 'In nine cases out of ten the difficulty of pulling the trigger makes the soldier open the whole of the right hand in order to aid the action of the forefinger; this gives full scope to the recoil: the prospect of the blow makes him throw back his head and body at the very moment of giving fire; and as no aim is ever required he shuts his eyes, from the flash of the pan, at the same instant, so that the very direction of the shot becomes a matter of mere accident.' Small wonder that Charles Napier wrote: 'The short range and very uncertain flight of shot from the musket begets the necessity of closing with the enemy, which the British soldier's confidence in superior bodily strength, due to climate, pushes him to do.' He added: 'No troops in the world will stand the assault of British troops, if made with the bayonet and without firing. Firing is a weapon . . . of defence, not of attack.' The British soldier's affection for the bayonet as a trustworthy weapon outlived the century. Its reputation in retrospect seems misplaced: various types either bent or fell off, and they were all unwieldy. The bayonet was no match against pikes or the long Chinese spears at Canton. At Merthyr in 1888 the 93rd Highlanders with bayonets fixed confronted Welsh dissidents with staves – and were defeated. And bayonets had bent at the battle of Abu Klea in 1885, causing a public outcry over the quality of British weaponry.

Gradually firepower improved. In 1830 muskets were converted to percussion cap ignition, which reduced misfirings. From 1851 the foot soldiers were rearmed with the Minie rifle, although initially in an unrifled model so that massive stockpiles of musket balls would not go to waste. The Minie was sighted to 1,000 yards and was accurate to 800. At that range 77 out of 100 hits were registered on a target 8 ft square. At ranges between 300 and 600 yards the experts calculated that 150 men armed with Minies could equal the

The 9th Lancers at Delhi, 1857

slaughter achieved by 525 equipped with the musket. It was a muzzle-loader, so still slow, but its effective range of more than ¼ mile dramatically changed the nature of ground engagements. Colonel F.T. Maitland described the universal adoption of the rifle as 'a complete revolution in the art of warfare'. William Napier said it 'must paralyse the action of cavalry against infantry and artillery within that range'. In 1866 there was a long-overdue breakthrough. The Snider breech-loading rifle began to be issued. Although still a single-shot weapon, it allowed soldiers, for the first time, to fire lying down, from behind defensive positions. The Snider was replaced by the metal-cartridged Martini-Henry during the 1870s. By the 1890s the Army was using the bolt-action, magazine-fed Lee Metford .303 rifle which would remain the basic infantry weapon up to and beyond the Second World War. In 1891 smokeless powder was introduced, a vital improvement because soldiers firing from cover were not given away by a puff of white smoke.

The vast improvements in firepower slowly changed the nature of mounted warfare. It was the beginning of the end of the proud cavalry regiments. Tactician Captain L.E. Nolan concluded ruefully: 'The great improvements made in firearms, and the increased range of the infantry musket, leave but little chance for cavalry, unless the speed at which they can pounce upon the infantry lessens the number and the effect of the discharge to be received during their advance.' Earlier he had written: 'With the cavalry officer almost everything depends on . . . the felicity with which he seizes the happy moment of action. There is little time for thought, none for hesitation. . . .' Increasingly, however, the cavalrymen, armed with lance, sword and pistol, and, later, carbines, were used for reconnaissance, skirmishing and attacking convoys, and as advance guards. George Cathcart, commander of the King's Dragoon Guards in Canada in 1838, stressed in orders that cavalry should take up advance positions with 'great promptness', then dismount and hold their ground until they could be relieved by the slower-moving infantry. The charge could still be deployed (although it rarely was) in open country against natives; for this reason the long sword was developed for use against tribesmen who fired their weapons from prone positions. Mounted infantry proved to be well suited for the colonies, especially for police duties. A small number of mounted men could garrison and patrol much larger tracts of remote countryside than a greater number of foot soldiers.

The development of field artillery was steady throughout the century but for the colonies the mainstay was the six-pounder. It was light and manageable, with a range of 1,200 yards at 4 degrees elevation. The main types of ammunition used were round shot (which bounced off the ground causing carnage among a column of men), grapeshot, common shell and shrapnel. Common shell included a time fuse which exploded a hollow round, despatching fragments in all directions. Shrapnel incorporated round shot but technical problems delayed its introduction. Once these problems were ironed out it proved devastating against a massed foe. After shrapnel was deployed to halt a river-crossing during the Second Sikh War a witness wrote: 'Never was it more clearly demonstrated that shrapnel, when directed with precision, is one of the most formidable and effectual inventions of modern times.' Rockets were often used during the first half of the century but were deemed inaccurate, unreliable and useful only for frightening the horses.

Fighting, the ultimate task of any trained soldier, was generally only the culmination of any campaign. A teenage Lieutenant Samuel Thorpe wrote of the 1808 retreat to Corunna: 'When we reached Astorga . . . want of shoes and food and long marches had much altered the appearance of the Army; the number of sick and stragglers was immense, and the men generally bare-footed.' The Welch Fusiliers' Official History, recording a South African campaign as the century closed, said: 'Averaging nearly 17 miles a day, over apparently endless prairies, in blazing sun and bitter cold, swept now by hot and choking dust storms, now by rushes of icy hail, fording rivers and floundering through sand, with scanty food and shelterless bivouacs, their toil unenlightened by anything but hope. Marching is the true rigour of campaigning. Of fighting, the welcome relief, they had too little to lighten the dullness of their task.' Astonishingly it was not until 1843 that soldiers were issued with left and right fitting boots. Previously, identical footwear had been issued with instructions that they should be swapped over on alternate days to ensure even wear.

Unsuitable uniforms and heavy equipment added to the soldiers' misery on the march, especially on other continents. By the start of the century powdered wigs had been phased out and heavy greycoats issued for winter wear. But most foot soldiers wore scarlet tunics, heavy felt shakos and the hated 'stock', a stiff leather support for a high collar. After Waterloo uniforms became more ornate. The infantry of the Line saw their sensible grey trousers replaced with white ones which were impossible to keep clean. Garnet Wolseley, writing of the 1853 Burmese expedition, said that the Queen's Army took an 'idiotic pride' in dressing for Asia as though it were an English parade ground. He wrote: 'We wore our ordinary cloth shell jackets buttoned up to the chin, and the usual white buckskin gloves. Could any costume short of steel armour be more absurd in such a latitude?' It was not until the 1870s, thanks to enlightened commanders like Wolseley, that scarlet could be put aside in hostile climates and replaced with grey serge jackets and Indian sun helmets.

Marching was, of course, rather different in peacetime, especially for the officers. General Sir Charles Dobell described a march across Northern India in 1887: 'Full Officer's Mess furniture accompanied us as we entertained in the usual way at all stations on the line of march. Transport consisted of camels or bullock carts . . . We were followed by 60 polo ponies, the property of the officers. We played wherever there was a ground and did a little mild pig-sticking as well. At each station cricket and football matches were arranged against the local regiments and there was frequently some shooting to be enjoyed.'

Food was a constant cause for complaint among the men. The standard daily ration was 1 lb bread eaten at breakfast with coffee, and 12 oz meat for dinner. The meat was boiled beef or mutton thickened into a broth in large copper vessels. Cash was deducted – 6d a day until 1854 – from the soldier's basic pay of one shilling a day for such rations. Extra vegetables were bought and paid for by the men themselves.

Incompetence and, it was often suspected, corruption caused appalling hardship and contributed to the epidemics that often devastated armies and expeditionary forces. In home barracks soldiers could expect to be hospitalized once every thirteen months but in overseas stations the numbers of cases swelled immeasurably. Between 1825 and 1836 the mortality rate among soldiers on the Gold Coast was 668 per 1,000. Soldiers in Jamaica, Ceylon, South Africa and North America were sick enough to be hospitalized several times a year. Between 1839 and 1853 the British Army suffered 58,139 deaths at home and abroad, the vast majority of them through sickness. The mortality rate among officers was half that of NCOs and men.

Major Daniel Lysons wrote of his camp in the Crimea: 'The food is very bad and insufficient. A lump of bad beef without any fat, boiled in water, and a bit of sour bread are not sufficient to keep men in good condition. We can get no vegetables whatsoever, and the people in the village here will not sell us anything.' Cholera broke out and his unit lost thirty-seven dead in three months. Later, after the battles of Balaclava and Inkerman, Lysons wrote home: '12 December 1854. Unfortunately our commissariat transport has broken down and we only get short rations; sometimes a quarter of a pound of salt pork and half a pound of biscuit a day, very short commons for men at hard work . . .

14 December. We had 73 deaths last month. This month we have had an average of two a day, till the day before yesterday when there were five, yesterday eight . . .

24 January 1855. I have only 206 men now left fit for duty; there were seven deaths yesterday.'

The Welch Fusiliers lost 754 men during the Crimean War, 530 of whom died of disease. Such an attrition rate, not caused by enemy fire, caused a scandal at home and conditions gradually changed with improved regulations covering hygiene, medical care and resources. Wolseley was able to sanction seventy doctors for 2,400 men on the Ashanti expedition.

Earlier in his career, when stationed in the West Indies, Lysons found some light relief during a cholera epidemic: 'One poor fellow, who was given over by the doctors and supposed to be dead, was measured for his coffin, and the coffin was made. In those hot climates there is no time to be lost. The man, however, disappointed the doctors and recovered. Then came the question, who was to pay for the coffin? It was charged to the man, but he refused to sign his accounts with this charge against him, saying that he had not ordered the coffin and did not want it.' A compromise was reached – the soldier paid for the casket, provided he could keep it in his barracks where, fitted with shelves, it held all his gear.

Drink could be a comfort or a curse. The young Lieutenant Thorpe described the destruction of supplies to prevent them falling into the hands of the enemy: 'As we marched through the town, the rum was running down the canals of the streets, and with much difficulty we prevented the men from remaining behind and getting intoxicated; those who had shoes slipped them off their feet, and filling them with rum and mud drank it off at a gulp before the officers could prevent them; others filled their caps for the same purpose.' After the same campaign a private of the 71st Foot wrote: 'The great fault of our soldiers at the time was an inordinate desire for spirits of any kind. They sacrificed their life and safety for drink, in many ways; for they lay down intoxicated upon the snow and slept the sleep of death; or, staggering behind, were overtaken and cut down by the merciless French soldiers.'

At the height of the Raj in Karachi Corporal Andrew Morton recalled: 'The canteen was open all day . . . and you could buy over three pints of spirits for one rupee or two shillings, and this arrack or rum was over-proof . . . There was men dying every day from the effects of drink which did more for death than fever . . . At the time the battle money was served out there were about thirty men in hospital from drink . . . Drink was the rage in India.' Corporal Alexander Morton described regular drunken fights in the bazaars: 'The native police, under the superintendence of a European Inspector, would make haste to the scene of the disturbance and endeavour to put a stop to it. If a row was continued the native police carried nets which they threw over the drunkards' heads, knocked them off their feet and rolled them up.'

During the Opium War British and Indian soldiers plundered the island of Chusan after looting vast stocks of the Chinese spirit Samsu. An officer reported: 'Its effect on them was of the most dreadful nature and very different from that of the spirits we are used to in England. A man no sooner took a small quantity than he was in a most dreadful state and committing the most horrible atrocities.'

Desertion was always a problem, averaging 4 per cent among troops serving in Australia and New Zealand during the 1850s. Such frontier lands offered safe havens in which a man could disappear and earn his fortune in goldfields or land grabs.

Discipline was harsh throughout the century. The penalty for desertion, cowardice, armed robbery, mutiny and murder was death throughout the nineteenth century and into the twentieth, and every expedition had its executioners. During the fourteen months up to February 1813 it is estimated that forty-one men were executed in an army of 100,000. However, it was the cat-o'-nine-tails which kept the rankers submissive. In 1814 more than 18,000 men were flogged. During a Commons debate that year Lord Palmerston, then Secretary for War, argued successfully that only the lash could instill fear in men who were used to settling their own arguments with fists, feet and cudgels. Wellington asked: 'Who would bear to be billed up [confined to barracks] but for the fear of a stronger punishment?'

Up to 1829 courts martial had powers to impose unlimited flogging, which often amounted to a death sentence. In that year the maximum was set at 500 lashes; in 1833 this was reduced to 300, in 1836 to 200 and in 1846 to 50. The issue was hugely political, linked as it was to the abolition of slavery and the introduction of proper policing and penal reform. During the mid-1840s military prisons were built as an alternative to execution or the lash, although military authorities were keen to retain flogging as a punishment for insubordination and the theft of Army property. Flogging in peacetime was abolished in 1869, but continued on active service until 1881

Defence of the British Embassy at Kabul, 1879

– a century after it had been scrapped in France, Austria and Prussia. Its final abolition marked an acceptance that soldiering was now an honourable profession.

More emphasis was placed on rewarding good soldiers through good conduct pay, badges and medals, and recreation. Proper canteens and messes were introduced for all ranks. Reading classes and regimental schools were established despite the splenetic rage of the Old Guard who preferred to keep their troops ignorant in all things but personal sacrifice. Sporting facilities were improved to ease the deadly boredom of barracks life. Fines and loss of good service pay were imposed for drunkenness in lieu of the lash.

Barracks, both at home and abroad, were generally miserable places. Overcrowding and poor or non-existent sanitation were universal, whether a soldier was stationed in Dublin Castle or in a stilted cabin in the Hondorus swamps. Army regulations said that each man was entitled to 300 cubic feet of air; in British gaols the minimum was 600. In the West Indies the sleeping space allocation was 23 inches width per man. Ablutions were conducted at standpipes in the yards while inside the piss-tub overflowed at night. Many barracks were built over or adjoining sewage ditches. The barrack rooms, draughty or poorly ventilated, were used for sleeping, eating and killing time.

Living in the same barracks were the wives and children of those men permitted to marry, their numbers swelled by unofficial wives and smuggled-in girlfriends, some of whom earned a few pence by cleaning laundry, cooking and cutting hair. Privacy was, at best, a blanket slung over a rope and behind such makeshift curtains women lived, loved, washed and even gave birth.

In many regiments, however, only 12 of 100 men were allowed official wives and marriage was frowned upon among the rank and file. The rest took their pleasures when and where they could. There were camp followers behind most regiments, and native girls along the way, although the incidence of reported rape appears low compared with that of other armies. In a letter home Trooper Charles Quevillart described a Karachi brothel: 'The sight of the older women was simply disgusting for they were one and all deplorably ugly and little was left for the imagination as a yard of calico would have furnished a dozen of them with a full dress. Some had breasts hanging as low as their waists and I noticed one party with appendages so long that she was enabled to suckle her child by throwing them over her shoulders.' But then, he might have been reassuring his mother. Other soldiers, less restrained, wrote glowingly of the dancing maidens of India and Arabia, the delicate Chinese women of Malaya, Nigerian princesses, the mixed-blood women of the West Indies. E. Sellon wrote that native women 'understand in perfection all the arts and wiles of love, are capable of gratifying any tastes, and in face and figure they are unsurpassed by any women in the world'. In hotter climes there were fewer sexual taboos than at home, and British soldiers could use their money, their power and position, and their novelty to rampage sexually across the world.

Prostitution grew immeasurably wherever the flag was planted, and venereal disease mushroomed. In India so many men were laid low that British authorities sanctioned regulated prostitution. From 1860 to the late 1880s seventy-five cantonments were designated brothel areas with regular medical inspection, registration and hospital treatment centres. Such methods worked and the rate of syphilis in the army in India was lower than in the barracks back home. But in 1888 the 'moral purity' lobby forced the Army to suspend the arrangements. The result was a dramatic upsurge in cases, peaking at more than 25 per cent of Indian Army rankers in 1895.

Among officers sex scandals, particularly those involving the wives of fellow officers, ruined promising careers. An indecent act in a railway carriage halted the upward rise of Army modernizer Valentine Baker. Allegations of homosexual activity often resulted in suicide, as in the case of 'Fighting Mac' MacDonald (see Appendix).

When Victoria took the throne in 1837 the British Army was around 100,000 strong and consisted mainly of infantry. By 1859 the total stood at 237,000, of whom well over half were overseas, garrisoning the Empire. Of the 130 infantry battalions, around 50 were in India, 37 in the Colonies and 44 at home. Most soldiers came from rural communities and there was a high proportion of Scots, Irish and Welsh.

The last stand at Adowa, 1896 (*Illustrated London News*)

As the century grew older so too did the generals. Arrogance, out-dated methods, senile incompetence, laziness and corruption trickled down from the top. Politicians demanded glorious adventures to distract the unruly mob at home while cutting back on military spending. The result was unnecessary, bloody fiascos such as the First Afghan War and the Crimea, as well as the innumerable smaller wars that are the subject of this book.

During the middle part of the century the incompetence of commanders was endemic. Major-General Elphinstone, commander of the ill-fated Afghan expedition, was elderly, inexperienced and disinterested. One writer summed up a widely held view: 'I state unhesitatingly that for pure, vacillating stupidity, for superb incompetence to command, for ignorance combined with bad judgement – in short, for the true talent for catastrophe – Elphy Bey stood alone . . . Elphy outshines them all as the greatest military idiot of our own or any other day.' More famously William Howard Russell described the Crimean commander thus: 'I am convinced from what I see that Lord Raglan is utterly incompetent to lead an army through any arduous task.' But Elphinstone and Raglan were not alone, as we shall see.

In 1868 Edward Cardwell was appointed Secretary for War and began his long-awaited reforms. He introduced short-time enlistment which resulted in a younger and fitter Army. He built up the Reserves. Most importantly, he scrapped the long-established practice, endorsed by Wellington, allowing the privileged classes to purchase commissions and promotion regardless of ability.

To many British politicians the small wars of the frontier were despised as 'nigger-bashing'. Armchair strategists believed that the 'lower races' could not stand up to colonial superiority, in terms of morality, Christianity and firepower. The abolition of slavery had not been universally acclaimed and troublesome natives and released slaves had engendered racist attitudes which had transcended the patronizing traditional image of 'Sambo' on the world's stage. The ordinary British soldier, however, had ambivalent attitudes to native enemies. Racism and bigotry were prized attributes at home in those Empire-building days and the new recruits shared them. But seasoned campaigners, used to fighting alongside sepoys, native regiments and local levies, took a broader view. The 200,000-strong Indian Army, although British-officered, was made up of Sikhs, Mahrattas, Dogras, Rajputs, Muslims and Gurkhas, all of them volunteers. In many other parts of the Empire local levies were raised because they knew the territory, were more resistant to the climate and, most importantly, were cheaper and could be dismissed without pensions when no longer needed. Such forces, always officered by whites, were widely deployed in the Caribbean, Guiana, West and South Africa, Ceylon, Malaya, Java, Goa, Mauritius and Mozambique. Malay soldiers were reckoned to be efficient, cheerful and healthy. 'Hottentots' were valued for their tracking skills in the bush.

The battle of Arogee, Abyssinia, in 1868, pitted massed firepower against naked courage (*Illustrated London News*)

Furthermore, the British soldier respected a courageous and determined foe, whether he was African, American or Oriental. (In broad terms, that is; there were exceptions, of course, when vengeance or fear were involved: witness the incredible savagery of the British following the Indian Mutiny and the Jamaica 'revolt'.) Rudyard Kipling, who better than anyone understood the attitudes of the common soldier, wrote: 'So 'ere's to you, Fuzzy-Wuzzy, at your 'ome in the Soudan; You're a pore benighted 'eathen, but a first-class fighting man . . .'.

And the memoirs of British officers and men repeatedly record the acts of incredible bravery among their adversaries. The 18th (Royal Irish) Regiment, after an assault on a Chinese temple, found they had captured a butcher's-shop. Those Tartar defenders not killed in battle had slain themselves rather than be taken prisoner. William Napier described the charge of Sind troops at the battle of Miani in 1843: 'Guarding their heads with large dark shields they shook their sharp swords, gleaming in the sun, and their shouts rolled like peals of thunder as with frantic might and gestures they dashed against the front of the 22nd.' At Omdurman 50,000 natives 'streamed across the open to certain death'. At Ulundi, according to another participant, the Zulus 'fell in heaps' as they ran in waves through volley fire. In battle the Zulus sometimes threw their own dead before them to blunt the redcoats' bayonets. On the Aroji plateau Abyssinian warriors in

Abyssinian warriors, 1867 (*Illustrated London News*)

scarlet shirts merely ducked when fired upon by rockets and then ran headlong into massed rifle and cannon fire.

A civilian witness at the battle of Tamai in 1884 saw Muslims attack General Buller's disciplined ranks: 'Not one man could get near enough to use his spear. It was an awful sight, and as an exhibition of pluck, or rather fanaticism, it could not be equalled. Poor deluded Arabs! thinking that they could do anything with their spears and swords out in the open against disciplined British troops armed with rifles.'

Courage was not just displayed in the heat of battle but also in its agonizing aftermath. Lieutenant Robarts of the Victoria Mounted Rifles described the Zulu wounded after Nyezane: 'They were very quiet, and seemed to bear pain well, no groaning or crying out. We could not do anything for them except give them water to drink . . .'. Captain William Molyneux described a visit to a Zulu kraal after the 1879 War where he met an old man 'who had lost half his right arm . . . the bone had been smashed by a bullet below the elbow; but he had cut the loose part off, and the wound had healed now. The many little mounds covered with stones, told how many of the poor fellows had crawled home simply to die.'

All ranks respected the concept – myth or real – of warrior peoples and their effectiveness at unconventional warfare. One regimental history written during the 1840s said of the Pathan: 'For centuries he has been on our frontier . . . subject to no man. He leads a wild, free, active life in the rugged fastness of his mountains; and there is an air of masculine independence about him which is refreshing in a country like India.' Sir Percival Marling recalled that 'the black Soudanese fought like blazes' at Tel-al-Kebir. The Dervishes at El Teb, according to a sergeant of the 18th Hussars, were without doubt 'the most fierce, brave, daring, and unmerciful race of men in the world'.

In the 1890s Colonel C.E. Callwell praised the Pirah tribesmen for their grasp of partisan warfare – the ability to move quickly over hard ground, appear where they were least expected and disappear when faced with superior forces. He said: 'Such methods are bewildering to the commanders of disciplined troops opposed to them.'

It can be recognized now, and many soldiers knew it at the time, that such opponents were fighting for their freedom, their country, their faith: causes which they believed were worth dying for even when they themselves were ruled by bloodthirsty despots. It is for such men and women, whose stories are not recorded in regimental histories, that this book was principally written.

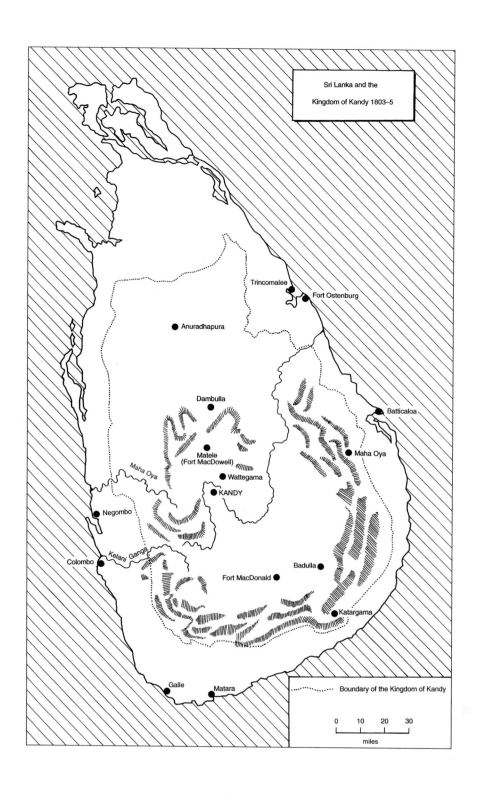

Sri Lanka and the
Kingdom of Kandy 1803–5

Trincomalee
Fort Ostenburg

Anuradhapura

Dambulla

Batticaloa

Matele
(Fort MacDowell)

Maha Oya

Maha Oya

Wattegama

KANDY

Negombo

Kelani Ganga

Colombo

Badulla

Fort MacDonald

Katargama

Galle

Matara

.... Boundary of the Kingdom of Kandy

0   10   20   30

miles

CHAPTER ONE

The First Kandy War, 1803–5

'The troops in Kandy are all dished, Your Honour'

'The Kandians had no sooner entered than they began to butcher indiscriminately everyone in the hospital, robbing them at the same time, cursing and reviling them, and spitting in their faces.' This description by one of the few survivors of the Kandy massacre reeks of horror. Yet Western travellers described the peoples of Ceylon as gentle and civilized. There is no contradiction. They were, and are, a peaceful people grown skilled in warfare. Scots wanderer Henry Marshall said they were 'hardy, brave and, like most mountaineers, passionately attached to their native hills'.

The British military disaster in the wild fastness of central Ceylon was a foretaste of many wars which dragged through the century. A modern Westernized force marched to the tunes of glory against a native population which was, to Western eyes, unsophisticated, ill-armed, medieval, craven, even corrupt. The invaders suffered hideously from that misjudgement. The campaign was ill-conceived and badly planned. Poorly equipped troops and raw recruits battled against the alien terrain and a people who well knew how to use it. The Kandyans used the landscape as a weapon of war. A people who would have been treated as exotic curiosities in the salons of London and Paris defended themselves against an army whose technology was more geared towards the battle plains of Napoleonic Europe than Ceylon's tropical rainforests, malarial swamps and saw-toothed mountains. It was a war like many others, marked by courage and cowardice, treachery and confusion, suffering and comradeship, brutality and nobility.

It was a small war but a costly one. For sheer savagery it has rarely been out-done.

* * *

Three thousand years ago King Solomon is said to have purchased elephants from Sri Lanka to woo the Queen of Sheba. Sri Lanka, 'the Blessed One', was the paradise designated by Buddha as the place where his religion would flourish. The Westernized history of the island was written in blood and fire. In 1505 the Portuguese discovered a treasure house of gold and spice on the prime trade routes: they found gems, king coconuts, a high grade cinnamon unique to the island, chillis, leopards, the white egret and beautiful women; they found excellent harbours, paddyfields, lofty mountains and a lushness that inspired awe even in eyes adjusted to the colours of the Orient. Inevitably it became a magnet for freebooters, explorers, soldiers, rogues and swindlers. The Sinhalese had suffered centuries of invasions from the Indian subcontinent but had created a civilization that the Romans had considered 'just and gentle'. Over 150 years the Portuguese created from the richness a ruin, a prize to be plundered and despoiled and fought over by the European nations.

The Sinhalese fought back against Portuguese armies made up largely of native allies and paroled convicts, perfecting guerrilla tactics from their mountain capital Kandy. They were years of carnage in which the invaders used every torture invented by the Inquisition. Finally the Sinhalese bottled up the Portuguese in Colombo and massacred columns loaded with booty from ransacked Buddhist temples. In one battle in 1638, 6,000 lives were lost. After another battle, fifty prisoners were returned to Colombo with only ten eyes between them and no testicles.

The Sinhalese then reached a deal with the Dutch to help them sweep the Portuguese into the sea in return for an overseas trade monopoly. That achieved, the Dutch simply renewed the plundering, corruption and land seizure under the guise of bureaucracy, and established a circle of coastal provinces protected by strong forts. In 1761 the Kandyans in the central mountains declared war on the coastal provinces, giving the Dutch an excuse to invade the highland kingdom. The first campaign saw the Dutch crushed by falling boulders, impaled by spears, trapped and slaughtered in ravines, lost in jungles. A second expedition captured Kandy City which the natives had abandoned, but monsoons forced the Dutch to retreat and a peace treaty was made. These campaigns were dress rehearsals for the British wars which followed. Western-led forces were able to control the coastal plains and paddyfields but the Kandyans were almost unbeatable in their mountain strongholds.

History repeated itself and the Dutch became victims of a deal between the Sinhalese and another foreign power. In 1795, 1,000 British infantry and four Indian battalions captured Trincomalee, the second city of the coastal provinces. Colombo surrendered bloodlessly and the Dutch withdrew ingloriously.

The British pact with the Kandyans proved an uneasy alliance from the start, with accusations of treachery and deceit on both sides. Partly to blame were the inevitable misconceptions which arose when East met West. The Kandyans could be an enigma. European chroniclers had described the islanders as a gentle and generous race, but one capable of great barbarity. Executions by trained elephants and by impaling did occur but their Buddhism made them reluctant to take life. Kandyan peasants lived in a

Frederick North, Governor-
General of Ceylon 1798–1805,
later Earl of Guildford
(The British Museum)

fruitful land and could live comfortably without too much effort. Most visitors agreed they were handsome, dignified and devout – yet capable of irrational rage. Even the more affluent lived in simple huts, although they built magnificent temples and palaces. Hardest for Europeans to understand was their love of ritual and ceremony for its own sake. This led to a delight in intrigue, bargaining and labyrinthine plotting which gave them a reputation for deviousness. Robert Knox, a seventeenth-century captive, wrote of them: 'In their promises very unfaithful, approving lying in themselves but misliking it in others.' It was a harsh verdict, and one based on ignorance, but the British soon came to agree.

Under the terms of the Madras Treaty the British inherited the coastal provinces but would allow the Kandyans access to the ports for supplies of salt and fish and for limited trade with the outside world. After two years the Treaty had not been ratified. The Kandyans belatedly realized that it gave the British the same coastal possessions and almost the same trade monopolies as the Dutch had enjoyed before them. By 1797 poor administration and British ignorance of local custom and land laws sparked a revolt in the provinces around Colombo. The Kandyans gave the rebels moral backing but stayed clear of the fighting.

Whitehall appointed Frederick North, third son of the Prime Minister, as Governor-General of the Ceylon territories in 1798. His task was to run them as a Crown Colony, against the wishes of the East India Company which retained the responsibility for trade and revenue. North was initially

Sri Wickrama Singha, King
of the Kandyans (Victoria
and Albert Museum)

successful. The revolt fizzled out as he reformed land laws, tackled
corruption, set up a legal code seen to be fair, and improved education and
health. However, he quickly concluded that the coastal provinces could
never be fully secure while the Kandyan kingdom posed a threat from
within. That kingdom was then in turmoil and gave North his most pressing
diplomatic problem.

Three months earlier King Rajadhi Raja Sinha had died. Pilima Talauva,
his *Adigar* (Prime Minister) wanted power for himself but was wary of
seizing the throne directly. Instead he installed as puppet monarch the
eighteen-year-old Kannasemy, who was the son of the dead king's sister-in-
law and perhaps, according to persistent rumours, also the *Adigar*'s own
child. The youth was invested with the sword of state as King Sri Wikrama
Raja Sinha. In manhood he was described as 6 ft tall with Herculean limbs,
his features handsome, his eyes intensely black and piercing. He was to prove
no puppet.

North began talks with the new regime, meeting Pilima Talauva with great
ceremony but reaching no conclusion. As the months dragged on North's
conviction grew that the kingdom was a barrier to progress. Meanwhile the
young king began to show his independence, much to the dismay of the
'king-maker' Pilima Talauva who began plotting his downfall. The full truth

Major-General Hay Macdowall, commander of the British forces (The British Museum)

may never be known but North undoubtedly began playing off the chief minister against the monarch, a diplomatic double game, confident that he could pick up the pieces to the benefit of Empire.

At a second summit meeting, North was allegedly shocked by Pilima Talauva's discreet proposal to kill Sri Wikrama and refused to send a British force to help him do so. Pilima Talauva, sick with VD and fistulas, grew increasingly desperate as his power at court diminished. He proposed that North should send an ambassador to Kandy City to negotiate a new treaty; he should be accompanied by a strong escort which would achieve a dual purpose: it would both intimidate the king and demonstrate British power and the benefits of living under its protection. North agreed and the ambassador chosen was the veteran Major-General Hay Macdowall. His orders were to offer support to whichever faction at court was most likely to reach a deal favourable to British interests.

In March 1800 Macdowall, with five companies of Madras foot, Malay infantry and Bengal artillerymen, was met just inside the Kandyan border by a reception force of 1,000 soldiers and seven elephants which was to escort them to Kandy itself. For 8 miles the men dragged the heavy guns through mud and fog, suffering blistering days and torrential nights. Progress was so slow that Macdowall left most of his column behind and continued with a few hundred Malays and Sepoys. Those he left behind at Ruwanwella were incapacitated by malaria, dysentery and other diseases known then by the catch-all 'jungle fever'. Of the men on the march with him one died from disease, another by drowning and another in the jaws of a crocodile. Officers described the track up to the Kandyan plateau as 'almost perpendicular' in stretches. It was crowded by the British column and their Kandyan escort. Baggage trains jostled with troopers cursing their ill-luck.

Four weeks after leaving Colombo Macdowall reached the royal palace at Kandy. He was graciously received with courtesy, sweet cakes, honey . . . and a maze of baffling protocol. The king's confidence and authority grew daily. Pilima Talauva demonstrated his wiles and cunning. The British ambassador could not penetrate the conflicting conspiracies. Neither could he perceive which faction to negotiate with. After several exasperating weeks his talks came to nothing.

Macdowall did achieve one thing. The £5,000 cost of the expedition had, in effect, financed a detailed reconnaissance of the hinterland, highlighting the need for proper transport and communication routes. It was a blueprint for future invasion. Valuable lessons were learnt, although most of them were subsequently forgotten.

The situation grew volatile. North, wearied by the endless negotiations, was moving towards a military solution. Kandy was also mobilizing for war. Troops were recruited from outlying villages and drilled in the defence of the city. The spark was provided by a seemingly trivial incident. Pilima Talauva, anxious to dispel rumours that he was a British agent and to promote his own authority, seized stocks of areca nuts from coastal traders and ignored British demands for compensation. There is much evidence that Pilima Talauva wanted to provoke an invasion. He may have hoped, after months of secret talks, that British action would destroy Sri Wikrama and leave him as a 'client king'. From that ambition a tragedy was born.

* * *

At the start of 1803 Macdowall was ordered to retrace his footsteps to Kandy, this time at the head of a full invasion force. Colonel Barbut led another force from Trincomalee, a longer route.

Marching with jaunty confidence from Colombo, Macdowall's force consisted of 1,900 fighting men: Britons of the 51st and 19th Foot, two companies of Bengal artillery, a company of Malays and 1,000 recruits to the Ceylon Native Infantry, plus many times that number of coolies, pioneers, drovers and ammunition carriers. Morale in the 51st was low after three years' garrison duty. Some, like Macdowall, were hardened veterans of the Corsican campaign but others were regarded as 'old men and boys'. The 19th was in better shape. Two of its companies had fought in the Mysore War a few years previously, while five more had seen action elsewhere and the rest had helped to suppress tax riots. They were relatively used to the climate, experienced and healthy. The Malay unit had a fearsome reputation for plunder and the swiftness of their krises. The Bengal gunners were battle-hardened. The Native Infantry, despite the name, consisted largely of recruits from India, Africa, Java and Malacca. Early attempts to recruit lowland Sinhalese had failed.

Macdowall chose a northerly route alongside the River Maha Oya, across level plains towards the massive escarpment that was their destination. The first stage was not arduous. The soldiers, hot and heavily laden, were greeted by friendly villagers anxious to sell them produce and cooling drinks. A supply depot was set up in the foothills and dubbed Fort Frederick. The next hilly stage proved more gruelling and the baggage train became an unwieldy burden. Even though most tents had been left at the depot the pack bullocks stumbled and the elephant handlers struggled to control their beasts. Macdowall was well aware of the need for a speedy and decisive campaign before the onset of the April rains, yet progress remained slow. Barbut suffered the same frustrations and setbacks as his column trundled slowly from the opposite direction.

First contact with the enemy came when troops surprised a Kandyan scouting party. A Malay was wounded but one prisoner was taken. He confirmed that the Kandyans were concentrating their forces around the capital, content to allow the mountains and jungle wear down the invaders. Macdowall met the first real resistance from a stone redoubt 50 ft above the track at Girihagama, close to the gateway to the plateau. Kandyans poured steady if inaccurate musket fire on a company of 19th Grenadiers before retreating through a rear door. They left a bloody trail as they dragged away their wounded. One Grenadier died, while another was lucky to survive a ball through a lung. The road to the capital was now open.

Barbut's smaller column, with five companies of the 19th, more Malays and one company of Madras artillery, saw no enemy at all until they reached the Balakaduwa Pass. A cursory shelling sent the defenders fleeing and Barbut reached the top with no casualties. He saw Kandy City burning.

The two columns met at the outskirts of the city. They found only ashes and half-burned buildings. All the inhabitants, the king and his court, had simply decamped for the mountains of Uva, taking with them their treasures, religious relics, arms and provisions. There was no one to fight, nothing to loot, no glory to be had.

Meanwhile North, in a calculated gamble, recognized an alternative candidate for the Kandyan throne A dignified Malabar called Muttusamy, who was brother-in-law to the old dead king, was despatched with an escort to the now British-occupied capital. Once there Muttusamy proved difficult and refused to cede land to the British. It hardly mattered. Few others recognized the pretender. He was ignored by the city garrison and neighbouring villagers. He sat alone, save for a few servants, holding pathetic court in the charred remains of the royal palace.

The acknowledged king, Sri Wikrama, was 18 miles away in another palace at Hunguranketa. The British learnt this from the double-dealing Pilima Talauva. Two columns of 500 and 300 men were sent across the steaming mountainsides to capture the king. Within a few miles they suffered heavy fire from native gingals or 'grasshopper' guns which were highly effective when aimed down the narrow tracks. Several troopers were mown down but the columns marched steadily through the high-altitude swamps and thickets, sweeping the areas ahead with light artillery in the text-book fashion. On the second day they reached their target . . . only to find the king and his entourage had once again decamped. The frustrated force returned to the capital under sporadic fire. This time the Kandyans concentrated on killing the baggage handlers, a classic tactic of mountain warfare. Many officers believed that the failed pursuit of the king had been a cunning trap laid by the wily Pilima Talauva.

Conditions for the garrison in Kandy deteriorated fast. Troops unused to the jungle, worn out by patrolling the sodden hills and harried by snipers, quickly lost their spirit. Stragglers and those who wandered too far foraging were butchered. Small parties of coolies, some Sepoys, the wives of several Malay soldiers and one unnamed European were found cut to pieces in gullies and underbrush. Sri Wikrama promised villagers a bounty of 10 rupees for the head of a European and 5 for that of a native soldier. Supply lines to both Colombo and Trincomalee were repeatedly severed. The worst enemy of all was disease. It spread through the insanitary ruins of Kandy as the rainy season began. Malarial fever and yellow-jack slew European and native alike. So did beri-beri, dysentery and infected wounds.

One officer wrote: 'Nothing is so apt to bring on that plague, the berryberry, as low living and exposure to heavy dews.' Of his company he reported 48 hospitalized and 4 dead. A few weeks later the death list had grown to 28. He wrote again: 'If they keep us much longer in this hole you will see very few of these fine fellows.' He warmly praised Barbut's efforts to improve the conditions of the enlisted men. Macdowall's force, pitifully reduced by disease and warfare, half-starved and demoralized, was no longer an army of occupation: they were prisoners in the Kandy rubble.

The Kandyans, though also suffering from fever, were moving freely. Large groups of warriors were sent into the Western and Northern provinces and the supply depot at Fort Frederick came under threat. The fort was abandoned although no enemy attackers were ever seen. By then most of its defenders, including the commander, Bullock, were dead of the fever.

North was unaware of the full danger but the campaign was proving miserable and costly. He dared not ask his overlords for reinforcements because of the more pressing priorities in India and war-torn Europe. His judgement in supporting Muttusamy was being called into question. Macdowall's force was being whittled away in the mountains and the garrisons in the coastal provinces were fully stretched. North and Macdowall agreed to withdraw a large part of the Kandy force to the coast but the return routes were treacherous. Pilima Talauva offered an apparent solution: a truce in return for help in deposing the king. Or so the *Adigar* alleged. The ceasefire was eagerly accepted.

On 1 April Macdowall left Kandy with the bulk of his force, leaving Barbut in command of a garrison of 300 Green Howards, 700 Malays and a considerable number of hospital cases. The Kandyans kept to the truce and the returnees went unmolested. Some 400 survivors of the 51st were given a hero's welcome in Colombo, having left 100 of their comrades dead or hospitalized in the mountains. Almost every man who returned was himself hospitalized and three months later barely 100 were left alive.

North opened new peace talks at Dambadeniya and Barbut briefly joined the parley. He gave a strangely positive report on conditions at Kandy, saying the fever would soon burn itself out. Barbut then collapsed, was taken delirious to Colombo and died some weeks later. At the peace conference Pilima Talauva agreed that the king should be handed over to the British along with much of eastern Ceylon. In return the *Adigar* would, with British blessing and support, rule over the reduced kingdom with the title Grand Prince. No one will ever know whether Pilima Talauva was serious. Some rumours suggest that the peace talks involved an unrealized plot to capture North. The Governor certainly believed the talks offered hope.

Macdowall was sent back, while the truce lasted, to replace Barbut in command in Kandy. What he found was shocking: the death toll was rising every day, the filthy hospital wards were crowded to bursting, the sick were too weak to stagger to the latrines. The rains were by now continuous and temperatures plunged at night. Food was scarce and rotten. Officers reported that few Europeans were capable of walking a mile. The coolies had fled. There were just three artillerymen fit for duty. The Malays lost thirty men dead in a month while others had deserted because of a dispute over 10 weeks' missing back pay, and opium.

North suspected that the fragile truce would not last much longer. Spies reported that Pilima Talauva's loyalty was suspect at Sri Wikrama's court. Macdowall decided to return to Colombo to emphasize the growing peril and to stress the need to evacuate Kandy while the truce still held. The General was sick when he headed down the mountain track, leaving the charnel city in the charge of Major Adam Davie. Reluctant to take command, Davie fully admitted that he was an inexperienced officer who had seen no previous action during his year in Ceylon.

North finally agreed to bury his pride and issued orders for a full retreat from Kandy. Sadly, his orders came too late to halt the remorseless drift towards disaster.

★ ★ ★

The Kandyans were ready to strike. Levies had been raised by the king and his generals throughout the mountains. As the forces encircling the city grew in numbers and boldness, Pilima Talauva informed the hapless Davie that the truce had collapsed and an attack was imminent. The outlying posts were abandoned without a shot and Davie concentrated his dwindling command

The King's Palace at Kandy, *c.* 1830, showing the main archway and the octagonal tower (Department of National Museums, Sri Lanka)

in the old royal palace, a rambling structure of interlocking compounds which included the makeshift hospital. He positioned four three-pounders to cover the main approaches. There were barely twenty European troops fit enough to join the Sepoys and Malays manning the defences. The palace would have been virtually indefensible even if Davie had had large numbers of operational troops under his command. The building was flanked on three sides by an ornamental wall, on the fourth by a flimsy stockade overlooked by a sheer cliff. That weak spot was covered by a three-pounder, a mortar and ten native troops. They were the first victims of a pre-dawn swoop.

Before daybreak on 24 June the little battery was overrun in total silence and the men captured. Two officers of the 19th who were talking on a verandah immediately below the outpost were unaware of the attack until by dawn's early light they made out several hundred Kandyans swarming down the hillside. The attackers, led by the Malay mercenary chief Sanguaglo, stormed the stockade. They slashed Quartermaster Brown to death with their krises. His companion, Ensign Barry, parried several blows and stuck Sanguaglo with his bayonet. Major Davie appeared in the mêlée and finished off the chief with his sword. The subsequent confusion halted the attack, allowing hastily mustered gunners time to fire a round of grapeshot from a three-pounder. At point-blank range the effect was devastating. A ragged hole appeared in the Kandyan ranks; twenty-four of them dropped in bloody heaps and the rest retreated.

The Kandyans were alarmed at the firepower still at the disposal of the enfeebled garrison. They held back but maintained steady gunfire on all sides of the 800-yard perimeter. This caused few casualties but the covering fire allowed infiltrators to slip into the tangle of palace buildings. Native defenders saw several of their former comrades – deserters or captives – among the attackers, offering proof of good treatment if they surrendered. Four officers of the Malay regiments approached Davie to urge capitulation. When Davie refused, one officer bizarrely tried to blow his own brains out. Such madness had the desired effect. Davie, weakened by sickness and fear, decided the position was hopeless. Together with the Malay adjutant Captain Nouradin he left the stockade under a white flag.

Davie and Pilima Talauva agreed surrender terms which would allow the fit survivors to march freely to Trincomalee and safety. Those too sick to be moved would be tended where they lay until they either expired or could be evacuated. They were generous terms, unbelievably so given the circumstances.

In the late afternoon 34 Europeans, 250 Malays, Muttusamy and his entourage, a few Bengal gunners, native wives and children followed Davie out of the city. With them went the garrison's two doctors, a sure sign that they regarded the surrender terms as too good to be true. The sick were left behind as the column marched off in torrential rain. The weather covered the sounds that emerged from the capital minutes later.

Thousands of Kandyans swarmed into the palace complex from all sides. In one long narrow room converted to hospital use they found 149 Europeans crammed side by side in cots and crude panniers, on stretchers and on the bare floor. Sergeant Theon, one of only two Europeans to survive, later described the horror: 'They mostly knocked out the soldiers' brains with clubs then pulled them out by the heels, the dead and the dying, threw many of them into a well and numbers of the bodies were left in the streets and devoured by dogs, but none were buried.' Theon was knocked senseless. He awoke naked under a pile of bodies in the palace courtyard. As he struggled free a Kandyan soldier discovered him and hanged him from a beam. Astonishingly the rope broke before he strangled and he crawled to a hut to hide. A week later he was found again, taken captive and treated well. He lived in Kandy as a royal pensioner for twelve years, raising a son by his Muslim bride. The only officer left behind, Adjutant Plenderleath, was beaten to death with his men. There is no sure record of what happened to 23 Malays and 17 Moorish gunners left in a separate wing of the hospital. Some sources suggest they were victims of the general bloody frenzy, others that they were spared.

Unaware of the carnage behind him Major Davie and his column reached the swollen banks of the Mahaweli Ganga just before nightfall. After a night's soaking they received an official delegation from King Sri Wikrama, who demanded that the usurper Muttusamy be handed over. Twice Davie refused, ignoring assurances that no harm would befall his charge. But his resolve collapsed on the third demand when he was told that 50,000 Kandyans were poised to attack. Muttusamy and his kinsmen were led away. They were later given a swift trial before the king. Muttusamy and three relatives were condemned and beheaded. Two servants were hanged and the rest released minus their ears and noses.

At the riverbank Davie's men built bamboo rafts for a crossing. The next day they awoke to find themselves surrounded by Kandyans led by the ferocious Joseph Fernando. After tremendous difficulties a rope was secured across the river waters, only to be cut by natives on the other bank before any raft could be hauled across. Emissaries from the king issued new demands. Davie and his men must give up their arms and return to Kandy. Word had by then reached them of the massacre in the city and several old campaigners protested that only death awaited them there. Nevertheless Davie, exhausted and in despair, agreed to the new conditions.

The British and Asian troops were disarmed and separated. The Asians were sent back towards the city. The British troopers were in turn separated from the officers and taken a short distance away. They were robbed of any valuables and marched in pairs to a hollow hidden by thick vegetation. There they were cut down by swordsmen working in relays. Only one British soldier, Corporal George Barnsley, survived, feigning death after a neck blow had sliced his tendons.

The officers were dying too, some by their own hand. Three shot themselves, a fourth threw himself into the river. The majority were brained with clubs or put to the sword. Two officers, one of them Doctor Greeving who had deserted the hospital, slid down the tangled hillside unobserved and hid in a pit. They remained there for four days, covered by the bodies of dead comrades. The last two officers, Davie and his second-in-command Captain Rumley, were led out for execution but were saved by the timely arrival of Pilima Talauva who ordered them to be sent to the King.

The Asian troops were given the choice of death or service in the Kandyan army. Some, including Bengal gunners, protested that they had sworn an oath to the British king and could not bend their knee to Sri Wikrama. They were swiftly killed. The remainder joined the Kandyans.

A column was sent to take the small Fort Macdowall on the British supply line. En route they captured the wounded Corporal Barnsley, who had been heading in great pain in the same direction. The fort was held by Captain Madge with two officers, a surgeon, 22 Malays and 32 soldiers of the 19th, of whom 19 were too ill to move and the rest sick on their feet. The Kandyans sent Barnsley into the fort to relay terms. His first words to the astonished Madge were: 'The troops in Kandy are all dished, your honour.'

His description of the mass murder by the river left Madge in no doubt that surrender was pointless and that he must do his best for those men capable of flight. He decided to evacuate the fort, leaving the immovable sick behind to certain death. Those who could walk, including Barnsley, crept out in the night after lighting lamps in the fort to fool the surrounding natives. They had been gone for some time before the Kandyans realized the fort was no longer defended. They followed in maddened pursuit, after first slaying the sick in their cots. Madge and his ill, weary and tattered little force fled through the jungle hills, harassed by the enemy all the way. It was a hideous and terrifying flight, with death snapping at their heels, but the soldiers kept their nerve and their luck held.

On the fourth day they met, by sheer good fortune, a column of 150 Malays. Together they were too strong for the Kandyans to tackle and the last three days to Trincomalee were unopposed. Perhaps the luckiest man of all was Barnsley. He survived the march and recovered from his gruesome wounds. He was promoted sergeant but quickly reduced to the ranks for drunkenness. In 1805 he was invalided home.

Among the British, Davie, now a pathetic, sick captive in Kandy, was held responsible for the whole military disaster. He was the obvious scapegoat. North was especially vitriolic, and was also determined to avoid any blame himself. In official reports North greatly exaggerated the strength of the garrison's defences in Kandy. He made hardly any reference to the weakened condition of the troops under Davie's command, the spread of epidemics and the strength of enemy forces fighting on their own terrain. Davie was certainly a poor commander, inadequate and indecisive, but he was not alone in that. Moreover, he had not sought out the job, fully recognizing his own shortcomings. His decisions to parley when in a hopeless situation and then to abandon Kandy were understandable. But his surrender on the riverbank, after hearing of the hospital massacre, was not.

There is still confusion over who ordered the massacre. Pilima Talauva could certainly be ruthless but he is an unlikely candidate. He was a crafty fox with his eye always on future negotiation, on keeping open avenues for intrigue. The evidence points at the hot-blooded young king, Sri Wikrama. According to some reports he was enraged at his chief minister's decision to allow the British to leave Kandy under truce, revoked the safe conduct and ordered the killing to assert his authority. Later each man blamed the other. Whatever the truth the savagery in the hospital and on the riverbank must have been in part due to the bloodlust which leaders can often harness but not control. The Kandyans were, after all, defending their mountain realm from an invader. So far they had been spectacularly successful.

Davie was at first badly treated, his illnesses and sores neglected. Later the king, perhaps with feelings of remorse over the spilt blood, gave him medical aid, cash, presents and household servants. Everything, indeed, but his freedom. Repeated British efforts to achieve his release failed. In one message passed to Colombo he said: 'Let not my friends know I am alive as I expect not to survive for many days.' He became a familiar figure in the kingdom, ragged and depressed and possibly half mad. He never tried to escape. His body broken by illness, his will-power sapped by the shame of ignoble defeat, Davie died still a captive in either 1812 or 1813.

⋆ ⋆ ⋆

One small fort, Dambadeniya, was left in Kandyan territory. It was a simple staging post. Behind its rough earth banks and a flimsy barricade of stacked rice bags were thirty-six troopers and Malays under Ensign Grant. All the

A typical hill fort, this one at Badulla

men had fever to varying degrees and Grant himself could barely walk. The fort soon came under strong attack. The besiegers under Migastenna kept up continuous sniping fire and each day emissaries were sent to demand surrender. Grant stubbornly – and sensibly – refused. After a two-week siege, rescue came with the arrival of Captain Robert Blackall at the head of a relief column. The Kandyans pulled back. Grant was ordered to return to Colombo after first destroying the fort's large store of provisions. In doing so several soldiers drank copiously from stocks of arak, a fiery native liquor. One drunken Briton and several Sepoys lagged behind as the column marched out of the fort. Their bodies were never found.

The British soldiers remaining in their coastal towns and garrisons were now seriously depleted by war and sickness. At the beginning of the year their forces had numbered more than 5,000 able-bodied men; just six months later 2,000 of them were dead or missing while most of the rest were ill. The hospitals in those pre-Nightingale days were full to choking and few men were fit for duty. Opposing them were tens of thousands of Kandyans who might at any time sweep down from the highlands and swamp the thinly spread garrisons. Fortunately the British were given a breathing space. The Kandyans suspended warfare to celebrate their Perahera, the biggest religious festival of the year. While the Kandyans rejoiced and caroused, Macdowall strengthened his defences. Convalescents dug ditches alongside the few fit men.

Their festivities over the Kandyans attacked and together with lowland Sinhalese swarmed around the British-held forts. The first strike was against Matara in the south. Its commander was paralysed with fear and North sent the remarkable Captain Beaver to replace him. Only just out of the fever-bed, the forty-year-old officer took sixty hours to cover 103 miles, some of that over sea. Within two days he had driven the enemy from the vicinity of the fort. A few days later he forced the Kandyans out of an outlying post previously abandoned to them. Within a few weeks, with only 60 European troops, 140 Sepoys and 170 Malays, Beaver had subdued the entire Southern province.

Colombo itself was threatened by a large force which halted 5 miles from the city. The beleaguered North had no effective troops, only a hastily raised militia of 500 men. From this, Macdowall put together a tiny strike force under Lieutenant Mercer and sent them out to meet the enemy head on. The Kandyans, taken by surprise, fled back across their border, leaving prisoners and dead.

Throughout the coastal provinces the pattern was repeated. Instead of waiting passively behind their rough barricades, the British commanders sallied out and harried the Kandyan attack columns, creating dismay, confusion and panic. Attack did indeed prove the best form of defence. The tactic was so successful that the Kandyans only managed to lay proper siege to one fort, a tiny outpost at Chilaw close to the kingdom's border. As many as 3,000 attackers faced two young civil servants and sixty native troops.

When their grapeshot ran out the defenders fired nothing but powder from their small cannon, hoping that the noise and smoke alone would dissuade the enemy from making an overwhelming frontal attack. The ploy worked and the Kandyans withdrew after four days.

Sri Wikrama now decided to lead a new attack on Colombo, marching in person at the head of an army of Malabar Guards, Malays and 12,000 Kandyans. In his path lay the ruined fort of Hanwella, commanded by the doughty Lieutenant Mercer. The king's men attacked on 3 September but were repulsed. A second attack the following day also failed, despite the ramshackle defences, but left most of the small garrison wounded. Mercer himself was extremely sick. Captain William Pollock rode from Colombo, dodged the encircling enemy, and took command of fewer than a hundred men in poor condition. The Kandyans bombarded the dilapidated stone walls with three- and six-pounders serviced by Bengal and Madras artillery lascars captured at Kandy. Those gunners deliberately loaded the cannon with grape instead of ball, which splattered harmlessly against the fort's walls. Others set the angle of fire too high so that the shot whizzed overhead. Unaware that the cannonade had been ineffectual, the Kandyans rushed to attack but halted 200 yards from the muzzles of the defenders crouched below the low parapets. The attackers were packed into the steel jaws of an ambush, caught in an open killing ground.

Mercer, with half the garrison, had crawled into the jungle bordering the clearing. Now they opened fire, tearing great holes in the Kandyan flank. Their volley was also the signal for the fort's cannon to open up with grapeshot, with brutal effect. Pollock and his infantry sallied out in orderly ranks, pouring volley after volley into the struggling, panicking, dying mass of humanity. The carnage continued for two hours. Only a handful of Malay mercenaries were able to return fire. At last the gunfire was stilled as the last survivors escaped. Eight Kandyan soldiers and much weaponry were captured. Much to their delight 176 gun lascars rejoined the British. The following day they helped bury 270 Kandyans where they had fallen in that awful field. The death toll was much higher. All paths leading away from the clearing were choked with the bodies of those who had fled mortally wounded. The garrison suffered just two casualties and both survived.

Sri Wikrama and his court followers took to their heels, leaving behind sharpened posts upon which he had intended to impale British captives. He blamed his general at Hanwella, Levuke Rala, for the disaster and had him beheaded. The leading troops, those who survived, were ordered to work on a 2,000-acre paddyfield as punishment. Three days later Pollock, reinforced by Europeans from Colombo, crossed the Kandy border in pursuit. Across the Kelani River the king's army was camped at Ruwanwella, protected by well-placed batteries. A British detachment forded the river under intense but ineffective fire, seized one of the gun emplacements and killed all twenty-six defenders. The Kandyans, hugely superior in numbers but dispirited and caught between military pincers, again fled in terror, narrowly escaping Pollock's attempt to entrap them in another killing ground. Pollock destroyed tons of stores at Ruwanwella and burnt over 1,000 huts, denying the enemy food and shelter. It was the start of a scorched-earth policy.

Pollock returned to Colombo a hero, the saviour of the city. His extraordinary verve, audacity and ruthlessness were matched in smaller episodes across the provinces. British officers led small forces deep into Kandyan-held territory using speed and surprise as their main weapon. They also savagely suppressed Sinhalese communities which showed any sign of rebelling and joining the enemy. Captain Robert Blackall boasted of burning ninety-three villages and extensive paddyfields without a single casualty among his men. Fishing fleets were burnt to the waterline and scuttled, crops were destroyed and several village leaders were flogged to death. No records exist to reveal how many died of famine or exposure but the numbers must have been high. The British were no doubt partly motivated by a desire to avenge the Kandy massacres. However, their brutal methods certainly worked in military terms. The Kandyans were denied the countryside and potential rebels were terrorized into submission. Much of the lowlands were laid waste but at least the coastal garrisons and trading ports were no longer under threat.

Reinforcements finally arrived from India and the Eastern Islands to defend Trincomalee, now virtually denuded of fighting men through sickness. To strengthen the other forts African slaves were bought at £37 a head, including purchase, 'freight', provisions and agents' fees, in the Mozambique markets to serve as mercenary soldiers. The purchase caused controversy. The negroes were regarded as a bargain: they were easy to administer and well suited to the tropics – and the natives of Sri Lanka viewed them with terror.

Macdowall's period of service now came to an end. He was often blamed for the Kandy disaster but his masterly conduct of the war in the provinces redeemed him in the eyes of his superiors. He was promoted commander-in-chief at Madras but quickly fell out with the civil authorities. He died in 1809, shipwrecked on his voyage home to Britain. His successor in Ceylon took command in March 1804. Major-General David Wemyss was, at forty-four, a veteran of campaigning in the Americas, Flanders and Italy. His military experience was never in doubt but he lacked the tact needed to deal with civilians. The delicate relationship between Governor and military overlord was shattered when Wemyss clashed with North over field allowances. He outraged Moslem Sepoys by ordering them to attend divine service. He quarrelled with judges over the use of a parade ground. He challenged civilian rivals to duels. Relations became so fraught that North drew up contingency plans to have Wemyss arrested if necessary. Such squabbling undermined the British counter-attacks. The raids continued with mixed success. Wemyss divided his forces into smaller units stretched around a 700-mile frontier. He maintained a blockade to deprive the Kandyans of salt and other commodities.

Pilima Talauva continued to play an apparent double-game. He kept up a regular correspondence with the British, at one stage proposing a peace conference at which his own most troublesome and war-hungry ministers could be snatched. North rejected all proposals which left Sri Wikrama on the throne. He was determined on a further offensive to depose the king and avenge the massacre. The coastal campaigns had shown how effective light mobile columns could be, even against an enemy fighting on home ground. North proposed a three-month campaign with British-led forces striking throughout the island in fast-moving columns up to 600 men strong. Preparations were made for September when the monsoon season ended. Until then warfare was suspended.

★   ★   ★

During a tour of the garrisons Wemyss met Captain Arthur Johnston, the commander at Fort Batticaloa. Johnston knew the country well and was experienced in jungle warfare. He had been one of the lucky ones evacuated from the hospital at Kandy before the slaughter. He must have made a good impression because soon afterwards he received secret papers ordering him to prepare a strong force to march on Kandy. Similar columns, he was told, would converge from other garrisons around the coast to meet on the heights above the city on 28 September. However, the wording of the instructions was ambiguous, the routes to be taken were vague and the timings imprecise. A second set of orders was even more confusing. It was the beginning of an almighty débâcle.

Putting aside any doubts Johnston set off on the 20th with two officers and 70 men of the 19th, a sergeant and 6 gunners of the Royal Artillery. They were joined upriver by 53 Malays and 175 Sepoys. In addition there were 550 pioneers and coolies with ponderous bullocks to carry the supplies. A fast-moving strike force it was not.

Johnston's column moved through a region devastated by smallpox and crossed the border into the wild uplands. The hills were desolate and empty. The Kandyans had learnt well from the British scorched-earth tactics. Every village on Johnston's route had been cleared, its stores and animals dispersed. The march was exhausting from the start and after a week some men were sent back with the fever. Ominously, a Kandyan sharpshooter, captured in a skirmish with snipers, told Johnston that there were no reports of other columns invading the kingdom from other directions. Puzzled, or perhaps dismissive, Johnston pressed on.

On the tenth day they reached the banks of the Mahaweli Ganga and crossed its turbulent waters by raft. Ahead lay a tortuous trail through jungle, jagged rocks and ravines to the royal city of Hanguranketa: it was a three-day slog, harassed by sniper fire which killed one soldier and uncounted coollies and bullocks. On the last day they traversed a narrow ridge, inching along artificial footways from which several pack animals crashed with their precious loads into the gorge below. That night Johnston camped in a state of almost total exhaustion. His men were roused by musket fire which was too high to do any harm. The attackers were beaten off by Sepoy pickets and suffered heavy casualties.

The column continued along the riverside, hemmed in between rock and stormy waters, and under continuous fire from the opposite bank. The noise maddened the bullocks and some broke free, adding to the confusion on the narrow pathways. After 3 painstaking miles their progress was blocked by a large house which had been turned into a fort, supported by a battery on the far bank. It seemed impregnable, but the defenders put up only token resistance before fleeing. After a night of intermittent cannon fire Johnston sent a small squad across the river to take the battery from the rear. The unexpected raid worked smoothly and the emplacement was abandoned. Within an hour Johnston captured a small palace nearby at Kundasale. The fine building was richly carved and gilded but its cellars were packed with munitions. Johnston reluctantly torched the lot.

Once again a British-led force found the road to Kandy City open. Apart from some long-range musket fire from the hills above it was undefended. Once again the city they found was deserted, save for a woman and a small boy. They marched into the eerie city streets on 6 October. There was no sign of any other British column. They encamped in the royal palace, long since cleansed of the blood of their forerunners. A Malay officer, captured by the Kandyans during an earlier expedition but now escaped, brought Johnston fearful news. Six British columns had indeed set out but the other five had either turned back or were beaten back. They were on their own.

Johnston was by now fully aware of his desperate predicament. He had succeeded only in taking an empty city. The Kandyans were gathering in the mountains around the city, waiting only for sickness and desertion to sap his strength before attacking. Already disease was cutting into his defences and the men were running low on ammunition and supplies. They were jittery and unnerved. Some raided arak stores and got dismally drunk. The native troops heard shouts from former comrades urging them to join them in the hills, to fight for riches rather than the Crown. A sensible and diligent officer, Johnston decided his first duty was to his men. Staying would be suicidal. So too would be a retreat along the route they had taken. Instead he decided to move his little army to the left bank of the Mahaweli Ganga where they could construct better defences. After just two days in the empty city they marched out at dawn and met a grisly scene: skeletons dangled brokenly from treetops. They were the remains of Davie's officers. The bones of his enlisted men lay where they had been butchered near the river ferry, a place known afterwards as the Shore of Blood.

Johnston's force crossed the river on two small rafts and established a bridgehead by dislodging enemy soldiers at bayonet point. The action caused him to think again. The difficult crossing, the increasing boldness of the Kandyans and the dwindling stocks of ammunition persuaded him it would be folly to stay. He set off in the opposite direction to his incoming route, towards Trincomalee. Each man was issued with six days' rations and the surviving bullocks were destroyed.

They fought their way up a hillside track, scrambling over tree trunks felled by the enemy, charging over a series of breastworks, and took the summit, with 13 soldiers and 30 coolies killed or wounded. Days of ferocity followed. They hacked and shot and clawed their way through the dense jungle of Matale. Kandyan raids became confused mêlées, with bayonet and musket butt matched against sword and spear. Powder was wet, the ammunition all but gone, and shooting was rare in the close-quarter fighting. A company of the 19th moved forward so fast it became separated from the rest of the column. Johnston and his men battled on through bloody encounters, sweltering days, rain-soaked dusks and cold nights, as sickness and wounds multiplied. Coolies deserted in terror, leaving behind wounded soldiers who were captured, trussed up like chickens and carried off to torture and eventual, welcome, death. More of the injured were abandoned when their comrades lacked the strength to carry them further. The march of death continued to Lake Minneriya where the column caught up with the missing vanguard and the Kandyan attacks diminished. By now Johnston was so ill with dysentery he had to be carried in a cloak, his body dangerously weakened, his spirits low, his mind troubled by fears that he faced a court martial for retreating from Kandy without orders.

Johnston's column marched into Trincomalee 'cold, wet, dirty and lousy,' according to one observer. 'Almost naked, many bare-footed and maimed, officers and all alike starved and shrivelled,' said another. Every soldier was admitted to hospital and there almost all of them died. Johnston's march had proved as deadly as the Kandy massacre. And it had all been for nothing. The epic and heroic adventure had been the result of a communications blunder. Johnston learnt that the second set of vague orders received from Wemyss weeks before should have cancelled the march on Kandy City. The British columns were merely intended to enter the kingdom, inflict the greatest possible devastation to avenge the massacre, and then retire. The other columns had done just that, suffering minimal casualties, and returned to the safety and comfort of their barracks.

Johnston was exonerated at a court of inquiry which praised his courage and skill. Indeed he was commended for the way he had held his disparate force together in seemingly impossible conditions and against massive odds. He survived his illness and served in Sri Lanka for another six years but the after-effects of his ordeal were blamed for his eventual death in 1824. In a bitter postscript to the march Sergeant Henry Craven was sentenced to transportation for life for abandoning four of his wounded men to certain death on the trail. He died of fever before he could be shipped to Botany Bay.

While Johnston had been fighting his way to and from Kandy other British forces had been busy on punitive raids. One column caused widespread destruction in the Western province to within one day's march of Kandy City. Another column made an unsuccessful bid to capture Pilima Talauva. The Kandyans in turn launched attacks on British regions but they were half-hearted and easily repulsed. A familiar pattern was repeated as the British counter-attacked across a lush countryside raped by war, starvation and smallpox. The war was dragging to an inconclusive end.

Governor North was exhausted by the effort. He wrote to London asking to be relieved because of his 'shattered and unstrung' nerves. He confessed uncertainty over whether he had acted 'like a good politician or a great nincompoop'. North had done his best and his achievements were fully recognized. He reformed the island's civil administration, improved revenue, abolished torture and established a modern system of public instruction. With hindsight he was often too impatient to see his changes through and it was his vision of ruling all Ceylon which had caused the war. On returning to England he came into the title Earl of Guildford and travelled extensively in Europe. He set up the Ionian University in Corfu. That experiment failed amid much ridicule and he died in 1827.

On 17 July 1805 he was replaced by Major-General Sir Thomas Maitland who, because of his extensive Army background and political contacts, took both full civil and military authority. Wemyss was ousted, much to his own disgust but to the relief of many others. Maitland was a Scots aristocrat, a veteran administrator and a realist. He set himself the task of ending the costly war, reducing all military spending and sorting out Ceylon's crippled economy. With warfare virtually at a standstill Maitland managed to both cut the armed forces and increase their efficiency. He tackled with gusto the corruption behind much of the discontent felt by lowland Sinhalese. He issued a statement rejecting any more 'foolish expeditions', adding: 'I shall not throw away the lives of His Majesty's subjects by disease in burning and destroying the defenceless huts of the innocent natives.'

Within two months he approached the Kandy priesthood seeking a peace treaty. Such a pact proved elusive, although 300 captured Malays and Sepoys were freed. Nothing was signed but tacitly the two warring neighbours agreed to leave each other alone. The disastrous war simply petered out and there was relative peace for ten years.

★   ★   ★

King Sri Wikrama grew in stature and power. He had begun his reign as the puppet of his chief minister but he became a self-confident autocrat as Pilima Talauva's influence waned. The two men quarrelled incessantly. The arch-plotter hatched a plan to assassinate the king and take the realm by force without the British assistance he had cultivated during years of war. The revolt was premature and easily crushed. Pilima Talauva and his son-in-law were captured and beheaded. Six minor chiefs were impaled in a circle around them.

Maitland grew sick of dealing directly with the Kandyan royal house. He and his envoys made deals with important chieftains and created a web of secret alliances which undermined the king. When war inevitably broke out again a British invasion force once more tramped the hilltop paths. This time it met little resistance and the campaign was over in forty days. The king was deposed and Kandy ceded to the Empire by a convention signed by the chiefs on 2 March 1815. It pledged the British to honour Kandyan customs, protect the power and privileges of the chiefs and guarantee as 'inviolable' the rites of Buddhism. Sri Wikrama himself was captured and in January 1816 he was sent with his wives to Madras. More than 2,000 years of Sinhalese independence was over. His kingdom was plundered. The king's personal treasure and royal regalia were dispersed among friend and foe. Part was later recovered by the authorities and sold by auction in Colombo. It raised £3,840 for the Prize Fund which, as was Army practice at the time, was to be shared out among the victors. Exquisitely crafted gold and jewelled artefacts were broken up for the worth of their base metal. Others simply vanished into the bags of officers and men. They can still be found in the dusty glass cases and vaults of British country houses and provincial museums.

Sri Wikrama lived in rich exile until 1832 when he died of dropsy. He was fifty-two. He had been condemned during his lifetime as a butcher and a despot. He had also been exalted as a protector of his people and culture against British expansionism, a leader who had defied the mighty Empire and slaughtered its armies. Both were true.

In 1818 a full-scale rebellion was suppressed, the power of the chiefs reduced and heavier taxes imposed. Minor outbreaks occurred in the Highlands throughout the 1820s, followed by a bloodless revolt in 1834 and more bloodshed in 1848. But it can be argued that colonial rule delivered a century of peace until rioting between Tamils and Sinhalese began in 1958. That violence escalated during the following decades into a vicious civil war.

Sri Lanka is a paradise ruined by greed and hatred. It is bleeding again.

CHAPTER TWO

The Falklands, 1833

'Rejoice, rejoice'

The first clash of arms on the remote, wind-lashed Falklands (or Malvinas) occurred almost 150 years before a much larger conflict. It was not a war, rather a brief outburst of butchery involving just a handful of men, but the passions involved had vastly bloodier echoes many generations later. It too involved sea voyages across huge distances, diplomatic bungling and a power struggle over specks in the ocean once thought worthless.

It is as a precursor of the 1982 Falklands War – itself considered the last of British Empire-style small wars – that it is included here.

★   ★   ★

The Falklands, or the Malvinas, those desolate, remote, beautiful, storm-tossed islands in the South Atlantic, have always been dogged by

Location map of the Falkland Islands

controversy, including who it was that first set eyes on them. Argentinians claim it was Spain's Amerigo Vespucci in 1502 but there is precious little evidence to support this. England's John Davies claimed to have seen them in 1592 but that may have been wishful thinking. The best contender was neither Spanish nor British, but the Dutch adventurer Sebald de Weert, on 16 January 1600, and for many years the Falklands were called the Sebald Islands by Dutch cartographers. But there is no doubt that the first landfall was made in 1690 by John Strong, a Plymouth sea captain.

During much of the eighteenth century the islands were used as a staging post for British and French ships heading for the Horn. Both nations established small communities because of their trade and political interests in the South American continent. Spain paid France to abandon all claims to the islands and the British withdrew their settlers in 1774.

The Spanish established a colony on the main western island and ships' captains registered the few babies born there as Spanish. But across the Falklands Sound on the eastern island the crews of British and American sealing and whaling ships put in regularly, establishing permanent encampments. They recognized no Spanish sovereignty, nor indeed any laws but self-preservation and the common good of their fellow seamen.

In 1820 the Argentinian Government in Buenos Aires sent an American, Colonel David Jewett, to take possession of the islands. He found fifty ships sheltering in the jagged coves, vessels registered from Liverpool to New York. His dictates were ignored by the tough, weather-forged seamen and, unable to exercise any control, he returned to Argentina.

In 1829 Buenos Aires contracted a Franco-German immigrant, Louis Vernet, to establish a settlement at Port Louis on the eastern island. He set off with several English families, Germans, blacks, gauchos, Indians and transported felons. He found seventy settlers, mainly English, ahead of him. He organized his workforce and rounded up the wild cattle, and paid an English seaman, Matthew Brisbane, to patrol the coast in his schooner *Elbe*, collecting taxes. The captain of the American vessel *Harriet* refused to pay the required levy and the ship was impounded pending a court hearing in the Argentine capital. In retaliation Captain Silas Duncan of the USS *Lexington* was despatched to the islands. He took a number of colonists prisoner and ordered his crew to destroy as much of Vernet's settlement as possible. He arrested Brisbane and took him to Buenos Aires where the legal ramifications of the whole affair were thrashed out.

Port Louis had not yet been properly rebuilt in 1832 when a sergeant, José Francisco Mestivier, was appointed Governor of what the Spanish now called the Malvinas. José María Pinedo, commander of the *Sarandi*, replaced Brisbane as guardian of the coastline. Mestivier found the small army of colonists in rebellious mood, demanding the back pay which Vernet had promised them. Numbers of felons mutinied and Mestivier was cut down and slain. Pinedo took command and captured the mutineers with a detachment of his crew. He had no sooner done so when on 2 January 1833

Captain John James Onslow of the newly arrived HMS *Clio* informed him that he was claiming the islands for the British Crown. Pinedo, his own force weakened and demoralized, did not resist. The Argentine flag was lowered at Port Louis. Argentina later described the 'invasion' as an act of colonial piracy, a view which continues to feature in its school books. Pinedo with his men, some settlers and his prisoners sailed for Buenos Aires. Seven mutineers accused of Mestivier's murder were swiftly executed.

Captain Onslow, thirty-six years old, had served off the coasts of Spain, Jamaica and South America. His ancestors included a former Speaker of the House of Commons. His father, Admiral Sir Richard Onslow, had been a doughty fighter in the Napoleonic Wars. After a period chasing smugglers as Commander of the Coast Guard at Great Yarmouth the younger Onslow had been put in charge of the 18-gun, 389-ton sloop *Clio* in 1830 as she was being fitted out for the South American station. After his success Onslow ordered storekeeper William Dickson, an Irishman not highly regarded by visiting British officers, to fly a Union Jack whenever a ship anchored off the colony. He called in the farmworkers and labourers employed by Vernet and offered them a deal: they would continue their work and if within five months no one returned to pay them they could take the equivalent of their wages in wild cattle. Onslow set sail, either unaware of or indifferent to the potential trouble he left behind him. His offer was effectively a licence to rustle.

The colonists tried to return to normal under the new flag, isolated from international power play. Brisbane returned as superintendent of Vernet's business projects. Charles Darwin called for a few days on board HMS *Beagle*. The workmen faced appalling weather and grumbled about their unpaid wages as their debts mounted in Dickson's store. After five months the men tried to claim the cattle they had been promised but Brisbane and Dickson prevented that happening.

The mood in Port Louis – by now reduced to 21 men and 3 women – turned ugly. Legitimate grievances spawned talk of violence. Eight men, led by 26-year-old Antonio Rivero from Buenos Aires, plotted to take forcibly what they considered their due. They were initially deterred by the presence of Captain William Low, a sealing sailor and businessman, and nine seamen who were awaiting repatriation after their vessel had been sold. But at dawn on 26 August 1833 Low and four of his men sailed out of Berkley Sound for a brief seal hunt. Rivero saw his opportunity and struck with his followers, two gauchos and five Indian convicts. Their targets were settlement leaders they believed had wronged them, and what followed was certainly premeditated murder. They armed themselves with muskets, pistols, swords and knives and headed for Brisbane's house.

Brisbane was shot and killed. The captain of the gauchos, an Argentine representative called Juan Simón, was hacked to death with swords, as was the storekeeper Dickson. A German named Anton Wagnar was also slain in the murderous spree. A witness to the killings, Ventura Pasos, tried to flee but was brought down by an Indian's bolas. He was stabbed to death by Rivero. The murdered men, all unarmed, were the principals of the settlement.

The other colonists, mainly Argentinians, escaped from Port Louis. A dozen men, the women and two children took shelter in a cave on Hog Island at the head of Berkley Sound a few miles away. The rebels rampaged through the settlement, looting every home, and then drove the disputed cattle inland.

It was another two months before relief came, on 23 October, in the shape of the British survey ship *Hopeful*. Its captain offered help to the settlers but was unable to chase the renegades inland. He found the settlement 'ravaged'. He sent a message, warning 'if an English ship of war does not arrive here soon, more murders will take place', to the British South Atlantic commander in Rio de Janeiro who despatched HMS *Challenger*. On 7 January 1834 Lieutenant Henry Smith, appointed Officer Commander of East Falkland Island, stepped ashore with six Marines.

Smith, who had volunteered for the Navy in 1810, had enjoyed a moderately distinguished war service. He had specific instructions to keep the British flag flying over the Falklands, for which he was given an allowance of seven shillings in addition to naval half-pay. He was just in time to save the colonists huddled on Hog Island, who had lived largely on seabirds' eggs, from further attack. The Union Jack was hoisted while *Challenger* provided a 21-gun salute.

Smith and his men set after the Rivero mutineers. They combed the Eastern islands on horse and foot, relying on informants and dogged pursuit. Rivero, meantime, was negotiating with the master of the US ship *Antarctic* the sale of a fat cow and six steers. Smith heard of the deal from a missionary but Rivero vanished. His escape did not last long: his hiding place was betrayed by friends seeking amnesty and he surrendered to Smith. There was no further violence.

Rivero and five fellow renegades were sent in chains to Rio de Janeiro and then on to London. A court there refused to accept a trial because of confusion over whose jurisdiction the crimes came under. The Argentinian Government had already lodged a strong protest over the British occupation of the Malvinas and Britain did not want to spark further complaints about abuse of Rivero's human and legal rights. To avoid further antagonism the Rivero party was quietly shipped back across the Atlantic and put ashore at Montevideo later that year. The murder and carnage they had inflicted on unarmed men was forgotten. The Commander-in-Chief in Rio, Rear-Admiral Sir Graham Eden Hamond, conceded, 'It is a very slovenly way of doing business.'

Smith, meanwhile, was left virtually unaided to make the islands both secure for Britain and self-sufficient so they would not be a drain on the Crown. That task he set about with gusto, raising potatoes and corn, taming cattle and horses, cultivating and improving soil, repairing shelters vandalized by American and British sealers. By the time he was recalled he had built up stockpiles of supplies and seeds, and 350 tame cattle for slaughter. He had also made the Crown 4,200 Spanish dollars by the sale of 850 hides.

The Falklands formally became a British overseas colony in 1841. Argentina offered to accept that provided a previous loan was cancelled. The offer was declined and the islands have been in dispute ever since, with tragic consequences in 1982. The British taxpayer has shouldered the burden.

CHAPTER THREE

The Flagstaff War, 1845–6

'Opening the doors of a monster furnace'

The Maori was arguably the Victorian soldier's most formidable foe, and one he never properly beat. Yet the story of campaigns in the stinking mud and dense jungles of New Zealand, as fierce as any, is now an almost forgotten chapter in the forging of an Empire.

The first Maori War on North Island erupted four years after New Zealand became a colony. It was, absurdly, sparked by the destruction of a flagpole but there was nothing comical about the way the natives fought. The British forces expected to subdue a band of naked, undisciplined savages. Instead they faced a sophisticated warrior class, as disciplined as any Empire troops and often better equipped with more modern firearms. Instead of hit and run skirmishes and mopping up operations against defenceless villages the British repeatedly found themselves laying siege to strong, intricate fortresses complete with gun emplacements, rifle pits and bomb shelters. It was in part a throwback to medieval siege warfare, in part a foretaste of the trenches in a later, bigger war.

The British fighting men quickly recognized an equal adversary and their journals lack the sneering contempt for natives found in other colonial wars. Despite instances of cruel torture and possible cannibalism the historian Sir John Fortescue could later write: 'The British soldier held him in the deepest respect, not resenting his own little defeats, but recognising the noble side of the Maori and forgetting his savagery.'

★   ★   ★

It was 800 years since the Maoris, a Polynesian people, had discovered *Aotearoa*, the land of the long, white cloud. In that time they had developed, through tribal disputes over land and honour, a fast and furious form of warfare. Fleet-footed warriors, armed with spears or clubs edged with razor coral, would charge straight through the enemy, striking only one blow and running on to another. The crippled enemy would be finished off by those coming behind. In a rout one man, if he were fast enough, could stab or club ten or more. To counter such raiding tactics the tribes built complex fortifications on hilltops, surrounded by ditches, palisades and banks. Over

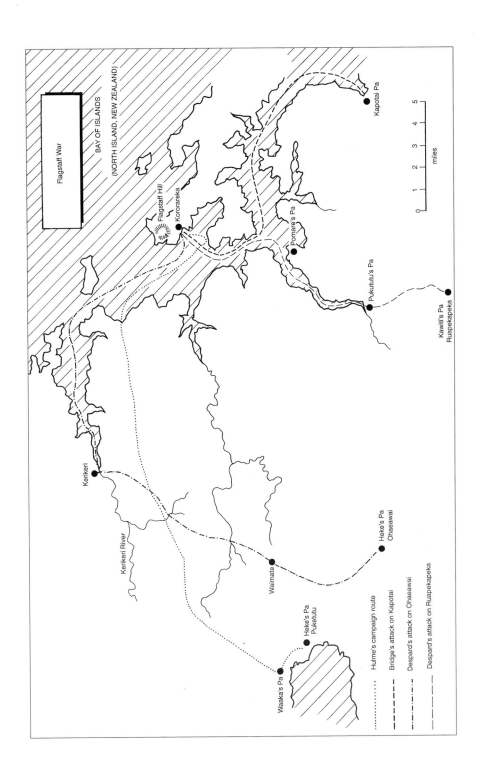

Flagstaff War

BAY OF ISLANDS

(NORTH ISLAND, NEW ZEALAND)

Kapotai Pa

Pomare's Pa

Flagstaff Hill
Kororareka

Pukututu's Pa

Kawiti's Pa
Ruapekapeka

Kerikeri

Kerikeri River

Waimate

Heke's Pa
Ohaeawai

Heke's Pa
Puketutu

Waaka's Pa

miles
0 1 2 3 4 5

.... Hulme's campaign route

– – – – Bridge's attack on Kapotai

–··–··– Despard's attack on Ohaeawai

— – — – Despard's attack on Ruapekapeka

4,000 such sites have been found in modern times, each providing evidence of communal defence and organized labour among forty tribes whose total population was somewhere between 100,000 and 300,000. The French explorer Marian du Fresne who sailed into the Bay of Islands in 1772 wrote: 'At the extremity of every village and on the point which jutted furthest into the sea, there was a public place of accommodation for all the inhabitants.'

Captain James Cook's 1777 journals described a fertile land of spectacular beauty inhabited by natives who, while aggressive, were intelligent and willing to trade. By the turn of the century European and American traders and whalers were using the Bay of Islands on the northern peninsula as a base. The settlement of Kororareka became a rowdy frontier town, a place of grog-shops, gambling dens and at least one brothel where pretty native girls exchanged their charms for liquor. It was known as the hell-hole of the Pacific. The Maori tribes traded extensively with the incomers and grew rich in the twin benefits of civilization – alcohol and modern firearms. The Colonial Office in London finally shook itself out of torpor and in 1840 the Union Flag was hoisted above the town, shortly before the rest of New Zealand came under the Crown.

The Maoris were – and remain – a tribal people with a strong sense of honour, of respect for the family, of a mystical sense of one-ness with their land. Children were taught that the land was sacred and that an insult must always be avenged. One proverb ran: 'The blood of man is land.' They were happy to trade with the white man but trouble flared when the Europeans began, slowly at first, to buy up, settle and fence off the ancient Maori homelands. More settlers flooded in. Land sharks from Sydney persuaded some chiefs to sell at rock bottom prices, creating a norm. It is a sickeningly familiar story of avaricious newcomers playing on the naive greed of individual chiefs at the expense of all.

The Colony's new Lieutenant-Governor Captain William Hobson set out in 1840 to defuse an explosive situation. He decreed that no land could be bought from the Maoris except through the Crown. He called a meeting of the chiefs at Waitangi and proposed a treaty in which they would cede their sovereignty to the British Queen in return for guarantees that they would retain undisputed possession of their remaining lands. Among the chiefs to speak in favour was Hone Heke Pokai of the Ngaphui. He argued that the only alternative was to see their strength sapped by 'rum sellers'. Five hundred chiefs signed the treaty.

A band of adventurers calling themselves the New Zealand Company had meanwhile established themselves near Wellington and declared that the treaty was not binding on them. After disputes over who owned what Hobson set up a land commission to investigate competing claims between the Company and the tribes. In July 1843 the Company clashed with two major chiefs, Te Rauparaha and his nephew Te Rangihaeata, over a slab of land just across the Cook Strait on South Island. Warriors harassed a survey team led by Captain Arthur Wakefield. The officer foolishly tried to arrest

Maoris from the Bay of Islands, 1845 (*Illustrated London News*)

the two chiefs but in a confused mêlée succeeded only in shooting dead Te Rangihaeata's wife. The enraged warriors took a terrible revenge and when the skirmish was over nineteen Englishmen and four Maoris were dead.

In the Colony's new capital of Auckland the Governor believed that the massacre had been provoked. The settlers, however, demanded military protection and Hobson sent 150 men from the North and further reinforcements from New South Wales. The tension quickly faded and there was no more bloodshed around Wellington. The reinforcements were sent back to Australia after missionaries complained about their drunkenness and fornication.

In the Bay of Islands the slaughter of the Englishmen had a profound impact on the mind of Hone Heke. He was a renowned warrior by birth and experience, in his mid-thirties, described by one officer as 'a fine looking man with a commanding countenance and a haughty manner'. He was not as heavily tattooed as other chiefs and had a prominent nose and a long chin. Like many of his people he was a Christian convert, having renounced youthful slaughter to train at Henry Williamson's mission station. Although he had backed British rule at Waitangi he had since become disillusioned. The new government encouraged the whalers to find new ports and trade with the Maoris subsequently declined. Customs duties on those ships calling into port replaced the native tolls. The living standards of his people suffered. American and French traders, jealous of British annexation, told Heke that the Union Flag represented slavery for natives and he began to see the flagstaff above Kororakeke township as a sign that the British intended stealing all tribal lands. It became an obsession with him. When Heke heard of the massacre in the south he asked: 'Is Te Rauparaha to have the honour of killing all the *pakehas* (white men)?'

In July 1844 he raided Kororareka to take home a Maori maiden living shamefully with a white butcher. The woman had previously been one of Heke's servants and at a bathing party on the beach she referred to him as a 'pig's head'. Almost as an afterthought a sub-chief cut down the flagstaff. His bloodless action triggered a bizarre charade. A new pole was erected by the garrison, now reinforced by 170 men of the 99th Lanarkshire Regiment sent from Australia. Heke cut it down. Another replaced it, only to be chopped down a third time. The matter became a test of wills when Governor Hobson died and he was replaced by Captain Robert Fitzroy, better known now as the captain of the *Beagle* during the voyage of Charles Darwin. He ordered a taller and stronger pole to be erected – an old ship's mizzen mast – defended by a stout blockhouse.

Fitzroy was particularly angered when Heke called on the United States Consul for support and later flew an American ensign from the stern of his war canoe. Between the toppling of the various poles the dangerous idiocy on both sides was almost ended several times. Heke guaranteed to replace the poles and protect British settlers. Fitzroy agreed to abolish the unpopular Customs charges which had hit Maori trade. But on the other side of the globe a House of Commons select committee chaired by Lord Howick, the future Earl Grey, decided to reinterpret the Treaty of Waitangi. They argued that the Maoris had no rights at all to the vast hinterland of unoccupied lands and urged that they should automatically fall to the Crown. The committee's report also criticized the 'want of vigour and decisions in the proceedings adopted towards the natives'. The implicit threat of a breached treaty was passed to the Maoris by helpful missionaries.

At dawn on 11 March 1845 Heke struck with unprecedented savagery. An officer and five men digging trenches around the blockhouse were swallowed by a flood of slashing, stabbing natives. As the troopers died the flagstaff was toppled. At the same time two columns of Maoris attacked the township below to create a diversion. Sailors and Marines guarding a naval gun on the outskirts fought hand to hand with cutlass and bayonet, pushing the attackers

Hone Heke Pokai, the Maori chief, and his wife, by J.J. Merrett (Alexander Turnbull Library, Wellington, NZ)

Kororareka Beach, Bay of Islands, 1845 (*Illustrated London News*)

back into a gully before themselves being forced back with their officer severely wounded and their NCO and four men dead. Troops in another blockhouse overlooking the main road exchanged fire with the attackers, as did civilians and old soldiers manning three ship's guns. Around 100 soldiers held the Maoris back as women and children were ferried out to the sloop *Hazard* and other ships anchored in the bay, including the US warship *St Louis*, an English whaler and Bishop Selwyn's schooner. Heke remained on Flagstaff Hill, satisfied with his day's work and not too anxious to press home the attack on the settlement if it meant too many casualties among his own men. Uncoordinated and half-hearted fighting continued throughout the morning, periods of eerie silence being shattered by bursts of gunfire and screams and the crackle of wooden buildings put to the torch. At 1 p.m. the garrison's reserve magazine exploded and fire spread from house to house. The cause of the conflagration was later attributed to a spark from a workman's pipe. Although Heke had shown no sign of attacking the township, save as diversionary tactics, the senior officer present, Naval Lieutenant Philpotts, and the local magistrate decided on a full evacuation of all able-bodied men. The remaining defenders scuttled for the ships and the safety offered by *Hazard*'s 100 guns.

The Maoris rampaged through the burning buildings, sparing two churches and the house of the Catholic Bishop Pompallier. When looters carried off some of the Bishop's household goods Heke threatened to have the thieves executed. Only a 3-mile hike by the Bishop to Heke's camp, after which he urged a pardon as enough blood had been shed, saved them. The Anglican Bishop Selwyn protested when Maoris calmly and soberly began to roll away casks of captured spirits. He said: 'They listened patiently to my remonstrances and in one instance they allowed me to turn the cock and allow the liquor to run upon the ground.' Other clergymen who later went ashore were well treated. Six settlers who returned to rescue valued possessions were not. They were butchered on the spot. In all 19 Europeans were killed and 29 wounded. The ships took the survivors to Auckland. To the Maoris, despite the reported loss of thirty-four of their own men, the white men had been humbled and the flagstaff, symbol of their pride and greed, lay in the mud.

★ ★ ★

Lieutenant-Colonel William Hulme, a sensible, no-nonsense veteran of the Pindari campaigns in India, was ordered to put down Heke's rebellion and avenge the deaths. He had under his command a small force of the 96th Regiment reinforced by a detachment of the 58th Rutlandshires, newly arrived from New South Wales: 8 officers and 204 men under Major Cyprian Bridge. Bridge was thirty-six, a literate and able commander whose journals contain a straightforward account of the frustrations and setbacks of the ensuing campaign. When they anchored in the Bay of Islands the regimental band played 'Rule Britannia' and 'The King of the Cannibal Islands'.

They were met by 400 friendly Maoris under Tamati Waaka Nene, a devoted ally of the British who saw Heke's revolt as a shameful breach of the oaths sworn at Waitangi. Hulme took great pains to ensure his troops knew the difference between hostile and friendly natives and promised severe punishment for any soldier who harmed a Maori ally. Many of the soldiers were uneducated country lads who were astonished at the natives' appearance: tall, fine-looking men, their bodies heavily tattooed, their cloaks richly decorated with feathers and pelts, their ears pierced with bone, ivory and brass. They were even more astonished to be joined by a few *pakeha* Maoris, white men who had 'gone native'. These included the colourful ex-convict Jackey Marmon from Sydney who boasted about the tribal enemies he had slaughtered in battle and eaten at cannibal feasts.

The flagstaff was quickly re-erected over the smoking and deserted settlement and Hulme's main force set off for the mouth of the Kawakawa river to deal first with Pomare, a local chieftain who had sided with Heke. The ships anchored off Pomare's *pa*, or fortress, which stood on an imposing headland. Pomare was arrested under a white flag. The chief was

Major Cyprian Bridge, officer and
war artist, in full dress uniform,
c. 1845 (*Illustrated London News*)

taken aboard the *White Star* and persuaded to order his men to surrender
their arms. The soldiers looted the empty *pa*, found a few rifles, and burnt it
to the foundations. It was an inglorious start to the campaign but those
thirsty for blood soon found it.

Hulme's next target was Heke's own *pa* at Puketutu near Lake Omapere
15 miles inland and close to the friendly Waaka's stronghold. The infantry
were augmented by seamen, Royal Marines and a three-pounder battery
under Lieutenant Egerton RN. They were ferried up the Kerikeri river and
then marched in good order through increasingly foul weather. Fierce and
sudden downpours added to the misery.

Hulme sent some men ahead with local guides to report on Heke's
position. They found a strong fortress with three rings of palisades made
musket-proof with flax leaves. The outer barricades were angled to pour
crossfire on any assailant. Between each line of defence were ditches and low
stone walls which offered shelter from bombardments. Maori riflemen
manned ditches behind the outer palisade, their guns pointing through
loopholes level with the ground.

Despite a lack of adequate artillery Hulme decided to attack the next
morning and his force advanced to within 200 yards of the *pa*. Three
storming parties were prepared. Hulme's plan depended on a terrifying

'The battle for Puketutu Pa', a watercolour by Cyprian Bridge (Alexander Turnbull Library, Wellington, NZ)

bombardment by Lieutenant Egerton's rocket battery. The Maoris believed the rockets would chase a man until he was killed. The truth soon proved rather more laughable. Egerton's first two rockets sailed hopelessly over the *pa*, carving crazy patterns in the still air. The third hit the palisades with a thunderous noise but when the smoke cleared there was virtually no damage. The remaining nine proved to be just as useless.

British troops and Waaka's Maoris were closing with the enemy when 300 hostile natives, led by Heke's ally Kawiti, dashed from concealment behind them, brandishing axes and double-barrelled guns. The men of the 58th turned around, fired and counter-charged with fixed bayonets. Kawiti's men later complained bitterly that the soldiers came at them with teeth gritted and yelling unseemly and unnecessary curses. The counter-charge shattered the enemy but the rest of the British force was then hit by a sally from the *pa* itself. Vicious hand-to-hand fighting around the Maori breastworks eventually drove the defenders back behind their palisades.

It was stalemate. British musket fire was ineffective against the strong defences, the rockets were used up, and Hulme realized that without heavier artillery he had no hope of a breakthrough. There was more inconclusive fighting amid nearby swamps but the first real battle of the war was over, a low-score draw. The British pulled back with 14 killed and 38 wounded.

Their enemy, by British accounts later disputed, lost 47 killed and 80 wounded, including Kawiti's two sons. The Maori's own flagstaff, carrying the Union Jack as an act of ironic derision, remained aloft above Heke's *pa*. The British returned, in low spirits, to their ships.

Hulme returned to Auckland leaving Major Bridge in command. Bridge decided to attack a *pa* up the Waikare river rather than allow his men's morale to sink even lower, kicking their heels in the Bay of Islands. His men barely rested, he set off with three companies of the 58th. At the river's mouth they switched to small boats, manned by sailors, with Auckland Volunteers and friendly Maoris as guides. Bridge intended to make a surprise attack and the raid was well planned at the start. The outcome was a messy if largely bloodless shambles.

Several miles upstream the boats stuck fast on mudflats. Small bands of soldiers were disembarked among scenes of noisy confusion. Some became bogged down in the mire, while Maori allies engaged in a running fight with natives who sallied from the forewarned *pa*. Waaka's men got the best of the skirmish but the enemy simply disappeared into the thick brush. The soldiers entered an empty *pa* and found only 'pigs, potatoes and onions.'

The *pa* was destroyed and, with the river's tidal waters high enough to float the boats off the mud, Bridge withdrew his tired and grimy force. There had been no British casualties but two of Waaka's men were dead and seven wounded. In less careful hands Bridge's expedition could have been a disaster. Misled by dubious guides and faulty intelligence Bridge had nevertheless behaved with calmness and common sense. Such qualities were not noticeable in the new commander of the British forces.

★   ★   ★

The forging of the British Empire saw its share of bone-headed bunglers. Colonel Henry Despard of the 99th is widely regarded as a prime example of that species. Despard received his first commission in 1799. His military thinking was stuck fast in the conventions of the Napoleonic era. He saw considerable action in India before taking up peacetime duties as Inspecting Officer of the Bristol recruiting district. In 1842 he took command of the 99th Lancashires, which had recently arrived in Australia. In New South Wales he outraged local civilians by snubbing a ball held in his honour, by blocking public roads around the barracks, and by having his buglers practise close to their homes. Despard insisted that his new command abandon its modern drill manuals and return to those of his younger days. The result was parade ground chaos which did not augur well for an active campaign. He was prone to apoplectic rages and rarely, if ever, listened to either advice or complaints. He had no doubts about his own abilities. Now aged sixty, it was thirty years since he had seen active service. He arrived in Auckland aboard the *British Sovereign* on 2 June with two companies of his regiment. Major Bridge's journal describes his mounting frustration at the arrogance and short-sighted stubbornness of his new CO.

Despard gathered his disparate force to move on the Bay of Islands. It was the biggest display of Western armed might yet seen by fledgling New Zealand: 270 men of the 58th under Bridge, 100 of the 99th under Major E. Macpherson, 70 of Hulme's 96th, a naval contingent of seamen and marines, 80 Auckland Volunteers led by Lieutenant Figg, to be used as pioneers and guides, all supported by four cannon – two ancient six-pounders and two twelve-pound carronades.

At Kororareka Despard was told Heke had attacked Waaka's *pa* with 600 men but Waaka had beaten them off with his 150 followers. Heke had suffered a severe thigh wound. Despard decided to launch an immediate assault on Heke's new *pa* at Ohaeawai, a few miles from Puketutu, despite foul winter weather which was turning tracks into quagmires.

Tamati Waaka Nene, Maori ally to the British (etching attributed to Robert F. Way)

During a miserable 12-mile march the cannon became stuck fast in the mud and the little army took shelter at the Waimate mission station. Despard was reduced to ranting fury. Waaka arrived with 250 warriors but Despard said sourly that when he wanted the help of savages he would ask for it. Luckily for him his Maori allies did not hear of the insult, and Despard must have changed his mind and the Maoris joined the British.

Most of the force stayed at the station for several days until fresh supplies were brought up. On 23 June, at 6 p.m., an advance detachment came within sight of Heke's *pa*. Alert Maoris swiftly opened fire but the scrub was up to 10 feet high and the skirmish line escaped slaughter, carrying back eight wounded comrades. The enemy marksmen retired to the safety of their stockade. The main British force caught up and encamped in a native village 400 yards from the *pa*. Waaka and his men occupied a conical hill nearby to protect the British from a flanking attack. A breastwork and battery for the guns was swiftly erected.

Heke's new *pa* was twice as strong as that at Puketutu. It was built on rising ground with ravines and dense forest on three sides, giving the defenders an easy route for supplies, reinforcements or withdrawal. There were three rows of palisades with 5-foot ditches between them. The outer stockade was 90 yards wide with projecting corners to allow concentric fire. The defenders, standing in the first inner ditch, aimed through loopholes level with the ground. The ditch was connected by tunnels to bomb shelters and the innermost defences. It was a sophisticated citadel and was well stocked. The Maoris had a plentiful supply of firearms and ammunition, some of it looted, the rest bought or bartered before the uprising. Four ship's guns were built into the stockade.

Officers, *pakeha* Maoris and native allies warned Despard of the fort's great strength. So too did Waaka. All such doubts were rebuffed. After one angry exchange Waaka was heard to mutter in his own language. Despard insisted on a translation. He was told: 'The chief says you are a very stupid person.'

The British battery opened fire at 10 a.m. on the 24th but 'did no execution'. The Maoris returned fire and until nightfall there was no let-up in the fusillades of shell, ball and grape. Bridge wrote that much shot burst within the *pa* and 'I fancy they must have lost many men.' The following day the bombardment continued but the flax-woven palisades made it impossible to see how much damage was done to the defences. The shot was simply absorbed by the flexible material.

Despard decided that only a night attack would breach the stockade. He prepared storming parties with ladders ready for 2 a.m. He ordered the construction of flax shields, each 12 feet by 6, to be carried by advanced parties. That night Sergeant-Major William Moir said: 'The chances are against us coming out of this action. I look upon it as downright madness.' Luckily for everyone concerned a storm in the early hours prevented the night attack. The following morning the flax shields were tested and to the surprise of few the shot passed clean through. After that demonstration few soldiers trusted Despard's ability and some doubted his sanity. Another of his bright ideas involved firing 'stench balls' at the enemy. That also flopped.

The physical condition of the British deteriorated as rain poured incessantly on their crude shelters. Their clothing was reduced to rags, in some cases barely recognizable as uniforms. There was no meat and little flour but a gill of rum was given to each man every morning and evening. Taken on an empty stomach and supplemented by local native liquor the result could be devastating. Drunkenness, a problem throughout the New Zealand campaign, increased. There were fights over the firm-limbed and cheerful native women.

A new battery was built closer to the *pa*'s right flank and quickly came under hot fire which wounded several soldiers and killed a sailor. An enemy raid was beaten off but the guns were withdrawn. Despard demanded that HMS *Hazard*'s 32-pounder be dragged from the mouth of the Kerikeri. After a brutal and agonizing haul it was manhandled into position halfway up the conical hill by twenty-five sailors. Despard planned to attack as soon as the big gun had softened up the outer defences. He told Bridge: 'God grant we may be successful but it is a very hazardous step and must be attended with great loss of life.'

On the morning of 1 July the enemy launched a surprise attack on Waaka's camp on the conical hill, aimed at killing Waaka himself. A number of Heke's men moved undetected through the forest and emerged behind the camp. Caught off guard, the native allies streamed down the hill with their women and children. Despard, who had been inspecting the cannon, was engulfed in the panic-stricken human tide. He ran into the British camp and ordered a bayonet charge up the hill. The soldiers came under crossfire from hill and *pa* but by then only a few of the enemy were left on the summit and it was quickly retaken. The attackers withdrew when they realized that Waaka had escaped.

Despard was driven to characteristic fury by his ignominious sprint into his own camp. His temper must have deepened with ill-concealed sniggers from the ranks of his tattered army. He decided to attack that same afternoon. The bombardment had clearly failed to leave gaping holes in the outer stockade and the enemy appeared unscathed. His troops and their Maori allies regarded a frontal assault as suicidal. But no appeals to caution would persuade him otherwise. The scene was set for tragedy.

His plan, such as it was, was to focus the attack on a narrow front at the *pa*'s north-west corner, which Despard believed had been damaged by the cannonfire. Twenty Volunteers under Lieutenant Jack Beatty were to creep silently to the outer stockade to test the defenders' alertness. They were to be quickly followed by 80 grenadiers, some seamen and pioneers under Major Macpherson, equipped with axes, ropes and ladders to pull down sections of the wood and flax perimeter. Behind these were to be 100 men under Major Bridge who were expected to storm through the gaps into the *pa*. They in turn were to be backed by another wave of 100 men under Colonel Hulme. Despard planned to lead the remainder of his force into the stockade to mop up and accept the enemy surrender.

The Maori plan of defence was less elaborate. One unknown chief called out: 'Stand every man firm and you will see the soldiers walk into the ovens.'

At 3 p.m. precisely on a bright and sunny afternoon the storming parties fell in. There was no surprise. They charged in four closely packed ranks, according to regulations, with just twenty-three inches between each rank. Fifty yards from the *pa* the men cheered. Corporal William Free later wrote: 'The whole front of the *pa* flashed fire and in a moment we were in a one-sided fight – gun flashes from the foot of the stockade and from loopholes higher up, smoke half hiding the *pa* from us, yells and cheers and men falling all around. A man was shot in front of me and another was hit behind me. Not a single Maori could we see. They were all safely hidden in their trenches and pits, poking the muzzles of their guns under the fronts of the outer palisades. What could we do? We tore at the fence, firing through it, thrusting our bayonets in, or trying to pull a part of it down, but it was a hopeless business.'

The Maoris allowed Macpherson's men to come within yards of the stockade before opening up with every gun they had. Their blistering fire was later described as like 'the opening of the doors of a monster furnace'. Only a handful of men with axes and ladders reached the barrier. Despard, supported by Bridge, later claimed that the Auckland Volunteers had dropped flat at the first fusillade and would not budge thereafter. The surviving men at the foot of the stockade scrabbled hopelessly at the interwoven flax, firing at the occasional glimpse of a tattooed face within.

Bridge was no slacker and he and his men were soon caught in the same murderous fire. He wrote: 'When I got up close to the fence and saw the way it resisted the united efforts of our brave fellows to pull it down and saw them falling thickly all around, my heart sank within me lest we should be defeated. Militia and Volunteers who carried the hatchets and ladders would not advance but laid down on their faces in the fern. Only one ladder was placed against the fence and this by an old man of the Militia.'

Despard watched the bloody shambles from the rear earthworks. Even he realized that such slaughter was worthless. A bugle call to withdraw was ignored in the heat of battle. A second call finally penetrated the brains of men conditioned to believe that retreat in the face of half-naked savages was unthinkable. The survivors dragged as many of their wounded comrades back with them as was feasible. Some soldiers returned two or three times through a hell of musket smoke and shot to rescue their mates. One wounded man was shot dead as he was carried on the back of Corporal Free, who dropped the corpse and carried another soldier to safety. Hulme's supporting party covered the retreat well with substantial fire which kept enemy heads down. But the casualties suffered in just seven minutes of fighting were fearful. At least one-third of the British attackers had been killed or wounded. Three officers, including Beatty, were dead and three injured. Some 33 NCOs and privates were killed and 62 wounded, four of whom later died. The Maoris lost ten at most. Bridge wrote: 'It was a heartrending sight to see the number of gallant fellows left dead on the field and to hear the groans and cries of the wounded for us not to leave them behind.'

The jubilant Maori defenders rejected a missionary's flag of truce and during that long night held a noisy war dance. The dispirited troops huddled in their camp and mourned their dead and tended their casualties and wondered who would be next. They were tormented by the 'most frightful screams' from within the *pa*, screams which haunted all who heard them.

Two more days passed before Heke allowed the British to collect their dead from the charnel field in front of his stockade. Several corpses had been scalped, beheaded and otherwise horribly mutilated. One, that of a soldier of the 99th, bore the marks of being bound, alive, by flax. His thighs had been burnt and hacked about. A hot iron had been thrust up his anus. The soldiers knew then the source of those terrible nocturnal screams.

Despard prepared to break camp and return, beaten, to Waimate. Waaka and his chiefs, hungry for loot, persuaded him to stay a few more days at least. More shot and shell for the cannon were brought up and the bombardment of the *pa* resumed. It continued ceaselessly for another day. That night dogs began howling within the *pa*. It was a sign, according to Maori allies, that the enemy were withdrawing. The following morning, while the British slept, Waaka's warriors slipped into the fort and found it empty. They looted everything, including weapons taken off the dead. They condescended to sell the outraged British the odd sack of potatoes. Everything else they kept for future trade. One officer missing in action, Captain Grant, was found in a shallow grave near the palisade. Flesh had been cut off his thighs, apparently for eating.

After inspecting the *pa*'s defences from the inside Bridge wrote: 'This will be a lesson to us not to make too light of our enemies, and show us the folly of attempting to carry such a fortification by assault, without first making a practicable breach.' The *pa* was burnt but there was no sense of victory. Heke had simply moved to build a new stronghold elsewhere, no great inconvenience. Too many lives had ended for no good reason.

* * *

Despard reported back to Auckland, anxious to pin blame for the carnage on anyone but himself, and taking with him the men of the 99th and 96th. Major Bridge was left in command of the 58th at Waimate. Back pay for all ranks was sent up to the mission station. Much of it was spent immediately on drinking and gambling by men anxious to blot out the horror and shame of Ohaeawai. Inevitably discipline grew lax. One private, a veteran who had been wounded at Puketutu, was accidentally shot dead on guard duty. The dead man, 22-year-old Private Ingate had been a Norfolk farm labourer before enlisting. His comrade Sergeant Robert Hattaway wrote: 'He allways told us he would never Be shot by a Maorie. It was true for him. . . .' One man was caught in the act of stealing rum from a barrel. But he was a family man and Hattaway, a newly promoted NCO, spared him a court martial. Another offender was not so lucky: an American Volunteer with a record for insubordination, he was found guilty at a drumhead court martial of cursing the British flag and immediately suffered fifty lashes.

Bridge tried to keep his men occupied by building stout earthworks and other defences around the camp as protection against an enemy elated by victory. These were almost complete when Despard returned, bubbling with his now familiar petulance. He said it was demeaning to build ramparts to defend a well-armed European force against a 'barbarian enemy'. He ordered the earthworks flattened. Bridge held his tongue but clearly believed that the slaughter in front of Heke's *pa* had taught his commander nothing.

Governor Fitzroy, anxious to get Heke to make peace, ordered the 58th withdrawn to camp among the ruins of the Kororareka settlement. His willingness to talk, and his careful conduct in the run-up to the Flagstaff War, were severely criticized in Auckland and London. He was accused of being over-protective of the interests of the aborigines and 'losing sight of the fundamental principles, that indulgence may be abused and forebearance misconstrued'. In his own defence he later wrote: 'Had I not treated them with consideration, and had not the public authorities been very forebearing, the destruction of Auckland and Wellington would have been matters of history before this period. An overpowering multitude have been restrained hitherto by moral influence.' He added: 'My object always was to avoid bringing on a trial of physical strength with those who, in that respect, were overwhelmingly our superiors; but gradually to gain the necessary influence and authority by a course of scrupulous justice, truth and benevolence.' Such sentiments did not match the thirst for revenge and Fitzroy was recalled.

His replacement was 34-year-old Captain George Grey whose early service in Ireland had convinced him that the frontiers of the civilized world must be widened to provide fresh opportunities for the poor, landless and hungry. He had served in Australia, and on the *Beagle*, and had impressed his superiors with his efficiency, diligence and courage. His remit was to punish the natives, end an increasingly costly conflict and bring 'financial and commercial prosperity' to the settlements. He told the Legislative Council: 'You may rely that my sole aim and object shall be to settle upon a sure and lasting basis the interests of yourselves and of your children, and to give effect to her Majesty's wise and benevolent desire for the peace and happiness of all her Majesty's subjects in this interesting portion of her empire, and upon which the regards of so large a portion of the civilized world are now anxiously fixed.' He also warned the settlers that he would, if necessary, use his full powers under martial law and aim to secure in any peace the 'freedom and safety' to which the aborigines were also entitled.

Grey decided he must see the troubles in the North at first hand. On reaching the Bay of Islands he made some attempts to parley with Heke and Kawiti. But becoming impatient, he demanded an immediate reply to Fitzroy's earlier peace moves. Further delays gave him the excuse to mobilize his forces. Those forces were now impressive as Grey had brought with him considerable reinforcements from Auckland. They included 563 officers and men of the 58th, 157 of the 99th, 42 Volunteers, 84 Royal Marines, a 313-strong Naval Brigade, 450 friendly Maoris – a total of just over 1,600 men plus six cannon including two 32-pounders, four mortars and two rocket tubes.

Between 7 and 11 December the British decamped and moved up the Kawakawa river to attack the 'Bat's Nest' – Kawiti's *pa* at Ruapekapeka, strongly built on a densely wooded hillside. Again drunkenness impeded the expedition. A few 'old troopers' were over-ready to blast away at anything that moved in the woods . . . wild pigs, birds and shadows. The advance faltered as bullocks, heavy carts and cannon stuck fast in the liquid mud. Christmas was celebrated by the men in teeming misery relieved only by rum. Officers noted in the diaries that the Christian natives showed great devotion in observing the day and attending mass.

By the 27th several cannon were in position overlooking the Bat's Nest and opened fire. Despard heard worrying reports that Heke had left his own refuge and was marching with 200 men to join Kawiti at Ruapekapeka. After exasperating delays which drove Despard into deeper rages, the big 32-pounders were dragged up to join the first cannon in a formidable battery 1,200 yards from the enemy *pa*. The Maoris, however, were well entrenched and their defences included solid underground bunkers which resisted every shot. After each bombardment they simply emerged to repair the little damage done to the stockades. Despard later wrote: 'The extraordinary strength of this place, particularly in its interior defences, far exceeded any idea I could have formed of it. Every hut was a complete fortress in itself, being strongly stockaded all round with heavy timbers sunk deep in the ground . . . besides having a strong embankment thrown up behind them. Each hut had also a deep excavation close to it, making it completely bomb-proof, and sufficiently large to contain several people where at night they were sheltered from both shot and shell.'

Most of the British column, including several cannon and mortars, were still on the trail. Bridge complained that the bombardment was pointless until all men and guns were in place and deployed to concentrate intensive fire on the *pa*'s weakest points. Instead Despard, bizarrely and to conserve ammunition, would not allow more than one cannon to be fired at any one time. Bridge wrote: 'How deplorable it is to see such ignorance, indecision and obstinacy in a Commander who will consult no one . . . and has neither the respect nor the confidence of the troops under his command.' He added: 'Our shot and shell are being frittered away in this absurd manner instead of keeping up constant fire.'

The lacklustre bombardment continued until another battery was built closer to the *pa*, protected by 200 men. This was swiftly attacked in a sortie from the stockade and the enemy were beaten back with only light casualties on either side. The fiercest fighting was between Kawiti's men and friendly Maoris on 2 January. In a confused and fragmented fight in thick brushland the enemy were driven back into the *pa*. From its barricades they taunted the white men, daring them to charge as they had done at Ohaeawai.

The siege dragged on through wet days and nights. Conditions in the British lines grew appalling. Disease and exposure put many men out of action. Reinforcements and fresh supplies were lost or abandoned on forest trails. Drunkenness continued and could not be curbed. Ammunition was wasted not just by Despard's tactics but by jittery soldiers who saw a foe behind every bush. Men and officers who had proved themselves ready to be heroes if given the chance sank into despair at their shabby leadership.

On 8 January eighty of the enemy were spotted leaving the safety of the *pa* and disappearing into the forest. Governor Grey urged Kawiti by message to send away the Maori women and children as he did not want them hurt in the bombardment. The British received more reports of small bands of warriors melting away with their families. The determination of those who stayed within the *pa* was stiffened, however, by the arrival of Heke, although he had with him only sixty men and not the reported 200.

At last, on 10 January, the entire British arsenal was in position – the 32-pounders, smaller cannon, mortars, rockets and small arms. They opened up a ferocious crossfire on the *pa*'s outer defences. Despard wrote: 'The fire was kept up with little intermission during the greater part of the day; and towards evening it was evident that the outer works . . . were nearly all giving way.' The stockade was breached in three places. Despard was almost delirious with excitement and prepared for a frontal assault. A Maori ally, guessing his intent, shouted at him: 'How many soldiers do you want to kill?' Other chiefs told Grey that an attack now would result in the same waste of life as at Ohaeawai, but if they waited until the following day the enemy would have fled. Grey listened, agreed and overruled Despard, much to the colonel's irritation.

On the following morning Waaka's brother William and a European interpreter crept up to the stockade. They heard nothing from inside except for dogs barking. The *pa* seemed deserted and a signal was given to the nearest battery. A hundred men under Captain Denny advanced cautiously with native allies. Some men pushed over a section of fencing and entered the *pa*.

It had not been deserted. The explanation for the eerie silence was rather more strange, and rich with irony. It was a Sunday and the Christian Maoris, the majority of the defenders including Heke, had assumed that

Christian soldiers would never attack on the Sabbath. Heke and the other believers had retired to a clearing just outside the far stockade to hold a prayer meeting. Only Kawiti and a handful of non-Christian warriors were left inside when the British stepped through the breach.

Too late Kawiti realized what was happening. He alerted the Maoris outside and threw up hasty barricades within the *pa*. He and his men managed spasmodic fire against the incoming troops. Heke and the rest of the garrison made a determined effort to re-enter the *pa*, firing through holes in its walls created earlier by the British cannon. Several British troops were killed and wounded but more troopers and native allies swarmed into the *pa*. In a topsy-turvy engagement the defenders became the attackers and vice versa within moments. Heke and the rest were pressed back to the tree-line of the surrounding forest and sheltered behind a natural barrier of fallen tree trunks.

A party of sailors, seeing action for the first time, charged this position and were shot down one by one. Three sergeants – Speight, Stevenson and Munro – and a motley band of soldiers, seamen and natives emerged from the *pa* and threw themselves at the makeshift barricade with such fury that the enemy withdrew deeper into the forest. The sergeants were each commended in orders and when, in 1856, the Victoria Cross was instituted Speight's name was put forward for a retrospective citation. The award was vetoed on the grounds that no VCs could be awarded for action prior to the Crimean War.

Kawiti and his stragglers fought their way clear of the *pa* and joined Heke and the other fleeing warriors in the forest. The battle was over. The British had succeeded because the Christian Maoris were more scrupulous in observing the faith than the Christian Europeans. It may have been farcical but it was not a bloodless victory. Friendly Maori casualties were not recorded but the British lost 12 men killed, including 7 sailors from HMS *Castor*, and 30 wounded, two of whom later died. Despard claimed that the enemy's losses were severe, including the deaths of several chiefs, but he was keen to add to the scale of the victory. He explained that a body count was not possible as the Maoris 'invariably carry off both killed and wounded when possible'. Ruapekapeka was burnt. The First Maori War, an unconventional campaign, had ended in a suitably offbeat way.

★ ★ ★

Despard did not enjoy popular acclaim for the victory. He exaggerated the scale and ferocity of the final battle in his despatches, although his reference to 'the capture of a fortress of extraordinary strength by assault, and nobly defended by a brave and determined enemy' contains some truths. His bravado cut no ice with the colonial press who lambasted him mercilessly. An editorial in *The New Zealander* condemned his 'lengthened, pompous, commendatory despatch'. Puzzled, angered and saddened by such barbs

Despard left for Sydney on 21 January. Bridge noted caustically that his departure was 'much to the satisfaction of the troops'. Despard retained command of the 99th until he was seventy but, happily for the men under him, never saw active service again. He died, a major-general, in 1858. He never, according to contemporaries, understood the ill gratitude he received. Many of his men, grieving for fallen comrades, would quite happily have hanged him.

Heke and Kawiti first tried to join up with their former ally Pomare but that wily old brigand knew which way the wind was now blowing and refused them aid. The rebel chiefs knew that the time to talk peace had now come. They opened negotiations with Governor Grey using their enemy Waaka as a go-between. Kawiti was prepared to agree peace for ever more. Heke, however, insisted that a Maori flagstaff should be erected alongside the Union Jack. Grey for his part rescinded all threats to seize Maori lands and granted free pardons to both chiefs and their men. He promised that all concerned in the rebellion 'may now return in peace and safety to their houses; where, so long as they conduct themselves properly, they shall remain unmolested in their persons and properties'. Her Majesty, he said, had an 'earnest desire for the happiness and welfare of her native subjects in New Zealand'.

The clemency shown by the Governor was not due to humanitarian feelings. Grey needed to bring the Northern troubles to a swift conclusion because his troops were desperately required in the South to deal with violence which had flared up around Wellington. The causes were familiar: a new clash between the land-hungry New Zealand Company and the chief Te Rangihaeata, whose earlier massacre of white men had so encouraged Heke.

The murders, sieges and inconclusive campaigning that followed in the South cannot properly be regarded as part of the Flagstaff War. Rather it was a foretaste of the bloodshed that was to follow with little let-up for another two decades. But in the North, around Auckland, the peace treaties were honoured by both sides and the occasional violent clash was small in scale.

Most of the 58th, which had done the lion's share of the fighting, left for Australia after a riotous ball organized by the grateful ladies of Auckland. Bridge and almost every other officer in the regiment were mentioned in despatches for their bravery, although these were the days before medals for courage were awarded. Bridge, after a long wait, took command of the regiment, at the age of fifty-one. His military career after New Zealand was uneventful. He retired in 1860, broken-hearted by the death of his second wife and of all but one of his many children. He died in Cheltenham in 1885, aged seventy-eight.

Corporal Free, who had written such a vivid account of the attack and tragedy at Ohaeawai, stayed in New Zealand and served with the Rifle Volunteers. He died, aged ninety-three, in 1919. Sergeant William Speight, the hero of Ruapekapeka, may not have been awarded a Victoria Cross but years later he was granted a Meritorious Service Medal and a £10 annuity for that action; he was the only veteran of the first Maori War to receive the medal. He stayed with the 58th and retired, a staff sergeant-major, in 1858 to settle permanently in New Zealand.

In 1848 Heke, who never fully accepted British rule, caught consumption which left him defenceless against other illnesses. He died two years later at Kaikohe, aged only forty. His one consolation was that the hated British flagstaff was not re-erected in his lifetime. Kawiti was converted to Christianity. He too died young, in 1853. It is likely, although impossible to prove, that had they lived longer both chiefs would have been leaders in the uprisings that devastated New Zealand through the 1850s and 1860s. The pattern set in their initial war was repeated with rising casualties and greater atrocity on either side.

The Maoris were never truly beaten but neither could they win against the tide of colonists who flooded to their green land. By 1858 there were 60,000 incomers, a decade later 220,000. The British Government decided they now sufficiently outnumbered the natives to be able to take care of themselves and the last troops were withdrawn in 1870. The wars were over but random butchery continued in isolated glades. Overwhelming numbers and disease crippled and contained the daring Maori. But the spark of resistance did not die out. In 1928 an anonymous Maori wrote: 'We have been beaten because the *pakeha* outnumber us in men. But we are not conquered or rubbed out, and not one of these *pakeha* can name the day we sued for peace. The most that can be said is that on such and such a date we left off fighting.'

CHAPTER FOUR

The Jamaica Rebellion, 1865

'Skin for skin, the iron bars is now broken . . .'

On 7 October 1865 at Morant Bay in Jamaica a black boy was convicted of assaulting a woman of his own impoverished village; the magistrate fined him two shillings with twelve shillings and sixpence costs. Over the next few days almost twenty officials and policemen, half of them white, were butchered and another thirty-five wounded. Within five weeks 439 blacks were killed in a merciless campaign of revenge. No fewer than 354, including seven women, were shot or hanged after summary courts martial, often on the flimsiest evidence. Fifty prisoners were killed without trial by soldiers and sailors, 25 by Maroons and 10 in other ways. Around 600 more were viciously whipped, some – including women – with cat-o'-nine-tails 'enhanced' with twisted wire. Fifty lashes were the norm but some received 100. Over a thousand homes were destroyed by fire.

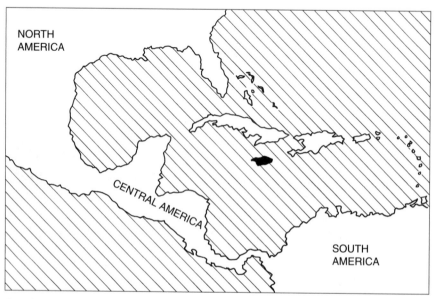

Location map of Jamaica

It is one of the worst stains on the history of the British Empire. Military might, religious fervour and blind fear combined together in a campaign of racist vengeance rare even by the cruel standards of the age. For many the possession of a black face in the wrong place was punishable by death. The origins lay in slavery, land rights and injustice. White arrogance and perceived black ignorance played their part in fanning a little local difficulty into such obscene over-reaction.

As insurrections go it was a small affair but it sparked a heated debate at a time when the queen and her privileged subjects prided themselves on the benevolent and paternal nature of British rule. A *Times* editorial said: 'Though a flea bite compared with the Indian Mutiny, it touches our pride more and more in the nature of a disappointment.' And the horrific aftermath divided public opinion bitterly. The *Annual Register*, not noted for its liberal interpretation of events, recorded: 'On the one side it is alleged that the severest measures were imperatively necessary to save the colony from destruction, and on the other it is clamorously asserted that a riot was mistaken for a revolt, and that the course pursued by the authorities implicates them in the crime of murder.'

* * *

Jamaica is another island paradise whose history has been shaped by the cutlass and the musket, in blood, anguish and greed. Lush and temperate,

Port Royal in the 1850s (*Illustrated London News*)

Jamaican slaves learn of their freedom on Emancipation Day, 1 August 1833 (*Illustrated London News*)

with mangrove, 200 species of orchids and a plateau of grey limestone, its central position in the Caribbean has always attracted adventurers.

It is alleged, but hotly contested, that the West 'discovered' the island when Columbus landed in 1494. During the Spanish conquest and settlement the native Arawak Indians were completely exterminated and Negro slaves were imported to replace them in the fields. Oliver Cromwell's commanders expelled the Spanish in 1660 after a five-year campaign and the slaves, whose blood had mixed with the Spaniards' and who were now called Maroons, took to the mountains. They fought to the end of the eighteenth century in fruitless attempts to gain their independence.

Under nominal English rule Jamaica became a haven for buccaneers, with planters and merchants supplementing their incomes with a bit of piracy. After a decade of mayhem the buccaneers were suppressed and in 1672 the Royal Africa Company, with its monopoly of the English slave trade, turned Jamaica into a huge market in human beings. In 1692 an earthquake destroyed much of the capital Port Royal and Kingston was built to replace it. French and Spanish invasions were beaten off in 1782 and 1806. During this period Jamaica was, for the white planters, at the peak of its prosperity. The sugar and coffee trade was booming and there were more than 300,000 slaves at work. But the abolition of the slave trade in 1807, together with a drop in sugar prices when the war ended, ended the boom days.

The 1833 Emancipation Act was a further blow although planters were paid £19 per slave compensation. Many of the freed slaves left the plantations to become hill farmers, leaving behind a chronic shortage of cheap labour. Sugar prices dropped further with the scrapping of tariff protection. White farmers faced an uncertain and impoverished future. Many went bust and between 1804 and 1854 the number of sugar estates fell from 859 to 330 and sugar production dropped by a half. Although their real grievance was with the British the planters, and therefore the Jamaican authorities, blamed the alleged laziness of the black labourers who had chosen to stay behind. Resentment against the blacks rose.

So, too, did the whites' terror of a black insurrection. A 1760 uprising resulted in the execution of one rebel by slow burning, starting with his feet, while two more were starved to death in a public hanging cage. The 1831 Baptist rebellion, encouraged by preachers, left hundreds of slaves dead.

After emancipation, renewed fears had been stoked by the creation of the black-ruled Republic of Haiti during the Napoleonic Wars. An abhorrence of blacks, possibly explained psychologically by fear of the unknown coupled with guilt at their exploitation, was reflected in the literature of the day. Sir Richard Burton compared Africans with animals; the explorer Sir Samuel Baker said they were 'not to be compared with the noble character of the dog'. The horrors of the Indian Mutiny remained fresh in British minds, as will be seen later. And Jamaica's Governor, Edward John Eyre, writing later to justify his actions, blamed the Press and rabble-rousers for

George William Gordon,
accused of inciting an
insurrection (Institute of
Jamaica)

leading an 'ignorant, excitable and uncivilised population' into 'rebellion, arson, murder'.

In 1860 Jamaica saw the 'Great Revival' centred on the local Baptist and Methodist Churches. Religious revivalists and political agitators made natural allies. White pastors and nonconformists had long supported their poor black congregations but the discontent expressed in church services developed overtly political overtones. One commentator reported 'fanaticism, disorder, delusion'. Foremost among the agitators was a self-ordained Baptist minister, George William Gordon, the illegitimate son of a rich white planter and a black mother. He was born about 1820 and his father, Joseph Gordon, was an attorney who represented absentee-owned sugar plantations, earning enough to be able to buy several estates in the foothills north of Kingston. He eventually rose to be an Assemblyman and Custos of St Andrews but offered little care, support or even acknowledgement to either his son or the mother. The young George taught himself to read and at eighteen he was well regarded as a bright, popular charmer with a gift for public speaking. He was also deeply religious but became dissatisfied with the structures of existing churches. He established a store selling local produce and was praised as a 'man of ready business habits'. The business prospered and by 1842 Gordon was reckoned to be worth £10,000. He sent his twin sisters to be educated at his expense in England and France, and married Lucy Shannon, the white daughter of an Irishman. Meanwhile his father's fortunes declined badly. Although his father had ignored him since infancy – George was never allowed into the family home – Gordon sorted out the elder man's tangled financial affairs. He paid off debts on his father's estates and helped support him and his 'legitimate' white family. Gordon was described as 'a man of princely generosity and unbounded benevolence'. He also never forgot his mother. On one occasion, with tears in his eyes, he pointed to a grassy mound in a copse and said: 'My mother is buried there. She was a Negro and a slave, but she was a kind mother to me and I loved her dearly.'

During the 1850s Gordon, by now the owner of several estates, was elected to the House of Assembly where he championed the cause of peasant farmers and newly emancipated slaves. He was for a period the owner of the *Watchman* newspaper, became a magistrate and helped found the Jamaica Mutual Life Assurance Society. He set up an independent Baptist Church and preached from his own chapel in Kingston. In both religion and politics he was renowned as a gifted orator. Never an advocate of armed rebellion or the overthrow of white rule, he did, however, get involved in petty disputes within his parish of Morant Bay. One, over the conduct of a fellow-magistrate, led to his removal from the bench. Another, involving his application to be a churchwarden, would have devastating personal consequences. He was rejected by the local Custos, Baron von Ketelhodt, on the grounds that he was not a member of the Church of England. Gordon challenged the Custos twice through the courts. He lost both times and costs were awarded against him. A third trial was pending in October. The Jamaica Commission later reported: 'All these proceedings had produced considerable irritation in the western part of the parish, and especially among the members of the Native Baptist Communion to which Mr Gordon belonged.'

It was hardly surprising that he clashed, often and vehemently, with the new Governor, Edward John Eyre. Eyre arrived in 1862 as stand-in for Captain Charles Darling, who was on leave in England. After two years Darling was dispatched to Australia and Eyre was confirmed as his successor.

Prior to his arrival in Jamaica, Eyre had a decent record as a colonial administrator among native people. As a young man he was a noted explorer of Australia. He was appointed Protector of Aborigines and was later promoted Lieutenant-Governor of New Zealand. In the West Indies he was Protector of Indian labourer immigrants in Trinidad and was again promoted Lieutenant-Governor, this time of the Leeward Islands. But he was also stubborn to the point of blindness and a fervent Anglican who hated dissenters, particularly Baptists, which perhaps makes it easier to understand his antipathy towards Gordon and his followers. Clinton Black wrote: 'He associated only with the white ruling class to whose interests he was sympathetic. He was incapable of mixing with and understanding the black population, nor did he understand the multi-racial future that was the only possible one for Jamaica.'

Eyre regarded Gordon as a dissenter and a rabble-rouser. He had Gordon removed from his post as a member of the St Thomas Vestry because he

Edward John Eyre, Governor of Jamaica (*Illustrated London News*)

dared to complain about the filthy conditions in the local gaol, where a vagrant was found dying, unattended, in a latrine. In January 1864 Gordon berated the Governor in the Assembly, declaring: 'If we are to be governed by such a Governor much longer, the people will have to fly to arms and become self-governing.' This was the typical rhetoric of the Assembly: outside Gordon advocated peaceful protest only.

The general grievances of the blacks were simple. The planters' pay was too little. The labourers felt that little had been gained from their emancipation save the right to live in poverty wherever they chose. They resented the different treatment afforded the Indian immigrants brought in to fill labouring shortages. The slightly more affluent black 'free settlers', who farmed the 'backlands' unwanted by the whites, demanded they should be allowed to do so rent-free. And the judicial system was designed to keep blacks poor and whites in power. Hardship and misery had been increased by cholera and smallpox epidemics during the 1850s which had killed 40,000. A severe drought ruined many plantations, unemployment rose and the outbreak of the American Civil War in 1861 raised the price of food previously imported in large quantities. By 1865 the position of the black population was desperate and they submitted a petition to the queen, begging for assistance, relief from poverty and permission to cultivate some Crown lands.

Governor Eyre would have none of it. He spoke for the planters when he later insisted: 'I know of no general grievance or wrong under which the Negroes of this colony labour. Individual cases of hardship or injustice must arise in every community, but, as a whole, the peasantry of Jamaica have nothing to complain of. They are less taxed, can live more easily and cheaply, and are less under an obligation to work for subsistence than any peasantry in the world . . . They ought to be better off, more comfortable, and more independent than the labourers of any other country. If it is not so, it is due to their own indolence, improvidence and vice, acted upon by the absence of good example and of civilising influences in many districts, and by the evil teaching and evil agencies to which I have already referred.' He said earlier: 'There is scarcely a district or a parish in the island where disloyalty, sedition and murderous intentions are not wholly disseminated, and in many instances openly expressed.'

Acting on Eyre's reports the Secretary of State replied to the blacks' petition, saying that the solution to their problems lay with themselves. He urged them to work 'not uncertainly or capriciously, but steadily and continuously at the times when their labour is wanted, and for so long as it is wanted'. It was in their own 'industry and prudence' that their salvation lay. There was no word of sympathy. It amounted to a victory for Governor Eyre and he had 50,000 copies of the document, known as the Queen's Letter or the Queen's Advice, pasted up across the island in July. The blacks, who revered Her Majesty as 'Missis Queen', were astounded. Many did not believe that she would write such a thing and regarded it as a forgery by the Governor. Gordon said she was 'too noble-hearted to say anything unkind even to her most humble subjects'. Others saw it as the death of their last hope of fair treatment. Some even feared it would be followed by a return to slavery.

Secret black militias were formed under the guise of Church activities, weapons were stolen, night exercises were organized and inflammatory sermons spoken from pulpits. Three weeks before the inevitable tragedy secret oaths were sworn at various meeting houses. The free farmers were the most vociferous. In the summer of 1865 one rent collector was told: 'Soon we shall have the lands free and then we shall have to pay no rent.' Most especially in the parish of St Thomas-in-the-East, Morant Bay, grew the 'vague expectation' that in future their rents would be lifted.

And it was a dispute over land rent which sparked the conflagration. A black farmer called Miller refused to pay rent on an estate near Stony Gut, not far from Morant Bay. He, like other occupiers, argued that the land belonged to the queen and should therefore be rent-free. He lost the case but stayed on the estate. He was summoned to appear before magistrates at Morant Bay on a charge of trespass. Local tempers were running high.

★ ★ ★

Paul Bogle, a prominent black agitator, was uneducated but driven by a belief that he had been chosen by God to bring justice to his people. Gordon had made him a deacon and he had raised enough cash in his district to build a large native Baptist church. In August he had walked 50 miles to Spanish Town at the head of a deputation to lay complaints to the Governor. Eyre refused to see him and Bogle, much embittered, walked all the way back. He was an admirer and political supporter of Gordon and advocated that blacks should set up their own system of courts, constables and justice.

On market day, 7 October 1865, Bogle led a group of up to 150 men, armed with sticks and preceded by a musical band, who marched to the court-house square at Morant Bay. They were determined that Miller should not be sentenced by the chief magistrate. That official was Baron von Ketelhodt, who was still in dispute with Gordon, and who was regarded by the free settlers as one of Eyre's toadies in the pocket of the white plantocracy. The touchpaper was lit even before Miller's case was heard. When the young boy was fined for assault a man called Geoghegan shouted that he should pay the fine but not the costs. Uproar ensued, the court was suspended and constables were ordered to seize the heckler. In a dispatch sent to Kingston the following Monday von Ketelhodt reported: 'A man having been ordered into custody on account of the noise he was making in the court-house, a rush was made by a body of men . . . and the man rescued from the hands of the police, one of whom was left with his finger broken, and several others beaten and ill-treated. In consequence of this outrage, warrants were issued yesterday against 28 individuals who had been identified, and the warrants placed today in the hands of six policemen and three rural constables for execution.'

The police officers set out on the morning of Tuesday, 10 October, to arrest Paul Bogle who, like Miller, lived at Stony Gut, a Negro settlement 5 miles away. They found Bogle in his yard but, having first insisted that the warrant be read out, he refused to be arrested. A confederate known as Captain Grant yelled 'Turn out, men.' At this signal more than 300 men armed with cutlasses, sticks and pikes rushed from a chapel where Bogle regularly preached and from an adjoining cane field. The police were swiftly and easily over-powered. Some were severely beaten. Three were held prisoners, two of them in handcuffs, but were released several hours later when they swore on a Bible produced by Bogle that they would join their captors. The oath said they must 'join their colour' and 'cleave to the black'.

According to one of the freed policemen Bogle said that he planned to attend a vestry in Morant Bay the following day. It was said, allegedly by others, that they intended to 'kill all the white men and all the black men that would not join them'. The threat was reported that night to von Ketelhodt and the Inspector of Police at Morant Bay. The Custos summoned the Volunteers of the parish to assemble and wrote to the Governor asking for military aid.

A document signed by Bogle and others was later used as proof that the original rioters were planning armed insurrection from the start. It read: 'Skin for skin, the iron bars is now broken in this parish, the white people send a proclamation to the Governor to make war against us, which we all must put our shoulder to the wheels and pull together . . . Every one of you must leave your house, takes your guns, who don't have guns take your cutlasses down at once . . . blow your shells, roal your drums, house to house take out every man, march them down to Stony Gut, any that you find in the way takes them down, with their arms; war is at us, my black skin war is at hand from to-day to to-morrow. Every black man must turn at once, for the oppression is too great, the white people are now cleaning up they guns for us, which we must prepare to meet them too. Chear men, chear, in heart we looking for you a part of the night or before daybreak.'

On Wednesday 11 October the Vestry, consisting of elected members and *ex officio* magistrates, assembled in the courthouse at noon and conducted their normal business. The Clerk of the Peace wrote: 'About three o'clock in the evening, and while the vestry was still sitting, a band of music was heard, and shortly after, from about 400 to 500 men appeared, armed with sticks, cutlasses, spears, guns and other deadly weapons.' They first ransacked the police station in search of firearms, taking some old muskets with fixed bayonets. By the time they reached the main square a guard of Volunteers had been hastily called and faced them uneasily across the dusty square. Baron von Ketelhodt stood on the courthouse steps and appealed to them to go home peacefully. When the crowd cried 'War' he read the Riot Act. While he was doing so, stones began to fly and one struck Captain Hitchins, commander of the Volunteers, on the temple. The Captain, having been given authority by the Custos, ordered his men to open fire. A volley rang out and several in the crowd fell dead or dying. There was later a dispute over whether the firing began *before* the stones were thrown but black civilian witnesses later attested that some women had sparked the bloodshed by throwing stones they had collected in their baskets.

The crowd reacted with fury to their casualties. They leapt on the Volunteers, some of who surrendered their weapons, before they could reload. Some of the Volunteers were swiftly battered or hacked to death, while others fled. A bugler guarding a bag of ammunition was harpooned with a fish spear. Most were forced back into the courthouse. Some escaped immediately through the rear windows but the majority were trapped inside. The building was pelted with stones and hit by musket fire, which the defenders returned. Cries were heard from outside: 'Go and fetch fire,' and 'Burn the brutes out.' The adjoining schoolhouse was set ablaze and the fire rapidly spread to the court-house roof. As the timbers began to cave in the defenders were compelled to leave the burning building under cover of darkness. Some were quickly butchered. Baron von Ketelhodt was 'murdered in the most brutal and savage way', according to the Clerk. The eyes and hearts of some men were torn out and 'the women showed themselves to be even more cruel than the men'.

Eyre's subsequent self-justifying dispatch to London claimed that the rebels cut out the tongue of the Island curate of Bath, the Revd V. Herschell, while he was still alive and 'an attempt is said to have been made to skin him'. Lieutenant Hall of the Volunteers 'is said to have been pushed into an outbuilding, which was then set on fire, and kept there until he was literally roasted alive'. Eyre added: 'Many are said to have had their eyes scooped out; heads were cleft open and the brains taken out. The Baron's fingers were cut off and carried away as trophies by the murderers. Indeed the whole outrage could only be paralleled by the atrocities of the Indian Mutiny. The only redeeming trait being that, so far as we could learn, no ladies or children had as yet been injured.'

During the night more people were dragged out of hiding places and slaughtered. Charles Price, a Negro and former Assembly minister, who 'had by his abilities raised himself to a position in life superior to that of most of his race', was among the victims. Some rioters argued that he should be spared because he was black and 'we have orders to kill no black, only white'. Another voice said: 'He has a black skin but a white heart.' He was beaten to death. According to Eyre's official report he was 'ripped open and his entrails taken out'. Others were beaten and left for dead. A few escaped. Four men were released unharmed: a Maroon, two doctors and another man who pretended to be a doctor and swore to Bogle he would never again dress a white man's wound. There were now 18 dead and 21 wounded, and the town was held by the rioters overnight. The town gaolers were forced to open the cells and fifty-one prisoners were released to join Bogle's 'army'. Stores were ransacked and a large quantity of gunpowder taken. An attempt was made to force the door of the magazine where over 300 stands of arms were stored, but the door stood firm. Bogle returned to Stony Gut and held a service in his chapel during which he gave thanks to God that 'he went to this work, and that God had succeeded him in this work'.

★   ★   ★

For three days Bogle's insurgents, numbering up to 2,000, rampaged around the countryside up to 30 miles from Morant Bay. A party of 200 armed men with bayonets mounted on sticks went first to Coley, a few miles from Stony Gut, and threatened fellow blacks with instant death if they did not join them. Estates in the Plantain Garden District were attacked. The small town of Bath was taken bloodlessly, most of the inhabitants, white and black, having fled to the bush. The insurgents themselves fled on hearing the horn of the Maroons who, at the request of the resident magistrate, relieved the town. (Bogle and his lieutenants made several attempts to recruit the Maroon communities to their cause, without success.) At one estate in Blue Mountain Valley, a few miles from Bath, about fifty men attacked the book-keeper who died of his wounds shortly afterwards. Only the intervention of the black overseer prevented the book-keeper's son being murdered also.

The Amity Hall estate, also near Bath, was attacked by 400 men. Mr Hire was killed and his son left for dead. Two more white men, including the stipendiary magistrate Mr Jackson, were severely wounded. When Jackson told the attackers he was a friend of Gordon's they 'rubbed him up and brought him back to life'. They set fire to Dr Crowley's bed, but on hearing he was a doctor they put it out. In most of the attacks the chief targets appear to have been judicial men and officials. Nevertheless the general cry heard across the parish was 'Colour for Colour'. The widow of one victim heard one of his killers say: 'We must humble the white man before us. We are going to take the lives of the white men, but not to hurt the ladies.'

More estates were plundered but in each case the whites had escaped well in advance, in some cases aided by their black labourers. At Hordley estate more than twenty women and children hid in woods for a day and two nights. The proprietor of Whitehall estate, Mr Smith, died of exposure after fleeing into the bush. Most of the houses were ransacked and fine furniture smashed. An exception, the subsequent inquiry was told, was the Great House at Golden-grove, one of the most valuable estates in the east of the island. One black leader said: 'That is to be saved for Paul Bogle – those are the orders of the general.' Throughout the short-lived insurgency many of the blacks were convinced that they would retain possession of the estates. The crops were left untouched and one of Hire's killers said: 'We are going down river to take up the crops.'

Bogle himself remained at Stony Gut the day after the massacre, giving sermons to his men in the little chapel and later drilling them. His followers were told that 'this country would belong to them, and that they were about getting it, to take possession, that they had long been trodden under sandals'. The following day Bogle was seen at the head of 200 men marching up the valley from Chigoe Foot Market. On the 15th he was at Mount Labanus Chapel with 100 men when the alarm was given that soldiers were coming.

Governor Eyre had not been idle. As soon as he received the initial plea for martial aid at Spanish Town he sent off expresses to Major-General O'Connor at Kingston urging 100 men be made ready for embarkation, and to the senior naval officer at Port Royal requesting that a man-o'-war should be made available to convey them to Morant Bay. This was done and the troops arrived at Morant Bay in time to prevent a second attack. News of the courthouse massacre was sent back to Eyre together with intelligence that insurgents were marching up the valley along the Yallahs River. More troops of the West India Regiment were sent to Morant Bay and Port Antonio where military posts were established. A party of the 6th Regiment was ordered to march from Newcastle towards Blue Mountain Valley to block the insurgents. Seamen and marines were landed at Morant Bay from the warship *Wolverine* to back up the regular troops. Maroons were deputized to protect Port Antonio as well as Bath.

Eyre called an emergency meeting of the Privy Council which unanimously agreed to declare martial law. Under law this required a Council of War which duly met on the morning of the 13th. It decided that martial law should cover the whole of the county of Surrey, which included the parish of St Thomas-in-the-East, but should not cover Kingston town. The proclamation referred to 'grievous trespasses and felonies' and declared that: 'Our military forces shall have all power of exercising the rights of belligerence against such of the inhabitants of the said county . . . as our military forces may consider opposed to Our Government, and the well-being of Our loving subjects.'

Meanwhile the swift deployment of troops by sea successfully contained the insurgents within the neighbourhood of St Thomas-in-the-East, preventing the spread of disturbances to other parts of the island. Troops were sent also to Linstead, 14 miles from Spanish Town, and Volunteers, pensioners and special constables enrolled to protect Kingston.

On the 13th Captain Luke left Morant Bay with 120 men of the 1st West India Regiment and marched overnight to Bath. At the Rhine estate they found nearly 100 women and children who had taken refuge from nearby estates. Many of them had suffered 'severe privations' and some were severely wounded. They were escorted back to Port Morant en route to Kingston. That same day, near the burnt-out courthouse, a black man, said to have been a rebel who had allegedly threatened the life of the Collector of Customs, was tried by court martial and immediately executed. The revenge had begun.

Also on the same day a party of fifty marines and sailors under naval Lieutenant Oxley advanced from Morant Bay westwards to Easington. Two Negroes seen running ahead on the road were shot dead after ignoring a command to stop. A prisoner was shot dead while trying to escape. A fourth man was tried and executed at Easington.

Ninety men were sent from Morant Bay to Bogle's village at Stony Gut. Shots were fired from within one of the huts. The culprit was fired on but escaped, although he was wounded. The troops held prisoner a black woman to act as a cook, tethering her with a cord tied around her wrist. The next day they burnt the chapel and eight cottages.

More parties were sent out by Brigadier-General Nelson, commander at Morant Bay. His orders were 'to make excursions in any direction supposed to be advantageous, care being taken that any firing of huts and buildings be not carried to excess'. At Leith Hall a prisoner accused of firing on Volunteers was tried and executed. Near Harbour Head a black, Charles Mitchell, was tied to be flogged for minor offences. Before the lash descended evidence was given that he had attacked a white man. He was tried on the new charge and executed in his own back yard.

Governor Eyre was himself busy, touring the military posts on the *Wolverine* and another ship, the *Onyx*. Although George Gordon was in Kingston throughout the disturbances Eyre reported that everywhere he found 'unmistakable evidence' that the member of the House of Assembly 'had not only been mixed up in the matter, but was himself, through his own misrepresentation and seditious language, addressed to the ignorant black people, the chief cause of the whole rebellion'. He told Edward Jordan, the Island Secretary, 'All of this has come of Mr Gordon's agitation.' Eyre obtained, under oath, a deposition that Gordon had sent seditious material to the rebel leaders through the Kingston post office – an unlikely way to foment revolt. The deposition contradicted itself, saying that the material was printed, and later that it was in Gordon's handwriting. Eyre ordered the Kingston Custos to issue a warrant for his arrest but Gordon, after a short time in hiding, surrendered himself to General O'Connor. He was placed on the *Wolverine* and sent to Morant Bay for trial. Eyre followed shortly afterwards with supplies of arms and ammunitions for the loyal Maroons.

Eyre received legal advice that Gordon should face a civilian court, but the Governor was determined he should be tried under martial law, a conviction and harsh sentence being certain. Eyre said in his report to London: 'Great difference of opinion prevailed in Kingston as to the policy of taking Mr Gordon. Nearly all coincided in believing him to be the occasion of the rebellion, and that he ought to be taken; but many of the inhabitants were under considerable misapprehension that his capture might lead to an immediate outbreak in Kingston itself. I did not share this feeling. Moreover, considering it right in the abstract, and desirable as a matter of policy, that whilst the poor black men who had been misled were undergoing condign punishment, the chief instigator of all the evils should not go unpunished, I at once took upon myself the responsibility of his capture.'

There was then, and remains, a question mark over the legality of his arrest in Kingston, where martial law did not apply, and his trial at Morant Bay, where it did. Eyre got around that by arguing that if it could be proved he took an active part in the insurrection such niceties were irrelevant. Moreover his house was within the parish where the blood was spilt. But most importantly the white planters feared his eloquency on behalf of the black peasantry, and any black victim was now reckoned fair game in their bloody thirst for vengeance. They accused him of calling for an end to white rule and the setting up of a New West India Republic. Gordon denied both charges, pointing to his record as a magistrate and Assemblyman and to his support for constitutional reform rather than armed revolt. It didn't do him any good. On 20 October Gordon was hastily tried before a military court consisting of two naval lieutenants and an ensign. He was found guilty of high treason and sedition, and inciting murder and rebellion. The court martial refused, however, to impose the death penalty. Their decision was overruled by Eyre who ordered that execution should follow almost immediately.

While awaiting his death Gordon wrote a letter to his wife which, when published in newspapers, aroused great sympathy. He said: 'I do not deserve this sentence, for I never advised or took part in any insurrection. All I ever did was to recommend the people who complained to seek redress in a legitimate way; and if in this I erred or have been misrepresented I do not think I deserve the extreme sentence. It is, however, the will of my Heavenly Father that I should thus suffer in obeying His command, to relieve the poor and needy, and to protect, as far as I was able, the oppressed . . . I certainly little expected this.' He told his wife: 'You must do the best you can, and the Lord will help you, and do not be ashamed of the death your poor husband will have suffered. The judge seemed against me; and from the rigid manner of the court, I could not get in all the explanation I intended. The man Anderson made an unfounded statement . . . but this testimony was different from the deposition. The judges took the former and erased the latter. It seemed that I was to be sacrificed. I know nothing of the man Bogle. I never advised him to the act or acts which have brought me to this end.'

Less than an hour after his trial finished, Gordon was hanged, with eighteen others, from a beam in front of the burnt-out courthouse. Their bodies were thrown into a trench behind the building.

★　★　★

Soldiers, militia and Maroons were meanwhile fully engaged in suppressing the insurrection. All searched for Paul Bogle, who had not been seen since the 15th when he had been dissuaded by one of his most active associates from attacking a body of soldiers coming over a grassy brow at Fonthill. On his failure to attack his followers became panic-stricken and fled. The fighting, what there had been of it, was over and the butchery just begun.

More troops were sent from Barbados and the Bahamas to reinforce the local troops. Another detachment was dispatched from Halifax but returned without landing. Two Spanish warships were sent from Cuba, but they were not required.

In the Blue Mountain Valley district 120 men of the 6th Regiment under Colonel Hobbs occupied the Monklands coffee estate and used it as a base to make incursions to small villages up and down the valley. Hobbs reported that 'numbers of the rebels had come in, having thrown away their arms, seeking protection; and though worthy of death [I have] shrunk from the responsibility of executing them, without first receiving the General's or Governor's wishes respecting them.' Major-General O'Connor's aide replied that he 'can give you no instruction, and leaves all to your own judgement'. A few days later, however, Hobbs received new instructions in which the Major-General, according to the Commission, 'expressed a hope that the Colonel would deal in a more summary manner with the rebels, and on no account to forward prisoners to Kingston.'

Hobbs did not need to be told twice. During the march to Chigoe Foot Market eleven prisoners were tried and executed. At the market were twenty-seven prisoners who were named as known rebels by a man who claimed he had been pressed into their company by Bogle. They were all sentenced to death. Sixteen were taken to their home village of Coley a few miles away where 14 were shot and 2 escaped. Nine others were shot and their bodies hung up in a chapel at nearby Fonthill. Hobbs also ordered a local 'Obeah' man, or witch-doctor, Arthur Wellington, be taken back to Monklands for trial. Following Wellington's inevitable sentencing, Hobbs decided to demonstrate the nonsense of the widespread belief that an Obeah's supernatural powers made him invulnerable. Wellington was marched up the valley side overlooking the estate to a spot visible from the surrounding heights. He was killed by volley and a constable, acting without authority, sliced his head off. Body and head were buried in a trench at the bottom of the hill but during the night heavy rain washed the head out of the grave and carried it along a stream, after which it was stuck on a pole. Hobbs released several prisoners, charged with minor offences, who told him they would never believe in an Obeah again. He was not lenient with suspected rebels. At Monklands nine men were made to kneel in a line above the trench that was to be their mass grave and then shot dead. One prisoner, showing signs of life, was allegedly hit on the skull with a pickaxe.

More than thirty were shot at the estate before the soldiers left and Major-General O'Connor informed the initially reluctant Hobbs 'I am much pleased by your adopting a decided course with regard to captured rebels.' The Commission later reported: 'During the operations along the Valley about eight casual deaths were inflicted without authority, on inhabitants in some of the villages. Some of these persons were shot in their houses, others while passing in the road, and two of the number were infirm persons, incapable of resistance. One of the two latter, however, suffered through a mistake. About 493 dwellings, situate in the various settlements of this district, were destroyed by fire during the same time.'

Hobbs went in hot pursuit of Paul Bogle, burning and killing as he went. In a dispatch to Major-General O'Connor he said: 'I found a number of special constables, who had captured a number of prisoners from the rebel camp. Finding their guilt clear, and being unable to either take or leave them, I had them all shot. The constables then hung them up on trees – eleven in number. Their countenances were all diabolical, and they never flinched in the very slightest.' He moved on to Stony Gut and utterly destroyed Bogle's 'vile and rebellious settlement'. Guiding him reluctantly was Bogle's unnamed valet: 'a little fellow of extraordinary intelligence; a light rope tied to the stirrups, and a revolver now and then to his head, causes us thoroughly to understand each other . . .'. The valet, Hobbs reported, 'knows every single rebel in the Island by name and face, and has just been selecting the captains, colonels and secretaries out of an immense gang of prisoners just come in here, whom I shall have to shoot tomorrow morning.'

On the 23rd Paul Bogle was caught by a party of Maroons and sent to Morant Bay for court martial. He chatted calmly to his captors and denied that Gordon had in any way incited violence. After the briefest of trials, he was hanged from the arch of the ruined courthouse. The slaughter of his followers, congregation and neighbours continued.

On the north side of the island at Port Antonio 54 prisoners were tried under martial law and executed. In the neighbouring villages 217 cottages were burnt. At Morant Bay and the Plantain Garden River district 194 were so executed, 68 at Monklands and 3 at Up-Park Camp. This 'reign of terror' was overseen by Captain Ramsay the Provost Marshall, a Crimean War veteran who had survived the Charge of the Light Brigade. Samuel Clarke was hanged simply for saying at a public meeting that the 'Queen's Letter' was a lie and Eyre should be recalled. Another black man, while being flogged, had the effrontery to glare at Ramsay full in the eye. The brave captain ordered the flogging to end and had the man hanged instead. Ramsay, almost certainly mad, later committed suicide.

On 17 October Captain Hole reported to HQ: 'On arriving yesterday at Long Bay I found the huts full of plunder. I had every house within a quarter of a mile of the road in which the plunder was found fired, and in doing so upwards of 20 of the rebels were killed.'

Captain Hole marched with 40 men of the 6th Regiment and 60 men of the 1st West India Regiment under Ensign Cullen the 20 miles from Port Antonio to Manchioneal. Their orders from Brigadier-General Nelson were 'not to leave the line of march in search of rebels, nor to allow prisoners to be brought in except leaders of rebels; and that those who were found with arms were to be shot'. Twenty-five blacks were killed along the line of march by 'casual shooting'. At his destination Hole immediately organized the execution of a man called Donaldson who was found with the horse and saddle of the murdered Mr Hire. A prisoner who had been released from Morant Bay gaol by the insurgents was shot for possession of a cutlass and another for carrying a flask of powder. During eleven days of courts martial at Manchioneal 33 people were sentenced and shot. Many more were flogged for trivial offences, twenty of them women. Hole argued that there were no prison cells for women who were often described as the 'principal plunderers'.

Three soldiers of the 1st West Indians were separated from their unit guarding a plantation. They returned with two wagon-loads of stolen property taken from Mr Hire and reported to Hole that they had shot ten implicated men. A black soldier of the same regiment who had deserted stopped three constables escorting four prisoners on the road near Long Bay. He took them off the policemen and shot them one by one. Later in the day, on the same road, a man presumed to be the same deserter shot six prisoners as a head constable looked on. Of this incident the Commission noted: 'These ten deaths were attended with such barbarity on the part of the soldier, and such cowardice on the part of the constables and other persons who witnessed what was done without interfering to prevent it, as to call for special notice and condemnation.'

Hole did his utmost to enforce military discipline in his own ranks. Two corporals were demoted for being absent. One soldier was sentenced to seven years' penal servitude for burning homes without orders.

Meanwhile Maroons under the command of Colonel Fyfe had received different orders from Brigadier-General Nelson: 'You are never to molest a woman or child, and you are not to shoot any man who surrenders.' During the operations Maroon detachments killed no more than twenty-five men, the majority in action. Seven were killed in an attack on a rebel makeshift fort at Torrington, and more at a barricade of felled tree trunks on the Stony Gut road.

By contrast the killings of blacks by British troops while on the march was later judged to be indiscriminate and in the face of 'no active resistance'. Blacks were executed on the flimsiest evidence – in one case the accused man had been seen beating a drum – while in some cases condemned men named others in the misplaced hope of a reprieve. One man was executed because, while in Kingston gaol, he had said: 'I have seen too much gun. If it had been in Africa we would have known what to do immediately.'

The Commission put the total number of blacks killed at 439 with more than 1,000 homes burnt, 100 men imprisoned for terms ranging from 6 months to 12 years, and no fewer than 600 flogged. One man was sentenced to fifty lashes and three years' imprisonment for travelling without a pass. Nearly fifty men suffered floggings in one day at Bath alone, and between thirty and forty on other days, until it was stopped by Colonel Fyfe on his return from leading the Maroons. The Commission reported: 'The mode of inflicting the punishment at Bath calls for special notice. It was ordered by a special magistrate, after a very slight investigation, and frequently at the instigations of book-keepers and others smarting under the sense of recent injury. At first an ordinary cat was used, but afterwards, for the punishment of men, wires were twisted around the cords, and the different tails so constructed were knotted.'

At the opening of the Jamaica Chambers, Governor Eyre spoke of a 'most diabolical conspiracy to murder the white and coloured inhabitants of this colony'. He said: 'The valuable lives of many noble and gallant men, who were ornaments to the land, have been sacrificed (while peaceably meeting in the discharge of their duties to the State) by a most savage and cruel butchery, only to be paralleled by the atrocities of the Indian Mutiny.' The rebellion had been 'fairly crushed' within the first week and the district had been scoured to capture and punish those of the guilty 'who had not yet met their just doom'. He went on: 'So widespread a rebellion so rapidly and so effectually put down is not, I believe, to be met with in history, and speaks volumes for the zeal, courage and energy of those engaged in suppressing it . . . One moment's hesitation, one single reverse, might have lit the torch which would have blazed in rebellion from one end of the island to the other, and who may say how many of us would have lived to see it extinguished.' He said that the colony remained 'on the brink of a volcano'.

His words were largely for consumption in Westminster and Whitehall, although if he thought they could quell the rising anger and shock at home over the brutality employed in suppression, he was wrong, but they worked well enough in the Jamaica Chambers.

The following day the Legislative Council thanked Eyre for the 'energy, firmness and wisdom with which you have carried the island through this momentous crisis'. The House of Assembly was even more fulsome and passed an address which said, in part, 'We desire to express our entire concurrence in your Excellency's statement that to the misapprehension and misrepresentation of pseudo-philanthropists in England and in this country, to the inflammatory harangues and seditious meetings of political demagogues, to the personal, scurrilous, vindictive, and disloyal writings of a licentious and unscrupulous Press, and to the misdirected efforts and misguided counsel of certain miscalled ministers of religion, is to be attributed the present disorganisation of the colony, resulting in rebellion, arson, and murder.' A bill was introduced for abolishing the Constitution and substituting a new one with just one Chamber in which dissent would be discouraged.

In his first dispatch to Edward Cardwell, Secretary of State for the Colonies, Eyre placed great stress on the perceived danger of the insurrection infecting the whole island, thereby justifying his harsh measures. He said: 'We have been singularly fortunate in capturing or shooting a large number of the principal ringleaders in the rebellion, and many of whom were personally concerned in the atrocious butcheries on the 12th of October, at the Morant Bay Courthouse, or in the subsequent destruction of life and property further to the eastward, as the rebellion extended in that direction. Very many acknowledged their guilt before the execution.' He added: 'It is a remarkable fact that, so far as we can ascertain, the rebels at Morant Bay did not proceed in any considerable numbers to the adjacent districts, but the people of each district rose and committed the deeds of violence and destruction that were done within it. This fact shows how widespread the feeling of disaffection is, and how prepared the people of each parish were to catch the spirit and follow the example of their neighbours. It shows, too, the extreme insecurity which yet exists in nearly all the other parishes of Jamaica, where the same bad spirit prevails. In the lately disturbed districts the rebellion is crushed; in the others, it is only kept under for the present, but might at any time burst into fury.'

Cardwell's initial reaction was to heartily endorse the Governor's actions. In a letter sent from Downing Street on 17 November Cardwell conveyed to Eyre 'my high approval of the spirit, energy, and judgement with which you have acted in your measures for repressing and preventing the spread of insurrection'. Later in the letter he said: 'I entirely agree with you that measures of severity, when dictated by necessity and justice, are in reality measures of mercy, and do not doubt it will appear that you have arrested the course of punishment as soon as you were able to do so. . . .'

A week later, however, Cardwell had received reports of the scale of reprisals and, in particular, Gordon's execution and its doubtful legality. He wrote twice on 23 November demanding from Eyre a fuller explanation of the evidence against the slain insurgents, without which explanation 'the severity would not appear to have been justified'. Of Gordon's case he said: 'I desire also to see it clearly established that he was not executed until crimes had been proved in evidence against him which deserved death; and that the prompt infliction of capital punishment was necessary to rescue the colony from imminent danger . . .'.

★ ★ ★

Indignation at the ferocity of the suppression, and in particular the judicial murder of Gordon, led to a heated political debate in England. The statesman John Bright said that the nation 'has never received a deeper wound or darker stain' on its reputation. John Stuart Mill wrote: 'The question was whether the British dependencies, and eventually, perhaps, Great Britain itself, were to be under the government of law or of military licence.'

Eyre had his defenders, including Charles Kingsley, Lord Tennyson and Charles Dickens, who argued that the Governor had acted by the rules of circumstance rather than malice, but the furore grew. Eyre was suspended and recalled to London. A temporary replacement, Lieutenant-General Sir Henry Storks, was sent hastily to Jamaica from Malta, and arrived there before the end of the year. The Government set up a Commission of Inquiry made up of Russell Gurney, MP, QC and Recorder of London, and J.B. Maule who were also dispatched to Jamaica to work together with Storks.

The Commission spent fifty-one days examining 730 witnesses, most of them 'uneducated peasants, speaking in accents strange to the ear, often in a phraseology of their own, with vague conceptions of number and time, unaccustomed to definiteness or accuracy of speech, and . . . still smarting under a sense of injuries sustained'. The Commission concluded that martial law had continued too long after the threat had passed, that the courts martial should have ceased, and the punishments were too severe in cases where the evidence of rebellion was flimsy. The death sentence was 'unnecessarily frequent' and the burning of 1,000 homes was 'wanton and cruel'. They recommended compensation to be paid to those families innocent of crimes whose homes had been burnt. They also expressed distaste at the method of flogging with wire: '. . . it was painful to think that any man should have used such an instrument for the torturing of his fellow creatures'. In general the floggings were 'reckless, and at Bath positively barbarous'.

Their report focused strongly on the trial and execution of Gordon. They found that although Gordon's writings and speeches might have influenced Bogle and other insurgents this was a long way from treason: 'We cannot see any sufficient proof either of his complicity in the outbreak at Morant Bay or of his having been a party to a general conspiracy against the Government.' In other words, Gordon had been wrongly executed.

But overall the Commission praised Eyre for his prompt action and accepted that there had been a planned resistance to lawful authority with roots in disputes over land and rent. Although the rebellion had been initially confined to a small portion of one parish the disorder quickly spread over a large tract. The report said: 'Such was the state of excitement prevailing in other parts of the Island that had more than a momentary success been obtained by the insurgents, their ultimate overthrow would have been attended with a still more fearful loss of life.'

As a result of the Commission's report the Government thanked Eyre for his prompt action in suppressing a revolt that could have consumed Jamaica and spread to other islands. (The Lieutenant-Governor of St Vincent stated that there had been much excitement on his island when reports were received and 'the sympathies of the lower orders were almost universally enlisted in favour of the malcontents'.) But ministers also blamed him for the savage reprisals. The Colonial Secretary, the Earl of Carnarvon, told the Lords: 'Promptitude, courage, fearlessness of responsibility, if not accompanied by a sound judgement on the part of the person who possesses them, become faults rather than virtues . . . The first attribute demanded of a Governor is not only justice but perfect impartiality and the power of rising above panic and the apprehensions of the moment. It is to the fatal want of this quality in Mr Eyre that we may trace at least half of the mischief which arose after the outbreak . . . Much has been said respecting the case of Mr Gordon. It is a most terrible case and one that is indefensible.'

Eyre was charged with murder at the instigation of the Jamaica Committee chaired by John Stuart Mill, but the case was dismissed by local magistrates in Shropshire, where Eyre was living. Lieutenant Brand, the naval officer at Gordon's trial, and Colonel Sir Alexander Nelson who confirmed his sentence, were also charged and committed for trial at Bow Street. The Chief Justice, Lord Cockburn, pressed the prosecution case strongly but a Grand Jury refused to find a true bill against them. In 1868 the case against Eyre was revived and he too was charged at Bow Street, but again a Grand Jury threw it out. The following year a Jamaican called Phillips took out a civil action against Eyre, charging him with false imprisonment, but Eyre took refuge behind an Act of Indemnity passed by the Jamaica Legislature.

Eyre was awarded a state pension by the Disraeli Government in 1874. During his long retirement he kept his silence, refusing either to defend or to justify himself outside a court of law. He died in 1901 and his *Times* obituary said that 'he did many good and brave things and atoned for one error in his life by a silence so dignified and so prolonged'.

The old, terrified Jamaica Assembly had voted for its own extinction after 200 years in existence and London duly complied. An 1866 Act created a Crown Colony. The new permanent Governor, Sir John Peter Grant, swiftly set to work reorganizing the entire island. He sacked the local planter-justices and replaced them with stipendiary magistrates, created a proper police force, introduced a public medical service, irrigation schemes for infertile areas and a public works department, and reformed land tenure laws. Education was improved and by 1867 there were 379 schools on the island, of which 226 received financial aid from the Government. Grant encouraged the trade in bananas which quickly became the colony's biggest export trade and principal crop. There were no more revolts, although poverty and discontent continued.

The Jamaican Rebellion, its suppression and subsequent controversy, gave the British an excuse to abolish the old and fundamentally corrupt administration which had become dominated by white planter power. More Crown colonies were established throughout the West Indies, with only a handful of exceptions. In the short term this meant direct rule from London but it reduced the power of an arrogant white minority and paved the way for more responsible Government and, much later, independence.

In 1962, however, when Jamaica finally won full independence George William Gordon and so many other innocents had been long cold in their graves.

CHAPTER FIVE

The *Arracan* Expedition, Andaman Islands, 1867

'No ordinary exertion'

They may have been the 'Good Spirit' islands mentioned by Ptolemy; they were certainly referred to by the fifth-century Chinese Buddhist I'Tsing, while Marco Polo, passing within sight in 1292, called them the 'Angamans' and said that the natives were cannibals with the heads of dogs. Nicolo dei Conti translated their name as 'Islands of Gold', although it probably derives from the monkeys which populated the forests. The Andaman Islands were the epitome of tropical paradise: the tips of a range of submarine mountains scattered like a necklace with 204 jewels across almost 2,500 square miles of the Bay of Bengal. Their countless natural harbours

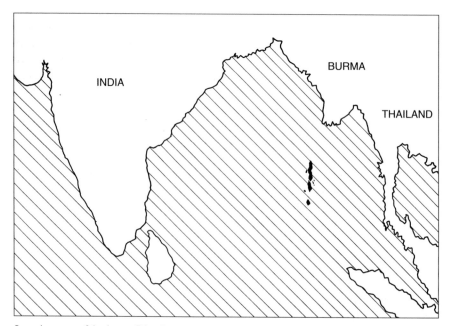

Location map of Andaman Islands

and rugged inlets were laced in turn with dazzling coral, while dugong and turtles swam the crystal waters. There were mangrove swamps, hills gashed by narrow valleys, forests of valuable redwood. At the start of the nineteenth century the islands lay on the main trade routes and offered shelter from the cyclones which lashed the Bay but never seemed to touch the islands.

The native people were largely untouched by the civilizations with which they came into contact. They had a policy of killing all foreigners. The people traced their blood lines to the pygmies of the Philippines and the Semang of Malaysia. They were hunters and gatherers, never farmers, on rocky outcrops where irrigation was unheard of. They fished from canoes with nets and four-pronged arrows. Their weapons were made of shell and broken shards of iron collected from shipwrecks. Sailors, merchants and explorers noted their ferocious hostility: hostility that was created, not inherent. Conti and Cesare Federici, who visited the islands in 1440 and 1569 respectively, wrote of peaceful natives in canoes. But hideous raids by Arab slave traders changed all that. The coastal tribes, who greeted strangers with simple gifts, were virtually wiped out. The inland Jarawa tribes were also friendly at first but clashed with foreign sailors who accused them of theft, a concept alien to tribes who regarded property as communal. A later British ambassador, M.V. Portman, said: 'It was our fault if the Jarawas became hostile.' An early incident on Tilanchong illustrates this point. In 1708 a vessel commanded by Captain Owen was shipwrecked and the crew ferried to nearby islands by courteous and kindly natives. Captain Owen put down a four-inch knife he had saved and it was picked up by an islander. Owen snatched it back, kicking and punching the native. Hamilton's *Voyages* records: 'The shipwrecked men could observe contention arising among those who were their benefactors in bringing them to the island . . . next day, as the captain was sitting under a tree at dinner, there came about a dozen of the natives towards him and saluted him with a shower of darts made of heavy wood, with their points hardened in the fire, and so he expired in a moment.' His crew, however, were protected and given two canoes with water and food. They were told not to return. One canoe, with three men on board, survived the journey.

In 1789 Captain Archibald Blair had established a penal colony for prisoners from Bengal at Port Blair on Chatham Island. Two years later, under Admiral Sir William Cornwallis, it was transferred with a naval arsenal to Great Andaman. This proved too costly in both cash and lives – most prisoners and many guards died quickly of tropical diseases – and it was scrapped in 1796. The local population did not welcome strangers any more. In 1844 they killed the stragglers from the troopships *Briton* and *Runnymede*, which were driven ashore in a gale. Attacks on shipwrecked crews and the huge numbers of prisoners taken during the Indian Mutiny of 1857 pushed the British into establishing a settlement and another convict colony close to the original site at Port Blair. Ravaged by sickness, many died before swamp reclamation created healthier conditions. During the early years deportation to the Andamans was considered a death sentence.

The English tried to deal with the war-like Jarawas by arming the remnants of the coastal tribes, the Arioto, with firearms. Given such unique power they began to slaughter every Jarawa they could find. Portman wrote: 'On our arrival the Jarawas were quiet and inoffensive towards us, nor did they even disturb us, until we took to constantly molesting them by inciting the coastal Andamanese against them.'

In 1867 some of the crew of the vessel *Assam Valley* were reported missing and captured by natives on Little Andaman Island. A detachment of the 2nd Battalion, 24th Regiment, South Wales Borderers, was dispatched on board the *Arracan* to find them.

★ ★ ★

The 24th Battalion had spent nearly six years in Mauritius, enjoying bathing, boating, cricket and local hospitality under balmy skies, before being sent to Rangoon. Three officers and 100 men were sent from there to the Andaman Island. Among them was a 26-year-old Canadian medical officer and four privates who were to join the most distinguished roll call in military history – the company of VC-holders.

Assistant-Surgeon Campbell Mellis Douglas, himself the son of a doctor, was born at Grosse Île, Quebec, and had been attached to the 24th in Mauritius. The privates, three of them Irish, were also in their twenties. David Bell, from County Down, had enlisted at Lisburn seven years before; William Griffiths, a County Roscommon man, had previously been a collier; and Dubliner Thomas Murphy had worked as a cloth dresser before enlisting. The fourth private, James Cooper from Birmingham, was illiterate when he signed up; he was the son of a jeweller and a stay-maker.

Shortly before the Andaman expedition Douglas, an accomplished boatman, had prepared a boat for entry into a regatta at Burma. The crew he trained for the event proved so strong that after winning the first race their boat was excluded from the competition to give others a chance. The names of his crew are not recorded but, given the later events, it is likely they included the Irishmen and the Brummie.

On 17 May 1867 the steamer *Arracan* reached Little Andaman, buzzing with rumours that the missing crew had been butchered by cannibals. On arriving at the scene of the alleged massacre, two boats were filled with armed soldiers and rowed inshore under the command of Lieutenant Much.

The *Regimental History* records: 'A heavy surf was beating but one boat's crew waded ashore through deep water and began moving towards a rock where the massacre was believed to have occurred, the other boat moving parallel to cover their movements. As they advanced natives began to show themselves and let fly their arrows freely but could not prevent the party from reaching the rock and finding the skull of a European, when, as they

Assistant-Surgeon Campbell Mellis Douglas VC leading the rescue in the surf of the Andaman Islands (RAMC Historical Museum)

had nearly exhausted their ammunition, the signal for recall was made. In trying to embark those ashore near the rock the shore party's boat was upset, so the men started back towards the original landing place, en route discovering the partially buried bodies of four more Europeans.' As the plight of the men on the beach became all too obvious, increasingly desperate efforts were made to reach them through the surf, first by boats and then by rafts from the *Arracan*. As more boats were battered to pieces Assistant-Surgeon Douglas and the four privates volunteered to man a gig to renew the attempt. Their first bid to get through the roaring surf failed when their little boat was half-filled with water. During another attempt Lieutenant Much and others were swept off a makeshift raft. A correspondent wrote: 'While in this critical and very dangerous predicament Dr Campbell Douglas showed all the qualities of a real hero. Being an excellent swimmer, and possessing great boldness and courage, he swam after the drowning men. Twice was Lt Much . . . washed off the raft, and, while struggling in the rolling waves, Dr Douglas flew to his rescue, and brought him back safe to the raft.' Chief Officer Dunn of the *Arracan*, confused and sinking, was also plucked to safety by Douglas, but Lieutenant

Glassford was less lucky. The correspondent, writing for the *Liverpool Gazette*, added: 'Dr Douglas, having struck his head against the rocks in diving after one and another of those he saved, felt himself confused and bruised, and his strength giving out. He could not follow Mr Glassford, who was carried some sixty or seventy yards away, and he was drowned. As night was rapidly approaching, the whole party had to make the most herculean efforts to save themselves from the risks and dangers which now beset them on every hand.'

On two occasions Douglas and his crew got through the surf and brought back seventeen men, 'the whole shore party being thus rescued from the virtual certainty of being massacred and eaten by savages'. The *Regimental History* added: 'The surf was running high and the boat was in constant danger of being swamped, but Assistant-Surgeon Douglas handled it with extraordinary coolness and skill and, being splendidly supported by the four men, who showed no signs of hesitation or uncertainty, keeping cool and collected. . . .'

The expedition, having discovered the fate of the missing Europeans, steamed away but the exploits of Douglas and his gallant crew reached the ears of the Commander-in-Chief in India, Sir William Mansfield. Hostile natives, though a threat during the early part of the incident, had not been evident when Douglas arrived on the scene but officers who were present, not least those who had been saved, wanted the rescuers awarded the highest honour. The newly created Victoria Cross was intended only for heroism in the face of the enemy, but the officers, and some newspapers, argued that the courage displayed in a boiling surf on a hostile shore was more than enough. A large factor was that very few Victorian Britons could swim and the sea was thus held in some terror. Luckily, an amendment in 1858 had made it possible for the Victoria Cross to be awarded for

Campbell Mellis Douglas VC   Private (later Sergeant) David Bell VC

Private Thomas Murphy VC

exceptional heroism far from the front line – Private Timothy O'Hea had previously won it for putting out a fire in an ammunition wagon in Canada.

On 17 December 1867 the War Office confirmed the queen's decision to reward all five men with the Victoria Cross. The citation for each was identical: 'For the very gallant and daring manner in which they risked their lives in manning a boat and proceeding through a dangerous surf to rescue some of their comrades who formed part of an expedition which had been sent to the island of Andaman, by order of the Chief Commissioner of British Burmah, with the view of ascertaining the fate of the commander and seven of the crew of the ship *Assam Valley*, who had landed there, and who were supposed to have been murdered by the natives.

'The officer who commanded the troops on the occasion reports: "About an hour later in the day Dr Douglas and the four privates referred to, gallantly manning the second gig, made their way through the surf almost to the shore, but finding their boat was half-filled with water, they retired. A second attempt was made by Dr Douglas and party and proved successful, five of us being passed through the surf to the boats outside. A third and last trip got the whole party left on shore safe to the boats."

'It is stated that Dr Douglas accomplished these trips through the surf to the shore by no ordinary exertion. He stood in the bows of the boat, and worked her in an intrepid and seamanlike manner, cool to a degree, as if what he was doing then was an ordinary act of everyday life. The four privates behaved in an equally cool and collected manner, rowing through the roughest surf when the slightest hesitation or want of pluck on the part of any of them would have been attended with the gravest results. It is reported that seventeen officers and men were thus saved from what must otherwise have been a fearful risk, if not certainty, of death.'

The five were the first of the 'Old Green Howards' to receive the Victoria Cross and the last to win it anywhere away from battle. By 1904 the regiment had sixteen VCs to its credit, of which seven were famously won at Rorke's Drift.

Assistant-Surgeon Douglas enjoyed a long and illustrious career. The Royal Humane Society awarded him a silver medal for the same act of heroism. He was Medical Office in Charge of the field hospital during the second Riel Expedition in 1885, during which he made an epic 200-mile canoe trip carrying dispatches. He wrote papers on nervous degeneration among recruits, and on military doctoring. His favourite recreation was, naturally, sailing. He reached the rank of Brigade Surgeon and married the niece of Sir Edward Belcher. In 1895 he made a single-handed crossing of the English Channel in a 12-ft Canadian canoe. He also patented a modification to a folding boat which was later put into general use. He died, aged sixty-nine, at his daughter's home near Wells, Somerset, on 31 December 1906. A painting displayed in the RAMC Headquarters on London's Millbank shows him standing bravely on the bows of the rescue boat.

Less is known of the four privates. Thomas Murphy emigrated to Philadelphia and died in March 1900 aged sixty. James Cooper left the Army, although he continued in the Reserves, and followed his father's trade as a jeweller. He died in Birmingham in August 1882. David Bell became a sergeant but was discharged in 1873. He was employed as a skilled labourer at no. 8 machine shop, Chatham Dockyard. He died, aged seventy-eight, in 1920 at Gillingham.

William Griffiths, still a private, was killed by Zulus at Isandhlwana on 22 January 1879. He was buried in a mass grave on the battlefield, far from the sound of pounding surf.

CHAPTER SIX

The Magdala Campaign, 1867–8

'The ruthless hand of war'

On a plateau below a great ruined fortress atop a mountain in modern-day Ethiopia a massive cannon lies on its side in the dust. In the royal palace of Windsor a brass plaque set in the Chapel Royal wall commemorates a young African prince. The story that binds them together covers one of the most remarkable military campaigns of the last century.

It is remarkable because its commander spared no monetary expense to ensure that none of his men died unnecessarily. His success did much to counter the shameful memory of the cruel shambles in the Crimea. It is remarkable because it mobilized armies from three continents and crossed some of the most savage terrain on earth for one purpose – to free a handful of unappreciative hostages. And it is remarkable for the main protagonist, Kassa – an African Emperor who was fanatically Christian, brave, educated, patriotic . . . cruel, barbaric and, certainly by the end probably raving mad.

At the heart of the story is a seemingly impregnable citadel perched on a mountain in the Abyssinian highlands and called Magdala.

★ ★ ★

Kassa, known to Europeans as Theodorus and to his people as Tewodros, Elect of God, the slave of Christ, Emperor of All Abyssinia, was born in 1818. It was a time of chaos and bloody carnage: the power of the hereditary emperors had declined while the barons or *rases* were out of control and divided the land. Kassa was the son of a local prefect and a peasant woman. When his father died he was sent to a monastery to train as a deacon in the Abyssinian Church which practised an ancient form of Christianity. Surrounded on all sides by Islam, the Abyssinian Church was forgotten or ignored by the rest of the Christian world. His training left Kassa with a profound love of the Abyssinian faith and a sense of his own mystic heritage which were to stay with him for the rest of his life.

When his monastery was destroyed in a raid Kassa was one of the few survivors. Aged around twenty, he took to the hills as a guerrilla, already

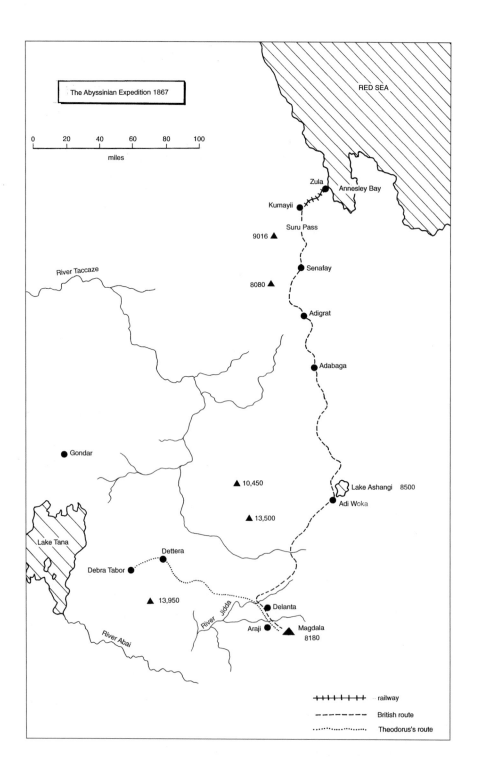

The Abyssinian Expedition 1867

0   20   40   60   80   100
miles

RED SEA

Zula
Annesley Bay
Kumayii
Suru Pass
9016 ▲
River Taccaze
8080 ▲ Senafay
Adigrat
Adabaga
Gondar
10,450 ▲
Lake Ashangi   8500
13,500 ▲
Adi Woka
Lake Tana
Dettera
Debra Tabor
13,950 ▲
River Jidda
Delanta
Araji
Magdala
8180
River Abai

++++++++ railway
- - - - - - British route
.... Theodorus's route

The Emperor Theodorus of
Abyssinia by Baudran from
*Theodore II Le Nouvel Empire
d'Abyssinie*, by C. Lejean (Paris,
1865)

well blooded in tribal warfare. He was by then a notable scholar, a
theologian, a fine horseman, marksman and spear-thrower. His wild
followers respected his courage and strength and loved his unusual habit of
dividing plunder equally with his men. His band caused so much mayhem
that in 1845 the region's governor, Ras Ali, offered terms including the hand
of Tewabach, the beautiful daughter of a northern nobleman. They married
and Kassa remained devoted to her.

Two years later he led a rebellion, snatching control of the imperial city of
Gondar. Ali, armed with British guns, tried to wipe out his younger
adversary. Both men were by now rival claimants to the vacant imperial
throne. After eighteen months of hard campaigning Kassa slaughtered Ali's
army at the battle of Gojjam. Kassa won the support of the Established
Church by promising to expel Catholic missionaries. The civil wars
continued but Kassa defeated his last rival at Deresye in February 1855. He
was crowned King of Kings in a small village church. He chose his new
imperial name from the legend of a Messiah called Tewodros who would
rescue the country from years of rule by idiots and women. Within a decade
he had united Ethiopia under his overlordship, although he still faced
encroachments from Egypt and the constant threat of rebellion by the
warlike Galla tribe.

Europeans who came into contact with the new Emperor were impressed
by the strong magnetism of his eyes. The British Consul William Plowden, a

colourful adventurer who had been appointed in 1848, told London: 'He is generous to excess and free from all cupidity. He salutes his meanest subject with courtesy; is sincerely though often mistakenly religious . . . When roused his wrath is terrible and all tremble.'

The first years of his reign were busy and fruitful. He abolished the slave trade and polygamy, with mixed success. He mobilized an army of 60,000 and subdued the troublesome Gallas, snatching their mighty fortress at Magdala. He subjugated the Tigrai province. After one battle he reportedly cut off the hands of 787 prisoners. He was far gentler with those he did not consider rebels, traitors or enemies. He dressed simply and lived in a tent of scarlet and yellow silk among his soldiers. When he was in residence at the palace of Gondar, the tent was pitched in the gardens. He identified with the common people rather than with the *rases*, whose power he reduced by dividing each province into small administrative areas with his own trusted men in key positions. He scrapped some of the more horrific criminal punishments, such as flaying alive, and simplified the penal code. He was merciless with corrupt judges.

His popularity among his troops and the poorer people grew swiftly. So too did the hatred of the *rases* and judiciary. During his first two years on the throne he was wounded six times in seventeen assassination attempts. He was never seen without a sword and revolver and he walked with a lance in his hand. As he grew older such plots, revolts and insurrections were crushed with increasing ferocity. The Emperor began to believe in his own Divinity. Only three people could with sweet reason calm his rages and curb his excesses: his wife Tewabach; Consul Plowden; and his friend John Bell. Within a few short years all three had died, and their benign influence removed.

During these turbulent times tensions grew between the Abyssinian Church, which had followed its own separate path for centuries, and Catholic and Protestant missionaries from Europe. Tewodros tolerated the missionaries as long as their missions included artisans who could bring with them such skills as mending firearms, making gunpowder and building roads. In 1858, when his beloved wife was stricken with illness, he viewed with gratitude the sadly unsuccessful efforts of mission doctors to save her. He rewarded them with land to build more homes and a school. The missionaries he liked and trusted the most were Swiss and German craftsmen. He promised they would never be 'molested or tormented' but at the same time warned them not to try to convert his Christian subjects.

Early in 1860 Consul Plowden was speared to death, reportedly by a runaway nephew of the Emperor who had joined Tigrai rebels. In a long apologetic letter to Queen Victoria, Tewodros told how he had pursued his young relative and his supporters and killed them all, '. . . not leaving one alive although they were of my own family, so that, by the power of God, I may get your friendship.' Plowden's death plunged Tewodros into a black despair which must have accelerated his decline towards insanity. His second wife, Terunesh, was comely but haughty and treated him like a peasant unworthy of her royal pedigree. The slide was mental, emotional and physical. He caught an unspecified disease of a 'peculiar and formidable nature'. He even suffered a broken leg. Excessive drinking and debauchery exposed the darker side of his nature.

Plowden's successor was Charles Duncan Cameron, a veteran of the Zulu campaign and a former diplomat to the Russias. He arrived with a goodwill letter from the British Government and a gift from Queen Victoria – a matched pair of engraved revolvers. After some delays Cameron was granted an audience with Tewodros in 1862. The Emperor received him 'in a reclining posture, with a double-barrelled gun and two loaded pistols by his side'. Despite his threatening appearance Tewodros treated the consul with kindness, although he also made it quite clear from the start that he could never replace Plowden in the royal esteem and affection.

Later that year Tewodros wrote a round-robin letter to the British Queen, the French Emperor and the Russian Tsar. It included an attack on Islam in general and especially on the Turks occupying much of coastal Ethiopia. He suggested a Christian alliance against his Moslem neighbours. In the version sent to London he specifically asked permission to send his own envoys to explain at first hand how the Turks were oppressing good Christians. Cameron was given precise orders to deliver the letter to the queen but instead relied on a string of messengers and it arrived in London early in 1863. By then the Foreign Office was incensed by its belief that Cameron was meddling in internal Abyssinian affairs. A combination of bureaucracy and bloody-mindedness left the Emperor's letter gathering dust in some Whitehall pigeon-hole. After eight months Cameron had no reply to convey. The French were a little more diplomatic – but only just. Tewodros found a convenient excuse to imprison the French consul, Lejean, until he received a reply. When it came it was signed not by Napoleon III but by his foreign minister. Tewodros stormed: 'Who is that Napoleon? Are not my ancestors greater than his?' Nevertheless he released the French consul, who, once safely across the border, let loose a flood of abuse against Tewodros, with little thought for those Europeans who remained within reach of the Emperor's wrath.

Into this explosive situation bumbled Henry Aaron Stern, a German missionary from the London Society for Promoting Christianity Among the Jews. A volatile and self-important character, he was unpopular among the other missionaries. During an audience with a heavily drunk Tewodros one of Stern's interpreters committed a blunder. Tewodros ordered that unfortunate man and another servant to be flogged so wickedly that they died. When the horrified Stern objected he was beaten unconscious and imprisoned. His baggage was searched and letters were found in which Stern and his colleague Rosenthal were critical of the Emperor. A book of travel writing by Stern included the insulting claim that Tewodros' mother had sold medicine for tapeworm. The two missionaries were chained up and their servants shackled to wooden yokes.

Meanwhile Cameron, embarrassed by London's tardiness, tried to steer clear of further trouble. It did him no good. Tewodros came to believe inaccurate reports that Britain and France were moving to support Turkish and Egyptian claims to Abyssinia's northern territories. The British consul and some of his staff joined the missionaries in chains.

London finally awoke to the urgency of the situation. Over a year after the Emperor's letter had been received a reply was drafted. It flattered Tewodros but insisted he could best demonstrate his affection for the queen by freeing the hostages. The task of delivering it was given to a Turkish Assyriologist called Hormuzd Rassam, a member of the British agency in Aden. The choice may seem strange, but no doubt the Foreign Office considered him expendable. After yet more delays he arrived at Massawa with Dr Henry Blanc of the Indian Army Medical Service and a regular soldier, Lieutenant Prideaux. They took with them 500 out-dated muskets as goodwill gifts. For weeks they were kept sweltering at the hot and humid coastal port while Tewodros played cat and mouse. It was not until January 1866 that they were permitted into the Emperor's silk tent to hand over the queen's reply – three years and three months after the original letter had been sent. Tewodros was pleased to see it had been signed and sealed by Victoria herself. Honour satisfied, he agreed to pardon the prisoners, by then being held in the Magdala stronghold. Blanc later wrote: 'The expression in his dark eyes was strange. If he was in good humour they were soft with a kind of gazelle-like timidity which made one love him; but when angry the fierce and bloodshot eyes seemed to shed fire.'

Rassam and company spent a pleasant month enjoying lavish court hospitality until the hostages were brought to them on the shore of Lake Tana. There were eighteen prisoners: Cameron and four of his European servants; five German missionaries: Stern, Rosenthal, Martin Flad, Staiger and Brandeis; the French messenger Bartel; two natural history collectors; the European wives of Flad and Rosenthal and three Flad children. Stern and Cameron, whom Tewodros had grown to detest, were in very poor physical condition.

Rassam, who realized his task was not complete until they were across the border, was determined that the captives should not come face to face with their imperial gaoler for fear of infuriating him again. He sent them on a roundabout route towards the border while he and his party crossed the lake waters by boat to pay their respectful farewells. They were ushered into the royal tent, only to find the throne empty. While Tewodros watched from behind a curtain the emissaries were seized. On the other side of the lake Cameron and the rest were again taken captive.

Tewodros claimed that Rassam had tried to spirit away the Europeans before they had formally made their peace. He also suspected that they would follow the Frenchman's example and shower him with abuse once safely out of range. But the chief reason for his action must have been the Europeans' continuing value to him as hard currency. In another letter to

Britannia: 'Now, then, King Theodore, how about those prisoners?'

Punch cartoon, 10 August 1867

THE ABYSSINIAN QUESTION.

London he held them openly to ransom in return for the skills, arms and equipment he needed to bring his divided, feudal country into the modern age. He specifically asked for 'a man who can make cannons . . . and an instructor of artillery'. The letter was delivered by Flad, who was forced to leave his wife and children behind as surety.

The Earl of Derby's new Conservative Government agreed to many of the Emperor's demands. A list of willing artisans was drawn up, including a gunnery sergeant. Six-pounders from Aden and arms worth £500 were collected as ransom, together with telescopes, field glasses and ornamental tumblers. A civil engineer and six technicians were sent towards Massawa before they were halted by disturbing reports.

At first the hostages had been treated well, especially the women. But then Tewodros set off on a series of marches to re-establish control over troublesome tribes. Cameron, Rassam, the original captives and some more were sent to Magdala where conditions were primitive and harsh. Three days later they were placed in chains. Blanc described their physical mistreatment as a great torture. Both he and Cameron were later accused of exaggerating their hardships. Rassam, who was proving himself to be a cool and courageous man, later wrote: 'Not one of the captives can justly complain that his imprisonment . . . was aggravated by privation. Nevertheless the chains were a great indignity for the Europeans even though their hands were free and their movements not seriously curtailed. They must have suffered considerable mental anguish when they considered that they were at the mercy of an unstable and unpredictable host.' Britain's Resident in Aden called for a rescue expedition. For a while the Cabinet resisted such pressure, despite growing public opinion and letters from the hostages themselves which suggested the Emperor was becoming madder by the day because of 'hot baths and concubines'. Finally Tewodros was given a three-month deadline to free the prisoners.

The ultimatum went unanswered. Tewodros was being threatened on all sides by internal revolt, desertions from his army and disputes with the Church. He seems to have convinced himself that the surest way of uniting his kingdom was to provoke a British attack which he could then claim was backed by Abyssinia's old Islamic foes. The Cabinet suspected such motives but agreed that Britain and her subjects could not be so abused. They were anxious, too, for a demonstration of British military power to dissuade the Russians from any encroachments on India. Chancellor Benjamin Disraeli proposed an extra penny on income tax to raise the £2 million thought necessary for a punitive expedition. All that was left was to find the right commander.

* * *

Lieutenant-General Sir Robert Cornelis Napier had been born a soldier. His middle name commemorated the 1810 storming of a fort in Java in which his artilleryman father had died. He was born that same year in Ceylon and after an English education sailed to India as an eighteen-year-old lieutenant in the Bengal Engineers. For the first seventeen years of his service he saw no action but built roads and bridges, painted, wrote poetry and collected rock and plant specimens. His devotion to art never left him and he was still taking lessons at the age of seventy-eight. That relatively peaceful life was shattered by the First Sikh War in 1845. Twice, in the battles of Mudki and Ferozeshah, horses were shot from under him. In the second engagement he continued his charge on foot until badly wounded, although his injuries did not stop him fighting at Sobraon. He saw more action in the Second Sikh War and in 1852 led a column in the Black Mountain expedition on the North-west Frontier. In the Indian Mutiny he saw both the first relief of Lucknow and its final capture. There was more fighting against rebels in Oudh and Gwalior and in 1860 he commanded a division in the China War. He had fifteen children by two wives. He excelled, too, at innovation and administration, bothering himself with such unglamorous but vital matters as camp latrines and the good health of his men. He was fifty-seven and the Commander-in-Chief of Bombay when he received orders to lead the Abyssinian expedition.

General Sir Robert Cornelis Napier, later Baron Napier of Magdala (*Illustrated London News*)

Napier realized from the start the enormous scale of the task facing him. The Foreign Office had envisaged a speedy dash into the wild Ethiopian heartlands, the snatching of the prisoners from an ignorant barbarian, and an equally swift withdrawal. The Duke of Cambridge suggested 'a flying column should be pushed forward . . . and finish the business before the rains set in'. The Cabinet certainly did not want an extensive, and therefore expensive, campaign. Napier knew better the logistical problems of fighting in hostile, rugged and largely unknown terrain. He believed that a flying column would simply be swallowed up and its men would perish in unnamed ravines. Instead he made detailed plans for a steady march with all supply lines defended. Given his glittering and successful campaigning career it would have taken a foolish man, even in the Cabinet, to contradict him. He got what he wanted.

His force was made up of 13,000 British and Indian soldiers – cavalry, infantry and sappers. The troopers included the 23rd Regiment of Foot, better known as the Duke of Wellington's. Its commander was Alexander Dunn who had won the Victoria Cross in the Charge of the Light Brigade. His men were largely Irish with a reputation for hard drinking and harder fighting although they included a good number of Germans who had signed on for the Crimea and never went home. The British troops and some Indian cavalrymen were armed with the latest breech-loading Snider rifles which had proved their worth in the American Civil War. The rest of the Indians, in line with Army policy since the Mutiny, carried the less efficient Enfield muzzle-loaders or the even older smooth-bores. In addition to the active soldiers there were over 8,000 auxiliaries: cooks, teamsters, grass-cutters, animal handlers and camp-followers. There were also eleven journalists, one of whom was Henry M. Stanley, yet to become famous for finding Livingstone, as well as a metallurgist, a geologist and a zoologist. The livestock amounted to 36,000 beasts, horses, mules, bullocks, beef cattle, camels and 44 elephants. Supplies included 70,000 lb of salt beef, 30,000 gallons of rum, 3,000 tins of condensed milk, 250 dozen bottles of port wine, 800 leeches in the medical carts and, especially for the Sikhs, a 'certain quantity of opium'.

It took 291 ships of every description to ferry them all from India, Aden and Europe to the Abyssinian coast. Napier travelled on the steam-powered naval frigate HMS *Octavia* and arrived at Annesley Bay to the south of Massawa on 3 June 1867. For three months the army had taken shape on the sandy shore. A constant supply of fresh water was ensured by the latest condensers and pumps from the United States. A photographic unit was established to copy maps. Two 300-yard piers were constructed to reach ships anchored in deeper waters. Stanley described his own disembarkation: 'It was as if a whole nation had immigrated here and were about to plant a great city on the fervid beach.'

The traditional reds and blues of the British uniforms mingled with the new and much more suitable khaki. The gaudy tunics of the Indians contrasted with the drab workclothes of Arabs, Africans, Turks. All struggled in the dust and the heat to bring that mobile city ashore. A score of languages competed with the braying of mules, the whinnying of horses, the trumpeting of elephants. In charge of all this organized mayhem was Major Frederick Roberts, a veteran of the Umbeyla expedition. It is a measure of the efficient job he did that, although he was to see no action in the campaign, Napier recommended him for a brevet lieutenant-colonelcy. It was another illustration of the prudent and methodical way Napier was determined to conduct this African adventure. Memories of the tragic waste of the Crimea were still vivid. Napier was determined that such cruel inefficiency would not be repeated.

He pestered London for more food and clothing before he would move out of his bridgehead. He busied himself with every detail, from the holes in his men's socks to camp sanitation which, one of his officers sniffed, was 'one of his pet hobbies'. He saw that dead mules were quickly replaced with fresh shipments, that sappers improved the roads, that a 10-mile military railway was built across a nasty stretch of coastal desert. Napier was criticized for his lengthy and detailed preparations. He brushed that aside and dismissed more talk of flying columns as dangerous, romantic nonsense. He had seen a lot of blood during his career. He was determined that not a single man would die because of his neglect. Christmas dinner that year was guinea fowl shot in carefully placed rows to conserve ammunition.

Meanwhile the hostages at Magdala were kept in two crude huts within the imperial compound at the heart of the mountain stronghold. After a few months they had turned these hovels into substantial homes with bedsteads, furniture and carpets given to them by Tewodros. Food was supplied by friends and relatives on the outside, augmented by tomatoes, potatoes and greenstuff from a garden and vegetable patch they planted themselves within the walls. They were weakened by the poor quality of some of their food, bored by the lack of variety, but they were far from starving as some of their champions had claimed in the British Press. Indeed they may even have fared better than their guards.

Those on the outside kept them informed through posted letters and clandestine messages. The first news they heard of a rescue expedition came shortly before Christmas. Any joy they might have felt must have been dissipated by news of Tewodros who had been away campaigning for a year. He and his army were on the move again, and heading towards Magdala. The war was to be a race to see which commander would reach them first.

Tewodros had failed to suppress the rebel tribes and his power was fading. He now gambled everything on beating the British in a glorious war. He told Martin Flad, who had risked the royal wrath by rejoining his family in captivity, 'I asked them for a sign of friendship which is refused to me. If they wish to come and fight let them come. By the power of God I will meet them and call me a woman if I do not beat them.' His Swiss and German artisans manufactured cannon and artillery pieces including a great mortar capable of propelling a 1,000-lb ball. He named this 7 ton monster 'Sebastopol'. It was the most cumbersome part of the army Tewodros led from Gondar towards Magdala. After desertions he was left with 5,000 fighting men, over 40,000 baggage-handlers, drivers and camp followers, the European craftsmen who still served him for pay, and several hundred native prisoners captured in his domestic wars. They made painstakingly slow progress through some of Abyssinia's wildest terrain. On the approaches to the high plateau of Zebrite thousands of men hacked and blasted a zigzag road for the new, prized artillery in which the Emperor placed so much faith. A contemporary engraving shows hundreds of men hauling Sebastopol with ropes while others placed logs and stones behind its

Captain Charles Speedy,
elephant hunter, mercenary
and soldier (*Illustrated
London News*)

wheels. Tewodros worked passionately alongside his workmen, lifting rocks with his bare hands. While this road was being constructed he heard the first firm news that the British were on the move. He said ironically: 'We must be on the watch as I hear that some are come to steal my slaves.' His toughest task was the crossing of the Jidda gorge, a deep gash which bisected the central highlands. It took eighteen days to cut a route to the floor of the ravine and another three weeks to scale the other side but by 20 February 1868 his entire army, including Sebastopol, was on the fertile plain of Delanta.

★   ★   ★

Napier had decided to divide his force into two separate parts. The larger division was to garrison and protect the long lines of supply and communications between their coastal bridgehead and their target. The smaller division, consisting of 5,000 fighting men, was to be the main striking force.

Advance parties set up a base 70 miles into the country at Senafay. As fresh troops reached it the first group, now rested, went forward to the next stepping stone at Guna Guna. In this methodical fashion the unwieldy army advanced in good order until the whole column was on the move. Napier aimed to take full advantage of the widespread discontent with Tewodros' rule and to win allies among the local barons, the *rases* who had their own reasons for hating the Emperor. These included Ras Kassai of Tigrai, a thirty-year-old warlord. In delicate negotiations Napier enlisted the aid of Captain Charles Speedy, who had first gone to Ethiopia to shoot elephants and who had once been part of Tewodros' entourage. He was 6 foot 6 inches tall, wore a bushy red beard and impressed the tribesmen with his ability to split a sheep along its backbone with one sweep of his sword. He spoke fluent Amharic and always wore native robes. Speedy used his inside knowledge of Ethiopian politics to steer the British commander through a minefield of tribal allegiances and vendettas to secure promises of safe passage through Tigrai, supplies and intelligence. By the end of January the British force was spread over 100 miles, the strike 'head' to the front, its long 'tail' guarding the supply lines back to the coast. Ras Kassai and the other barons could only be trusted so far.

The Europeans found the march easier than had been anticipated. They followed the crest of a watershed – rough going but not brutal for troops hardened in the boiling cauldrons of Afghanistan, India and Aden. They marvelled at pyramid rocks, fantastic stone columns, castles for giants with which nature mocked the puny efforts of mankind. Professional reportage

The Line of March of Napier's army (*Illustrated London News*)

Loading artillery on elephants (*Illustrated London News*)

and personal journals describe sheer precipices, gurgling crystal-clear torrents, the flowering of roses, violets, jasmine, the blurred wings of hummingbirds. The weather was clement but that would not last. Napier, who reached Adigrat on 6 February, knew he had to speed the march up if he was to complete his mission and bring his men back before the unbearable heat of July. At roughly the halfway mark the main strike force of 5,000 men had with it 1,356 horses, 518 regimental mules, 33 elephants, 1,969 camp followers, more than 5,000 baggage mules and 1,800 muleteers. Napier sent servants and many camp followers back to base with much of the baggage he deemed luxuries. There was much grumbling when he reduced the baggage allowance, even for officers. But the army's pace stepped up noticeably and began to average 10 miles a day. Two days ahead of the main force was a reconnaissance and pioneering party under Colonel Phayre. Napier led the vanguard of around 1,000 men, equally split between British and Indian. Then came the main strike force while the steady reliable elephants brought up the rear.

The land itself now began to fight for the Emperor. The route ahead was slashed by deep gorges and high ridges. Nevertheless Napier was confident he would reach Magdala by the end of the month. His intelligence reports told him Tewodros would reach the fortress at roughly the same time. It was going to be a close-run thing. An error by Colonel Phayre swung the race in the enemy's favour. He and his advance party had been striking far ahead.

Adi Woka, a mountain village
on the route to Magdala,
sketch by R.R. Holmes (From
*Record of the Expedition to
Abyssinia*, Holland and Hozier,
London, 1869)

He was directed by a rascally local chieftain called Wolde Jesus along some
of the worst tracks they had yet seen. Finally even those petered out in the
1,600-ft pass of Fulluk Eimuk Oonzool. They turned back and the main
column then took the obvious and direct route over the Amba Alajl Pass, but
Phayre's mistake cost them six precious days.

They marched on through the spectacular mountains of Wojerat
Province. The *Times* man reported: 'The country heaved with mountains in
every direction, like a rough sea.' The pace of the elephants and other
animals fell below 8 miles a day. Again Napier ordered officers and men to
shed more of their baggage, especially tents. Combined with fatigue and the
prospect of ever more saw-toothed mountains to cross, this led to more
restlessness in the ranks. One officer reported an increase in 'swearing,
grumbling and discontent . . . obscene and violent language'. Napier
paraded the Duke of Wellington's Regiment, gave the tough Irishmen a
severe tongue-lashing and switched them from their coveted place at the
head of the column to the inglorious rear.

Train of mountain guns crossing hilly terrain (*Illustrated London News*)

Weather and terrain worsened. Steep tracks, swollen rivers and hair-pin bends tested the ingenuity of the Sapper trail-blazers until Napier's column reached the relative ease of the Wadela plateau. On this high plain the tribesmen were reputed to be the best and fiercest horsemen in Africa. Aware of the danger Napier halted to allow stragglers to catch up. After a much-needed rest they marched the 40 miles across the plateau until they reached the Jidda gorge, 3,500 ft deep and 8 miles across. Napier was startled to see clear evidence that Tewodros was ahead of him: the mammoth new roadway that the Abyssinians had cut in the sides of the precipice. He was astonished also to discover that it was not blocked by the Imperial army or even by a rearguard. If it had been, Napier wrote home, he would not have had a chance of getting across. Instead the British column enjoyed a route made easy by the enemy.

Some 12 miles from Magdala Napier saw the outlying spurs which hid the fortress itself. He realized at once the 'formidable character of the whole position'. He wrote that he might need every man, on foot or steed, to scale its dizzy heights. Napier decided that the first flat-topped ridge at Fala should be his first objective. He aimed to muster his men on the level ground at Aroji, below a hill where, unknown to him, Tewodros had already positioned many of his heavy guns.

Tewodros had decisively won the race to Magdala. He entered the fortress on 27 March and carefully positioned his artillery on the ledge of Salamji

The Middle Sooroo Defile in the Senafe Pass (*Illustrated London News*)

and the twin peaks of Fala and Salassie which together overlooked the only viable approaches to the stronghold. For weeks while his army was on the move Tewodros had behaved like a general, a fine soldier, skilled tactician, a true leader of men. Once within the brooding, sinister Magdala fortress his unpredictable moods returned.

In a fit of belated generosity he ordered the prisoners freed of their shackles and given compensation of 2,000 silver thalers, 100 sheep and 50 cows. That order was quickly rescinded and Rassam was the only hostage unchained. Rassam used all his wiles to persuade the Emperor to unchain first Blanc and Prideaux, then Cameron and the other hostages. They were invited to stand with Tewodros to watch the heavy guns being dragged up the heights. He was in good humour even when the first British forces came within range of his telescope. He told one captive to take the glass and directed him: 'There thou will see thy brethren who had come from England to kill me. I am pleased to see those red jackets.' He was distressed only at the tattered appearance of his own men. He asked Rassam: 'How can I show these ragged soldiers to your well-dressed troops?'

In another generous fit he began to release some of the hundreds of native prisoners, a good number of whom were crippled and starving, who had also been held at Magdala. On the first day 186 women and children and 37 minor chiefs were freed. Seven men were executed. The next day Tewodros decreed that all the rest should be released, apart from a handful of political prisoners. The removal of several hundred sets of shackles inevitably took time and some Galla prisoners unwisely demanded food and water. Tewodros went berserk. He screamed: 'I will teach them to ask for food when my faithful soldiers are starving.' He speared several prisoners on the ground. His soldiers, fearful and infected by the same bloodlust, carried on the grisly work with swords and guns until between 200 and 300 lay dead or dying. Both corpses and wounded were thrown off the high cliff at Salamji.

The following day, 10 April, was Good Friday. Tewodros joined a concentration of gunners and troops on Fala. Below them were coats of red and khaki. He exhorted his men to smite the English as David smote the Philistines.

★ ★ ★

The British expedition had so far been almost faultless in its care, preparation and execution. Napier made his first major error when he allowed the unguarded baggage train to pass onto the Aroji plateau, under the false impression that Phayre's advance column would protect it. In fact Phayre was deep in a neighbouring ravine in search of a more suitable route for the pack animals and the heavy guns. The Abyssinians on the heights above saw the chance of easy prey. Napier quickly recognized his error and despatched the 23rd Punjab Pioneers and the King's Own Regiment to save the baggage. By this time Tewodros' tribesmen were swarming down the

Naval Rocket Brigade firing at Senafe (*Illustrated London News*)

mountainside. The cannons on Fala, Selassie and Salamji opened fire at maximum range. They were too far away to do much damage but one heavy ball landed yards from Napier as he sat on horseback directing his hastily assembled troops.

The Sikhs were first in position at the head of a ravine between the attackers and the train. The King's Own, with some engineers and members of the Naval Brigade, formed a line across the plateau just as the Abyssinians reached the level ground. The attackers, dressed in medieval armour and colourful cloaks, formed a solid mass of horsemen and foot soldiers 1,500 yards wide and seven men deep. The most reliable witnesses suggest they were 3,500 strong. They advanced not at some unruly ramble but at a steady, purposeful pace and with a cool courage that surprised the toughest British trooper. Facing them in the front line were perhaps 300 men of the King's Own, strung out across a shooting gallery as flat as a billiard table. Their firepower, including double-barrelled rifles, was awesome. The new Snider rifles were effective at 500 yards and their breech-loading mechanism made them capable of firing seven rounds a minute. What followed was not battle. It was butchery.

The first shots fired were the rockets of the Naval Brigade. They passed narrowly over the heads of the King's Own, causing more discomfort to the British than to the enemy. The British line opened fire at 250 yards. The first rank of Abyssinians fell. Among those initial casualties was the elderly

General Babri, dressed in a red tunic laced with gold, whom some of the British mistook for the Emperor. Neither the shock of the rockets nor the withering volley caused the attackers to slow their pace. They were battle-hardened troops and their tactics had always been to soak up heavy casualties in the first volley and then rush forward while their enemy was reloading. They had no experience of the Sniders, the first metal-cartridge breech-loaders generally issued by the British Army. There was no time between volleys for them to dash to the front line: no respite from the non-stop fusillade. Hundreds fell before the attackers took cover behind scattered rocks and returned fire with their elderly and inefficient muzzle-loaders. A group of sixty warriors scorned their comrades' good sense and marched to within 100 yards of the British lines until they too broke. The British counter-attacked as the day's light faded but Napier ordered a halt. He did not want this first proper engagement to deteriorate into a series of night skirmishes over unknown territory from which his own men could all too easily emerge as the losers.

In the meantime a smaller Abyssinian force launched a flanking attack on what they thought was the baggage train. In fact it was a light mountain battery whose guns were already limbered up. They opened fire at 500 yards but shot and shell failed to stem the onrush of warriors. Neither did two volleys from the out-of-date muskets carried by the Sikh Pioneers. The tough, hugely built Indians met the charge of savage but smaller Amhari warriors head on, with bayonets fixed. It was basic, brutal killing. The bloody hand-to-hand fighting all but massacred the attackers. A splinter group managed to get around the Sikh defences but were met by searing volleys from a detachment of the King's Own firing from behind the baggage. The survivors turned and fled, only to find themselves in a killing ground between the Sikhs and the mountain battery. Most died.

The night on the plateau was punctuated by the wails of women searching for their dead, the last death-throes of the dying and the snuffling of wild beasts. Stanley wrote: 'In ravenous packs the jackals and the hyenas had come to devour the abundant feast spread out by the ruthless hand of war.' British and Indian burial parties found that few Abyssinians had discarded their weapons as they attempted to flee the hail of shot. To the Victorian mind they had died like the very best kind of soldier. There was little rejoicing, much less gloating, in Napier's camp that night. They buried 560 Abyssinians. The true death toll was estimated at 700 minimum with 1,500 wounded, many of whom must have perished later. Napier lost 2 dead and 18 wounded.

Tewodros watched the slaughter from the Fala hilltop. He was furious at the ineffectiveness of the heavy cannon he had dragged, sometimes with his own blistered hands, over the mountains. One of the largest guns, his namesake Theodorus, splintered on its first firing. Tewodros was driven to despair at the defeat of his army by what he knew could only be the vanguard of the main British force. He returned to Alamji and told Rassam to compose a letter of conciliation to Napier. Prideaux and Flad were sent to the British camp in the early hours of the following morning. Napier showed both European and native emissaries his cannon, his elephants and the rest of his forces which had doubled overnight, with more men streaming in by the hour. Napier's letter of reply said: 'It is my desire that no more blood may be shed.' But his demands were tough. The prisoners must be released. Magdala must be given up. Tewodros must surrender unconditionally although Napier pledged 'honourable treatment' for the Emperor and his family. Tewodros was outraged. He scornfully described Napier as 'that servant of a woman'. The two Europeans were sent back to the British camp with a threat that all hostages might be executed and with the message: 'A warrior who has dandled strong men in his arms like infants will never suffer himself to be dandled in the arms of others.' Tewodros then fell back into one of his commonplace moods of black despondency. He put a pistol in his mouth and pulled the trigger. His retainers wrestled the gun from his hand but the bullet grazed his head. His few trusted advisers persuaded him to make a gesture of peace.

Hardly believing their luck Rassam, Cameron and forty-seven other prisoners were allowed to pick their way down the mountain slopes to the British camp. Mr and Mrs Martin Flad stayed behind, along with European artisans who worked under contract to the Emperor and who had never considered themselves hostages. The British soldiers were surprised at the captives' sleek, well-fed appearance. It had been assumed they had suffered horribly at the hands of the mad Emperor but there was precious little evidence of that. One of Napier's staff officers wrote: 'I must say I think they are a queer lot, taken as a whole. The rag-tag and bob-tail they have with them in the shape of followers etc., are wonderful to behold. They have about 20 servants of each sort, and the idea of being able to move with less than three mules for baggage seems to Mr Rassam as utterly impracticable.' Overnight the number of freed hostages swelled to fifty with the birth of a baby to one of the wives. The captives found that after years of living, albeit as prisoners, in some considerable luxury they were now expected to sleep on the ground under canvas, like any common trooper, and eat tough soldier's beef and chapatis. It was not a joyful reunion. Napier sent them grumbling to the rear where their dissatisfaction would not infect his troops.

Tewodros, by now desperate to appease, sent down the traditional Abyssinian gesture of peace: 100 cows and 500 sheep. They were rejected. Close to panic the Emperor ordered the remaining Europeans to descend to the British lines. They did so with 187 native servants, 323 domestic animals and large quantities of baggage, including more tents than were possessed by the British advance column.

Every European was now free and Napier had achieved everything except the surrender of the Emperor. He wrote to his wife: 'It is not easy to express my gratitude to God for the complete success as regards the prisoners.'

The 33rd Foot advance on Magdala from below Islamgee (*Illustrated London News*)

However, his strict military sense dictated that the war must end with the surrender, capture or death of Tewodros. His army had been unmolested, indeed fed, by various tribes on the understanding that the British would rid them of the despot. If he failed to do so he would probably have to fight for every foot of the road back to the coast. He reassured one of the rebel barons: 'We have come this far with an army to punish Theodorus for his ill-treatment of British and European servants.'

Tewodros gathered 2,000 followers within Magdala and planned to escape by a steep southern path to regroup elsewhere. Those of his supporters who elected not to fight with him 'to the end' he gave permission to flee or surrender. Many warriors did just that, including the commanders of the batteries on Fala and Selassie who agreed to surrender their positions in return for safe conduct. Thus Magdala's outer defences, for which Napier had planned tough and bloody frontal assaults, fell without a shot. The way was clear for a direct attack on Salamji and the mighty Magdala fortress beyond.

★ ★ ★

The attack began at 9 a.m. on 13 April 1868. The Duke of Wellington's Regiment led in fine drill formation, the band playing 'Yankee Doodle

Dandy' as they marched. They were met not by a hail of fire but by a disorganized flood of refugees and warriors who threw down their weapons as they fled down the track. One British trooper likened the scene to the flight of the Israelites. Napier's men found the Salamji plateau abandoned. Peering over the far edge they saw heaps of naked bodies, piled brokenly several corpses deep, the prisoners who had fallen victim to the Emperor's earlier rage. The stench was horrible. The gruesome sight stiffened resolve among the horrified onlookers and did much to counter the stories of Tewodros' civilized grace and courage which had circulated among the troops. The 300 twisted corpses were an eloquent vindication of the entire expedition. In the middle of the small plateau lay the giant gun Sebastopol. It had proved too heavy to drag the last stretch to the fortress. It, too, was a silent witness to the Emperor's grandiose dreams, now lying in the dust.

As the British and Indian troops were assembling on the level ground ten or twelve horsemen burst from the fortress in a wild dash aimed at carrying off some small, abandoned brass cannon. Leading them, clad in a white tunic and lionskins, and carrying rifle, spear and sword, was Tewodros himself. It was typical of the man: gallant, medieval, hopeless. He shouted a challenge of single combat, preferably with Napier. The British commander was not present and the most senior officer on the plateau answered the challenge with a salvo of artillery fire. Tewodros, his robes swirling, his steed's hooves raising a cloud of dust, screamed abuse at the British ranks. He and his wild warriors used their swords to make the sort of rude gestures that are universally understood, fired their rifles in the air, wheeled around and galloped back to the ancient fortress.

The storming of Magdala, as seen from the heights of Salamji (*Illustrated London News*)

Private James Bergin VC

Drummer (later Corporal) Michael Magner

At 3 p.m. Napier ordered the final assault. A steep track flanked by sheer rock and thorn hedges climbed the final 300 feet to the twin gateways of Kokit Bir. After surveying the defences by telescope he assumed that defenders were concealed behind rock slabs overlooking the narrow approach and hidden within the craftily designed hedges. Napier's artillery, 4 twelve-pounders, 12 seven-pounders, two 8-inch mortars and 16 rockets, bombarded those positions for an hour with little clear evidence of success. Napier recognized it could be a risky business which would mean heavy casualties if the fortress was heavily defended. He later wrote: 'If simply old women had been at the top and, hiding behind the brow, had thrown down stones, they would have caused any force a serious loss.' Colours flying, the attack was led by the scarlet-jacketed Royal Engineers and a detachment of Madras Sappers, followed by ten companies of the Duke of Wellington's in their khaki. Two further regiments and two more companies of Indian Sappers – the Baluchi and Punjabi Pioneers – were lined up in support. Napier's plan was for the Wellingtons (33rd) to give covering fire while the engineers blew the main gate.

A heavy downpour turned the path into a slippery mudbath. The attackers came under lacklustre musket fire which suggested that the morale of the defenders was broken. There were not even old women hurling rocks. The Irishmen of the 33rd were 'firing and shouting like madmen'. So enthusiastic were they that some of the Sappers ahead were grazed by British bullets. The defenders on the gate were more spirited and inflicted nine casualties, none of them fatal, on the engineers milling in confusion below them. The Sappers were unable to force the gate because the Abyssinians had piled heavy stones to a distance of 15 feet behind it. They could not blast their way through because, through an incredible oversight, no one had brought gunpowder, axes or even ladders.

The commander of the 33rd, Major Cooper, sent his men around the right side of the ramparts to find a weak spot. One massive Irishman, Private James Bergin, got a handhold on the wall and used his bayonet to hack an opening in the wicked thorns that surmounted it. He asked drummer boy Michael Magner to give him a heave up but he was too heavy for the lad. Instead he hauled the boy on to his shoulders and then pushed him up the final few feet with his rifle butt. Sitting astride the wall in clear view of the Abyssinians Magner coolly pulled up his comrade and then more of the 33rd while Bergin poured shot after shot into a knot of defenders behind the outer gate. Ensign Walter Wynter, who carried the regimental colours, later wrote: 'It was a tough pull up, but I was hardly ever on my feet as the men took me and the colours and passed us on to the front. I shall never forget the exhilaration of that moment.' As more troopers added their rifle power to Bergin's, the warriors at the gate broke and retreated across the outer bailey, taking casualties all the way. They ran through the inner gateway without bothering to lock it behind them.

Unknown to the Irish on the wall the warriors had included Tewodros. It was the final humiliation. It later emerged that only 250 men had stayed with him inside the huge fortress. He had been further disheartened by seeing his chief minister, Ras Engada, blown to pieces in the opening

Theodorus lying dead after shooting himself as Magdala fell (*Illustrated London News*)

bombardment. The Emperor of All Abyssinia, Elect of God, King of Kings, sat down behind a hayrick and again put a pistol barrel in his mouth. This time there were no loyal retainers to deter him. With the last shot of the siege he blew an enormous hole in the back of his head. The pistol was silver-plated with an inscription on the butt declaring it had been presented to him by Queen Victoria 'as a slight token of her gratitude for his kindness to her servant Plowden'.

When the British reached the inner fortress, passing through the unlocked gateway, they met no further resistance. The remaining warriors had laid down their weapons, with the Emperor's permission, during his last moments of life. The burial parties got busy. The artillery bombardment killed 20 Abyssinians and wounded a further 120. Another 45 had been slain by British rifles, most of them in the turkey shoot between the two gateways. Napier's forces suffered 10 wounded and 5 scratched by rock splinters. Most British reports admitted it had not been the most glorious or hard-fought battle in the history of the Empire. No one, however, begrudged Bergin and Magner the Victoria Crosses they were awarded on their return home. The citation read: 'For their conspicuous gallantry on the 13th April last. Lieut.-General Lord Napier reports that, whilst the head of the column attack was checked by the obstacles at the gate, a small stream of officers and men of the 33rd Regiment, and an officer of Engineers, breaking away from the main approach to Magdala and climbing up a cliff, reached the defences, and forced their way over the wall and through the

The head of Theodorus, sketched after his death by R.R. Holmes

The burning of Magdala (*Illustrated London News*)

strong and thorny fence, thus turning the defences at the gateway. The first two men to enter, and the first in Magdala, were Drummer Magner and Private Bergin.'

★   ★   ★

The British and Indian troops plundered Magdala, guzzling many gallons of captured honey beer. Their loot included brand-new English rifles, silver-mounted spears, toy soldiers, photographic equipment, state umbrellas and Persian carpets. All such items were auctioned within the fortress and the £5,000 raised was divided among the troops, who each received 25 shillings or 15 rupees. A representative of the British Museum, one of the scholars who had gone with the expedition, spent £1,000 on 350 beautifully illustrated religious books, lovingly and piously collected by the dead Emperor. All but two remain in the Museum. The imperial crown of gold was sent back to London and presented to Victoria. Many years later George V returned it to Ethiopia as a goodwill gesture to Haile Selassie.

The Emperor's wife Terunesh was discovered – a 'pretty, fair girl of about 25 with large eyes and long hair', according to an officer. She remained haughty in manner and treated the soldiers as servants. As a result she suffered the indignity of having her bottom smacked by coarse British hands until Napier took her under his protection. Tewodros' eight-year-old son Alamayu was treated well. Napier respected his father's wishes that he be given an English upbringing and education.

Tewodros' body was cleaned and laid out briefly in state, then buried alongside a ramshackle church known as the Madhane Alam or Saviour of the World. His shallow grave was in unconsecrated ground as he had died by suicide, a poor end for a man who, however fatally flawed, had shown himself a devout and zealous patriot.

Napier ordered the destruction of fifteen smooth-bore cannon on Magdala's ramparts and the dismantlement of the fortress walls. They were never rebuilt. Sebastopol was too heavy to move and lies there still. Everything else not looted by the victorious army was put to the torch. Napier recorded: 'Magdala, on which so many victims have been slaughtered, has been committed to the flames, and remains only a scorched rock.'

Napier's force retraced their steps, dragging a huge tail of refugees. Terunesh sickened and died on the march, despite the efforts of British doctors. She was buried with full honours. The column was hit by storms and by marauding bands of their recent allies, the war-like Gallas. Provisions ran low, although there were always daily issues of rum for the men, port and brandy for the officers and Press. Mules died in their hundreds and five of the elephants had to be shot. Other tribes were less friendly now that the tyrant was dead. Some even forgot past hatred and regarded Tewodros as a fallen hero, a martyr. Finally the exhausted and tattered force reached the coast and by 10 June the entire army was embarked on the waiting fleet. The drifting sands covered most signs of their passing. The *Illustrated London News* reported: 'The military expedition to Abyssinia . . . so reluctantly determined upon, so carefully organised, so wonderfully successful, has come to a close.'

Napier returned home in triumph. Disraeli praised the campaign's 'completeness and precision'. He told the Queen: 'So well planned, so quietly and thoroughly executed, the political part so judiciously managed, the troops so admirably handled during the long, trying march, the strength of Anglo-Indian organisation so strikingly demonstrated in the eyes of Europe, wiping out all the stories of Crimean blundering – the Abyssinian expedition stands apart.'

Napier's casualty rate had been astonishingly light. Just thirty-five Europeans had died, mainly through illness and exhaustion on the long marches. Three hundred were ill or wounded. Losses among the Indian troops, although not precisely recorded, were much the same. Such a carefully planned and well-provisioned campaign did not come cheap and there was some political disquiet in London about the financial cost. Parliament had voted £2 million but the final bill came to £8,600,000. A Commons select committee found that some profiteers had made a fortune from the supply of mules. Almost 28,000 animals, most of them mules, had been lost, stolen or destroyed. The P & O Steamship Company was also criticized for its excessive transport charges. Disraeli replied: 'Money is not to be considered in such matters – success alone is to be thought of.'

In his address to his troops Napier wrote: 'You have traversed, often under a tropical sun, or amidst storms of rain and sleet, 400 miles of mountainous and difficult country. You have crossed many steep and precipitous ranges of mountains, more than 10,000 feet in altitude, where your supplies could not keep up with you . . . A host of many thousands have laid down their arms at your feet . . . Indian soldiers have forgotten the prejudices of race and creed to keep pace with their European comrades . . . You have been only eager for the moment when you could close with your enemy. The remembrance of your privations will pass away quickly but your gallant exploit will live in history.'

In a dispatch from Suez he summed up his late adversary: 'Theodorous had acquired by conquest a Sovereignty which he knew only how to abuse. He was not strong enough to protect his people from other oppressors, while yet able to carry plunder and cruelty into every district he himself might visit. I fail to discover a single point of view from which it is possible to regard his removal with regret.'

Napier asked for and was given a peerage, becoming Lord Napier of Magdala. He was given a pension of £2,000 a year and the Freedom of the City of London. He was made an honorary citizen of Edinburgh and honorary colonel of the 3rd London Rifles. He received the thanks of Parliament, an honorary degree from Oxford and fellowship of the Royal Society. He was made a Knight Grand Commander of the Star of India. Although he saw no more action he served for several more years as Commander-in-Chief in India, becoming a field-marshal, before being appointed Governor of Gibralta. He died, aged eighty, of influenza in 1890. The German Emperor praised his 'noble character, fine gentlemanly bearing, his simplicity and his splendid soldiering'. R.H. Vetch wrote: 'Napier was a man of singular modesty and simplicity of character. No one who knew him could forget the magic of his voice and his courteous bearing. He had a great love of children . . . He never obtruded his knowledge or attainments and only those who knew him intimately had any idea of their extent and depth.' He was buried in St Paul's. No state military funeral since that of the Duke of Wellington in 1852 had been so imposing a spectacle.

Cameron received no honours on his return. His behaviour up to and including his ordeal as a hostage fell well short of what London expected of its overseas emissaries. He was pensioned off as consul and died shortly afterwards, complaining bitterly of his treatment to the end. By contrast Rassam, the expendable Turk, was given much well-deserved praise. He was awarded a special payment of £45,000 for services rendered. (Blanc and Prideaux received £2,000 each.) Rassam married an Englishwoman and died peacefully in Brighton. Magner and Killbricken-born Bergin continued

Almayu, the young prince, sketch by William Simpson (*Illustrated London News*)

their service with the West Riding Regiment although the latter eventually joined the 78th Highlanders. He died at Poona in 1880. Magner died in 1897.

With the British gone from Abyssinia the Egyptians occupied the coastal regions while bloody anarchy and civil war reigned inland. Various overlords fought to fill the throne left vacant by the death of Tewodros. It culminated in the savage battle of Adowa in 1872, won by Kassai of Tigrai who was aided by modern arms bought from the British. He was crowned Emperor Vohannes IV. His seventeen-year reign was not peaceful and the country was carved up between himself and Menelik, King of the Shoa, who by common consent succeeded Vohannes on his death. Both men inflicted crushing defeats on the Egyptians, subdued the Gallas, and reinstated the conditions for religious tolerance. For a time tensions faded and mass slaughter ceased until the Italians appeared on the scene – but that is a twentieth-century tragedy.

Alamayu was treated as an honoured guest and was brought up as a young English gentleman. He was schooled on the Isle of Wight, in India, in Cheltenham and finally at Rugby. He was thoroughly unhappy with the rigours of public school life and his mood did not improve when he was sent to Sandhurst to train as an officer. He took ill and became convinced he was being poisoned. He refused all food and medical aid and on 14 November 1879 he died, a sad and lost nineteen-year-old.

The queen was 'grieved and shocked'. A brass plaque was set in the wall of the Chapel Royal at Windsor. It reads: 'Near this spot lies buried Alamayu, the son of Theodore, King of Abyssinia . . . He was a stranger and ye took him in.'

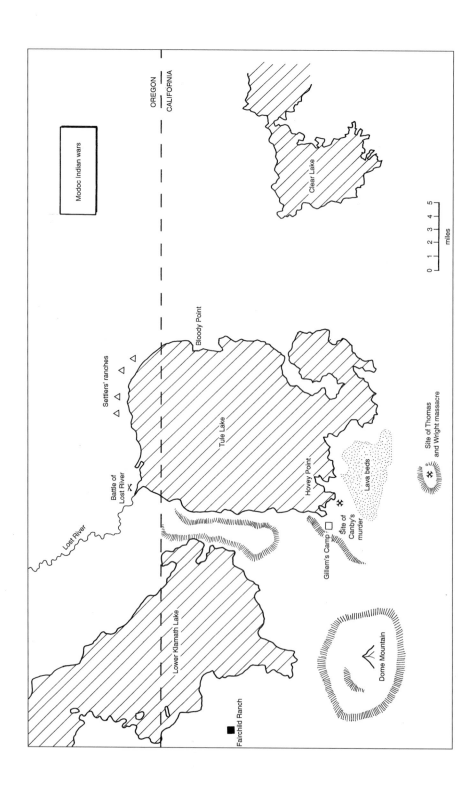

Modoc Indian wars

OREGON
CALIFORNIA

Lost River

Settlers' ranches

Battle of
Lost River

Tule Lake

Bloody Point

Lower Klamath Lake

Fairchild Ranch

Dome Mountain

Gillem's Camp

Hovey Point

Site of
Canby's murder

Lava beds

Site of Thomas
and Wright massacre

Clear Lake

0 1 2 3 4 5
miles

CHAPTER SEVEN

The Modoc Indian War, 1872–3

'All must suffer'

The Modoc War was a bloody shambles that has some claim as America's most inglorious conflict. The US Government engaged more than 1,000 Regular soldiers, over 100 California and Oregon militiamen, and around 80 Indian scouts yet still failed to humble a band of 'degenerate' Modoc tribesmen never numbering more than seventy-five warriors and their families. In skirmishes, raids and open battle numerically inferior natives repeatedly thrashed well-trained soldiers, veterans of the Civil War, and enthusiastic Volunteers. In the end it was internal dissent and betrayal which beat the Modocs, not force of arms. By then the US had lost 65 killed, including 2 scouts and 16 Volunteers, 67 wounded and £500,000, making it proportionately the nation's costliest war. Among the army dead was Edward Richard Sprigg Canby, the only Regular army general to be slain in the history of Indian wars. The Modocs lost 11 men, including their chief Captain Jack and three confederates executed after hostilities had ceased, at least 11 women and an unknown number of children. It is hardly the stuff of regimental honour, to be toasted at military academies. But the ironies and the individual tragedies involved make this war rather more than a ferocious footnote in the development of the American West. It echoes the wider brutalities, misunderstandings and mutual suspicion which soured every stage of the settlers' dealings with the native population and it has a resonance with the conflicts which erupted during the forging of the British Empire. Its two chief protagonists, more victims than heroes, were both decent men who tried to avoid bloodshed. General Canby and Captain Jack were fine men by the standards of their respective tribes. Their words retain dignity across more than a century. If matters had been left in their hands alone the war could never have happened, but both lost control and allowed themselves to be swept along to a bloody finale. Both died by treachery, ill-served by lesser men.

★   ★   ★

The Indian wars of the Pacific North-west have never received the attention given to the more glamorous sweep of the Plains or the dust-dry ferocity of

Apache country, but they were every bit as savage. The native inhabitants of this, the last frontier, were unaware of the encroachment of the white man's civilization until relatively late. They enjoyed a bountiful land, teeming with game. When the first settlers came they were welcomed, as there was more than enough for all. Then the miners came northwards from California, bringing with them the soldiers. The Pacific seaboard gave the Indians nowhere to go in their search for new lands. The newcomers had crossed a vast continent and were in little mood for compromise or accommodation. Their demands for land and access turned Northern California and Oregon into a place of bitter grudges, prejudice and occasional violence. It was likened to a kettle constantly coming to the boil. There was the Cayuse War of 1848, the Rogue River Wars of the 1850s, the Yakima War of 1853–6 and its successor the Coeur d'Alene War of 1857. General Cook's victory over the Paiutes in 1868 ended war in the rough lakelands until settlers began to complain about the 'apparently hostile dispositions' of a sizeable splinter of the Modoc tribe led by Kintpaush, known by the whites as Captain Jack.

The Modocs were a division of the once-powerful Lalacas who split from their brothers the Klamaths after a dispute over fish from the Lost River at around the time of the American War of Independence. The Modocs won their own independence but remained at odds with the Klamaths. Their land straddled the present Oregon–California boundary around Tule Lake and the Lost River basin. When white settlers began to squeeze on to their territory the Modocs numbered around 600 under the head chief, Old Schonchin.

During the 1850s the Modocs regained the warlike reputation of their forefathers with a series of attacks against white and Indian interlopers. But they were on good terms with some of the miners at Yreka, 50 miles to the west, with whom they traded. Old Schonchin (who should not be confused with his brother John) displayed great courage in early skirmishes with the whites but grew tired of conflict and remained neutral in the final war. A series of murders and small-scale massacres near the shore of Tule Lake, at a place thereafter called Bloody Point, claimed many lives but the local tradition that more than sixty settlers died in a single attack is a myth. After one raid two white girls were taken captive and adopted the dress and customs of the tribe until they were killed by jealous Modoc women. The citizens of Yreka decided to punish the tribe for the deaths of the girls, and Ben Wright was put in charge of a Volunteer company. On reaching Modoc land Wright claimed he had found the bodies of twenty-two white people. He invited the Indians to a parley under a flag of truce and a feast was prepared. Witnesses later testified that Wright had brought strychnine with which to poison his guests. (Later Wright's men admitted that they had planned a massacre, but not by poison which would have been 'unsportsman-like'.) Fearing treachery the Modocs refused to eat before the whites had themselves tucked in. Wright and his men then opened fire, killing around forty unarmed Indians. Only a handful escaped. This

Kientpoos, better known
as Captain Jack, 1873
(US National Archives)

treacherous act was not forgotten by the Modocs and greatly influenced
their behaviour twenty years later. Their own subsequent acts of treachery
must be weighed against this white precedent.

Purple-prose writers later claimed that Captain Jack's own father died in
the Ben Wright affair. In fact he was the son of a Lost River chieftain who
died in battle with Warm Springs and Tenino Indians when Kintpaush was
an infant. This gave him a claim to royal blood. He was born at
Wa'Chamshwash village on Lower Lost River around 1837. His Indian
name means literally 'He has water brash' (pyrosis). Little is known of him
until he was twenty-five, when he appears as an advocate of peace, a cool-
headed realist who believed that further warfare would destroy his people.
He befriended some prominent citizens at Yreka and carried documents
from them attesting to his good character. He became known as Captain
Jack either because of the brass-buttoned coat he wore, a gift from an
officer, or because of his resemblance to an earlier 'character' of the little
mining town.

In 1864 North California's Acting Superintendent of Indian Affairs, Elisha
Steele, concluded an informal treaty with the Modocs in which the tribe
relinquished their lands and agreed to settle on an ill-defined reservation on
Klamath territory. At a council the two tribes, feuding for so long, agreed to
keep the peace between themselves as well as with the whites. It was at this
peace meeting that Jack was first recognized as a sub-chief.

Almost immediately Jack regretted signing the treaty and told Old Schonchin so. However, the Modocs did their best to settle on the new ground, struggling with homesickness and trying to ignore the resentment and hostility of the Klamaths who, despite the treaty agreement, bullied the newcomers. Indian Affairs Commissioner Edward P. Smith, in his later report, made it clear that at this stage the Modocs were the victims, not the perpetrators, of antagonism: 'There is evidence that Captain Jack and his band were prepared at this time to remain upon the reservation and settle down in the way of civilisation, if there had been ordinary encouragement and assistance, and if the Klamaths, who largely outnumbered Captain Jack's band, and who were their hereditary enemies, had allowed them to do so. This band began to split rails for their farms, and in other ways to adopt civilised habits; but the Klamaths demanded tribute from them for the land they were occupying which the Modocs were obliged to render. Captain Jack then removed to another part of the reservation, and began again to try to live by cultivating the ground. But he was followed by the same spirit of hostility by the Klamaths, from whom he does not seem to have been protected by the agent. The issue of rations also seems to have been suspended for want of funds, and for these reasons Captain Jack and his band returned to their old home on Lost River, where they became a serious annoyance to the whites who had in the meantime settled on their ceded lands.'

Old Schonchin and most of the tribe remained on the reservation near Fort Klamath while Jack and his followers found themselves hemmed in on their old lands. There they stayed for almost four years as pressure for their removal was put on the military and the Indian Bureau.

Contemporary reports differ greatly as to the band's behaviour and the attitudes of their white neighbours. Considerable commerce was done with respectable white citizens and a farmer called Miller voluntarily paid the Modocs grazing rent for his livestock. Jack made some distinguished white friends whose affection outlasted the subsequent bloodshed. But inevitably on both sides there was deep-seated suspicion and prejudice. The encampment was described as a 'degenerate band', prone to getting drunk and 'selling children'. Another commentator wrote: 'They were a degenerate tribe, by common standards, whose men forfeited all claim to local esteem by profiting in the immoralities of their women, while affecting to be affronted by the proposal that they themselves be put to work.' Such is the language of bigotry, though doubtless it was substantiated by a dissolute and unruly minority of the Modocs. Among the whites old fears and the memory of Bloody Point and other raids must have been vivid, while they were determined to hold on to the Modoc lands given to them by the Government.

In 1865 Fort Klamath's commander Captain MacGregor made an unsuccessful and bloodless bid to return the Modoc band to the reservation. Two years later Jack and his men threatened to fire upon Superintendent

Huntingdon who was on the same mission. Jack consolidated his leadership of the band by showing such resolution while curbing the bloodlust of his most warlike followers.

In December 1869 Superintendent Alfred Meacham again urged Jack to return to the reservation. During the negotiations Jack dubbed all white men 'liars and swindlers' and refused to touch Meacham's proffered food for fear of poison. Nevertheless the parley continued, aided by the white trapper Frank Riddle and his Modoc wife Winemah, a cousin of Jack also known as Tobey. At one point in the delicate negotiations Meacham feared that Jack was planning murder. He said: 'I am your friend but I am not afraid of you. Be careful what you do. We mean peace but we are ready for war. We will not begin, but if you do it shall be the end of your people.'

Among the Modocs Schonchin John, the old chief's brother, urged the deaths of Meacham and his party. Jack once more insisted on peace and honour. Their wrangling was ended by the arrival of 200 soldiers, summoned by Meacham, who encircled the camp. The Modocs, disarmed but granted face-saving gestures by Meacham and the Army officers, agreed to return to the despised reservation.

It was a short-lived solution. The Modocs met the Klamaths for another peace ceremony. Meacham told them: 'This country belongs to you all alike. Your interests are one. You can shake hands and be friends.' Within three months such hopes had been shattered. Impetuous young Klamath warriors repeated their taunts and insults, and the bigger band tried to exploit the outnumbered and dispirited Modocs. The two tribes simply could not live together. Jack called a council and led the majority of his followers, around seventy families, back to Lost River. He remained convinced of the justice and common sense of his decision and won verbal support from some of his white friends.

Meacham, by most accounts – particularly his own – a reasonable man, now believed that the band should be forcibly returned to the reservation. The new Commander of the Department of the Columbia, General Canby, disagreed. Canby would not commit his troops to such dangerous and disruptive action while the Government dithered over the site of a permanent home for the Indians. Even the informal treaty of 1864 had remained unratified for two years and waited a further six before it was proclaimed by the President. Canby believed it would be 'impolitic if not cruel' to force the Modocs back. In the winter of 1870–1 Canby, a humane man, authorized a limited issue of food from Camp Warner to Jack's band.

Such an uneasy peace could not endure. The flashpoint, unusually, did not involve a clash with the white settlers. In June 1871 Jack was the arbiter in a matter of Indian justice. A shaman, paid in advance, failed to save the life of a sick child. Thus his own life was forfeit and, urged on by the child's relatives, Jack either killed the medicine man himself or authorized his execution. Friends of the dead man invoked the white man's law. An attempt to arrest Jack for murder failed, and Meacham knew that the territory was close to war. In a last bid to prevent the kettle exploding Meacham forwarded to Canby a scheme from a noted surveyor to create a small new reservation on Lost River for Jack's band. Canby saw it as a possible route towards permanent peace and revoked the order for Jack's arrest. Two Commissioners and two guards met Jack's force on his home ground. Again the militant faction among the Modocs – led by Schonchin John, Hooker Jim and another shaman, Curly-Haired Doctor – urged assassination. They were overruled by Jack with the aid of his lieutenant Scarface Charley.

Tragically the plan came to nothing. Jack agreed to the proposed new reservation, as did the Commissioners, and Canby himself. The proposal was sent to Washington. It was filed in some dusty cubbyhole of the Indian Department and there it remained. The failure of the faceless bureaucrats in Washington to grasp this sensible opportunity can now be seen as a major cause of the now inevitable war.

Jack authorized a raid on a cattle train to underline the urgency of the situation. The leader of that raid, Jack's half-brother Black Jim, was to be one of the victims of the final tragedy. Antagonistic whites continued to agitate for the removal of the Modoc band. The Modocs gave them little cause but every theft in the neighbourhood was laid at their door. One petition from Jackson County, Oregon, called on the 'strong arm of the Government' to be used against this 'petty Indian chief with 20 desperadoes and a squallid [sic] band of miserable savages.'

In spring 1872 the sympathetic, if cynical, Meacham was replaced as Superintendent of Indian Affairs by Thomas Odenal, a stubborn and self-satisfied official who understood little of Modoc grievances and appeared to care less. Odenal saw himself as a new broom, determined to sweep away such Modoc nonsense, and strongly recommended a forced return to the reservation without further delay. In July the Indian Bureau agreed with him. Canby had his orders and forwarded them to Fort Klamath and Camp Warner. The stage was set for conflict. Two Yreka judges advised Jack not to resist further and even offered their services as attorneys. Jack refused but clearly felt that such friends would help him if it came to a head-on collision with US authority.

Canby, always a stickler for obeying both the spirit and the letter of his orders, cautioned Lieutenant-Colonel Frank Wheaton of the 21st Infantry and Major 'Uncle Johnny' Green of the 1st Cavalry that if troops had to be used 'the force employed should be so large as to secure the result at once and beyond peradventure'. Odenal waited until November before moving. Jack refused to talk to him, claiming the protection of natural justice and his influential white friends. Odenal clearly underestimated the strength of Modoc resolve not to be shifted again. On 27 November he asked the Army to carry out the July order 'at once'. Both Canby and Major Green, the senior officer closest to the scene, accepted Odenal's judgements uncritically. But the Army's obligation to follow Odenal's directive was questionable then and seems even more so now.

Scarface Charley (Western
History Collections)

Green ordered Captain James Jackson and forty-three officers and men of
B Troop, 1st Cavalry, to take charge of Jack's band. The detachment
approached the west bank of Lost River, where Jack and fourteen Modoc
families were camped, while a force of around twenty-five Linkville citizen
Volunteers aimed for the east bank portion of the Indian village, where
Hooker Jim was sub-chief and Curly-Haired Doctor the shaman. The
troopers reached their target at dawn on 29 November and would have
taken the Modocs completely by surprise if it had not been for a solitary
gunshot from an early morning hunter. The two sides agreed to parley, the
Modocs wiping the sleep from their eyes under the barrels of Army guns.
Jackson's demand for the surrender of weapons began to be obeyed and an
Indian Department messenger, One-Armed Brown, was despatched to
Linkville to report the success of the mission. On the far shore the
militiamen had met with similar success, their charges sheepishly
acquiescent.

All that changed when Scarface Charley, on Jack's side of the river,
refused to give up his rifle, swearing and waving his weapon in Jack's face.
A lieutenant was instructed to disarm him and advanced on Charley
'calling him vile names'. Charley then fired the first shot of the war,
missing the foul-mouthed officer but setting off a mutual fusillade. The

Hooker Jim (Western History
Collections)

ensuing sage brush battle lasted three hours. Jackson claimed sixteen
Indians slain but in fact only one, Watchman, died. The Army lost two
dead and six wounded. Jack directed his force, firing for the first time an
ineffectual shot at an Army messenger. Jackson withdrew, burning the
Indian encampment as he left. Meanwhile on the far river bank the
militiamen tried to stop the Modocs running to their canoes to go to the aid
of their brothers. In the fight that followed several citizens died, while the
Modocs lost one woman, her dead infant cradled in her arms. The
Volunteers broke and ran.

The Modocs gathered to survey their short-term victory and hopeless
prospects. Jack took the majority of his band to the natural fortress of the
lava beds to the south of Tule Lake. Scarface Charley, whose shot had
sparked the battle, insisted on staying behind to warn friendly white
farmers, including the noted rancher John Fairchild, of the danger. But
the militants, once again led by Hooker Jim and including Curly-Haired
Doctor, Steamboat Frank and others, wanted a vengeance raid. Their war
party took a longer route to the lava beds, around the east side of the
lake, attacking every homestead along the way. They did not touch the
women or children but dragged out the men, most of whom Odenal had
neglected to warn of the impending action, and butchered them. At least

fourteen died, including the farmer Miller who had been on such friendly terms with the band. His supposed friend Hooker Jim shot him dead, later claiming that he had not recognized him. The killers, laden with plunder, scalps and stolen ponies, reached Jack's stronghold with blood on their hands and a taint of dishonour that was to remain with the tribe forever.

Jack bitterly denounced the murderers, perhaps sensing the scale of white vindictiveness about to be unleashed. Jack wished to hand over Hooker Jim and the others to the white authorities but he was overruled by a large majority vote after Curly-Haired Doctor vowed to 'take medicine' to protect them. Jack settled back to await the onslaught. His band was joined by fourteen more families from Hot Creek, led by Shacknasty Jim, who were fleeing from the violence of outraged Linkville citizens. In one of the many ironies of a messy war this group had been saved from lynch mob fury by the timely intervention of John Fairchild: the same rancher who had been warned of danger by Scarface Charley.

★ ★ ★

Jack's refuge was a superb natural stronghold, a portion of the lava beds rippling to the southern shore of Tule Lake, likened by Army officers to 'an ocean surf frozen into black rock'. Formed of the roughest type of lava, its ridges and escarpments, up to 50 feet high, provided battlements while its pitted surfaces provided natural rifle pits and trenches. Countless caves and tunnels provided shelter and lines of escape. Crevices, gorges and sinuous canyons made it impossible to traverse in good military formation, the broken landscape perfectly designed for absorbing cannon blast. Circular soil mounds and grass patches provided pasture for the Modoc cattle. Sagebrush gave them fuel. Water could be obtained, for a time, from winter ice in the darkest caverns, and more could be sneaked from the lake shallows. The rough terrain was ideal for the sort of fighting that the Modocs excelled in. They also knew every square yard of it.

Major Green tracked the band to what became known as Jack's Stronghold. He was joined on 21 December by Colonel Wheaton from Camp Warner, who assumed command. They waited for more reinforcements, including troopers from as far away as Vancouver, and three companies of Volunteers from both sides of the Oregon–California line. Wheaton's force grew to more than 325 men. He seriously overestimated the number of warriors facing him, putting it at 150, more than double the actual number.

On the night of 16 January 1873 the Government force split into two, commanded by Major Green and Captain Reuben Bernard, and approached the Stronghold from north and south. These officers and other seasoned Regulars knew what to expect. The callow recruits and over-enthusiastic Volunteers expected an easy, exhilarating victory. Most did not even bother to take blankets and bedrolls, expecting to be tucked up safely in camp the following night.

A dense fog fell around them and at 4 a.m. on the 17th the bugles sounded the attack. Two 12-pound mountain howitzers dropped shells ahead of the skirmish lines. Cavalrymen dismounted and joined the infantry and Volunteers, tramping over ground that grew increasingly hard and treacherous to the foot. Men crashed into each other in the murkiness, their yells destroying any sense of surprise, their positions pinpointed by the clatter. From the fog ahead there was only silence; there was no sign of the Modocs and it was assumed that the enemy had fled. Then, without warning, the fog was sliced by yellow streaks of rifle fire. The first soldier to fall was hit in the neck. A second dropped and the soldiers responded with indiscriminate firing, fog and rocks their only targets. Army howitzer shells began to fall too close for comfort to the advancing bluecoats and the cannon were silenced. Green called a charge but after several hundred yards in which more men fell the Modocs remained invisible. The accuracy and intensity of their sniping continued throughout the day as the two US columns floundered about ineffectually. Both columns came upon chasms wide open to Indian fire which the officers thought suicidal to cross. An attempt to unite the two Army groups almost succeeded but the fog lifted and the sunshine exposed even further the vulnerable troopers to enemy fire. Colonel Wheaton called a council of his senior officers as bullets whined overhead. Everywhere soldiers were in retreat or pinned down by murderous fire. The dead and wounded lay scattered among the rocks, lost to their comrades. Two troopers turned back for a wounded friend, but one was shot as they reached him. After further attempts to rescue them, both wounded men were left for the scalping knives. Trapped pockets of frightened men waited until nightfall before slipping away in the dark.

It was a humiliating rout. Some of the soldiers did not stop running. Many Volunteers drifted home shame-faced. The men they left at the Army camp were disheartened. They faced the prospect of cold, miserable winter billets and a long campaign with little glory. The confusion in the camp makes a true assessment of the US casualties difficult. Some reports put it at up to forty dead but that figure includes some missing men who may have deserted. More reliable reports put it at 11 dead and 26 wounded. Not one Modoc was hurt in the battle. Few troopers claimed to have even seen a single warrior. One brave who took part was suffering from wounds inflicted in an earlier skirmish.

That night the soldiers' bodies were stripped and scalped. The sound of the victory dance was carried on the night breeze to the ears of the chastened soldiers. Jack did not dance. Curly-Haired Doctor, supported by Schonchin John, boasted of the protection his medicine had given the Indians and Jack knew that he could soon face a challenge to his authority. He told his men that only the first battle was won and the white man would

General Edward Richard
Sprigg Canby, photographed
just before he was murdered
(US National Archives)

come again in greater numbers. But he pledged to fight on himself and
would not make peace until 'the Modoc heart says peace'.

* * *

General Canby, who commanded the Department of the Columbia from
his headquarters in Portland, was neither an Indian-hating martinet nor a
self-seeking careerist thirsty for personal glory, unlike so many of his
contemporaries. The testaments of fellow officers and men who served
with him throughout his career describe a compassionate, devout man,
zealous in his sense of duty, brave but not foolhardy, a born administrator
although lacking in imagination and handicapped by an awe of greater
authority.

He was born in 1817 and graduated from West Point in 1839. His
promotion, though steady, was not meteoric. He did not enjoy the privilege
of an influential family but relied instead on a gruelling series of tough

campaigns and thankless tasks in some of North America's most inhospitable corners. As a lieutenant he waded through Florida swamps, fever-ridden and deadly, to the battle of Palaklakaha Hammock. As a captain in the Mexican War he was pinned down in the sandhills around Vera Cruz, witnessed the taking of Mexico City and fought in the battles of El Telégrafo, Cerro Gordo, Contreras and Churabusco, being twice breveted for gallantry. In various frontier postings he hunted deserters heading for the California goldfields, and took part in the expedition sent to subdue rebellious Mormons. He advocated that troublesome Shawnee and Kickapoos should be treated 'with kindness and compassion'. Colonel Riley reported that he was 'at all times active and zealous in the performance of his duties'. As Colonel of the 19th Infantry in 1861 he opposed General Sibley's Confederate invasion of New Mexico. He fought and lost the battle of Valverde and from then on avoided combat, drawing the invaders deeper into the desert and letting hunger, heat and thirst whittle down the enemy. His tactics were wholly successful. Sibley lost half his force and the survivors staggered back into Texas. In 1864 as Major-General commanding the Division of the Mississippi he was shot by a Confederate sniper while sailing the White River on the gunboat *Cricket*. He was reported killed in Washington and obituary notices were printed, but he recovered quickly enough to assemble his forces to attack Mobile. The city fell on 12 April 1865 and the finest moment of his Army career came when he took the surrender of the armies of Taylor and Kirby Smith, the last Confederate forces on the field.

For five years Canby was switched around the South, smoothing the path of Reconstruction following the war between the States, unblocking administrative bottlenecks. He fed freed Negro slaves and protected them from assault, while trying to stop unscrupulous northern firms stealing southern cattle markets. 'Wherever he went order, good feeling and tranquillity followed his footsteps,' enthused soldier-author General George Washington Callum.

A Colorado Volunteer in an earlier campaign described him: 'Canby is usually seen near the head of the column, attended by his staff and a few mounted troopers as an escort. Tall and straight, coarsely dressed in citizen's clothes, his countenance hard and weather-beaten, his chin covered with a heavy grizzly beard of two weeks' growth, a cigar in his mouth which he never lights – using a pipe when he wishes to smoke – he certainly has an air of superiority, largely the gift of nature, though undoubtedly strengthened by long habits of command. His person is portly and commanding, his manner dignified and self-possessed, his whole appearance such as to inspire confidence and respect . . . I think of him as a man of foresight and judgement – patient, prudent and cautious – of great courage, both moral and physical, and as true to the Government as any man in existence.' There were some too who considered him a prig and a cold fish, dull and pedantic, smug. Yet the variety and diligence of the career which took him to the desolate lava beds of Modoc County tend to belie such views and only highlight the tragedy that was to end it.

Captain Jack told the friendly rancher John Fairchild, one of the few men trusted by both sides, that despite the brave words uttered at the scalp dance he wanted no more war. Former Superintendent Meacham agreed and others argued in Washington that a peace commission had a better chance of bringing the Modocs to heel than further force. The Secretary of the Interior, Columbus Delano, agreed also and in turn persuaded President Ulysses S. Grant, whose own wider-ranging peace policy was now largely discredited. Canby was told that the President 'seems disposed to let the peace men try their hands on Captain Jack'. Meacham was appointed head of the peace commission and in late March Canby was put in overall charge, his orders giving him 'the entire management of the Modoc question'. Other commission members were a Methodist minister, the Reverend Ezekiel Thomas, and the Indian Agent of the Klamath Falls Agency, LeRoy Dyer. The interpreters were Frank and Tobey Riddle.

Canby set up his field headquarters at Fairchild's ranch and the Commissioners made contact with the Modocs, initially through the Indian women Mathilda Whittle and One-Eyed Dixie, then again through Fairchild. For weeks second-hand negotiations proved frustrating and inconclusive. An apparent willingness by the Modocs one day was reversed the next. The cause was not any deceit by Jack, as was then supposed, but increasingly damaging dissent in the Indian ranks. Jack's leadership was under constant challenge from Curly-Haired Doctor and Hooker Jim and he could not afford to bend too far towards peace and an honourable surrender. He demanded an amnesty for all his people and a reservation on Lost River. Canby and his civilian colleagues demanded that Jack should hand over those who had committed the Lost River massacres. In a freelance bout of negotiations authorized by Canby the sympathetic Judge Steele mistakenly believed that the Modocs had agreed to unconditional surrender. He waved his hat in the air and shouted: 'They accept peace.' He was lucky to escape with his life when he returned to the lava beds the following day and Hooker Jim and his cronies discovered that under the Judge's proposals they were to be handed over to white man's justice. But they need not have worried – Jack had no intention of handing them in.

Fairchild, one of the few men to emerge with credit from the next sad chapter, explained to Jack the terms of an armistice while negotiations continued. Jack agreed, pledging that the white men would be safe if they met him on neutral ground, scrubland at the foot of a bluff just outside the lava beds. He insisted that there should be no soldiers with the commission and promised in return that his warriors would keep their distance and 'we will not fire the first shot'.

Two Modocs, Boston Charley and Bogus Charley, returned with Fairchild to Canby's headquarters. The commissioners agreed to Jack's proposals for talks but sent the two Charleys back to Jack with the proviso that the delegations must be either both armed or both unarmed. The Charleys added their own observations. They told the rest of the band about gossip in the Army camp of a Grand Jury indictment against the Lost River killers, of the lynch-mob temper of Linkville citizens, of the white man's desire for revenge. Such talk fostered among the Modocs the belief that the commissioners were plotting treachery. That belief was strengthened by the very visible build-up of Canby's forces as reinforcements arrived almost daily. The troops facing the Stronghold had moved to bivouacs closer to the lava beds and were now under the command of Colonel Alvin Gillem, 1st Cavalry. The Modoc militants advocated the assassination of the commissioners as a pre-emptive strike. Canby for his part wrote to his wife that the only hope of permanent peace was to remove the tribe as far as possible so that they could never again come home to Lost River.

Frank and Tobey Riddle, in constant touch with Modoc friends and relatives, were keenly aware of the intentions of Hooker Jim and the war-mongers. They repeatedly warned the commissioners to be on their guard. On 4 March the Modocs invited Meacham and several unarmed companions to a meeting inside the lava beds. Meacham believed the proposal 'undoubtedly means treachery' and refused. By April, however, hopes of a settlement had blossomed again. Modocs wandered freely about the Army camp. The commissioners' tent was erected on the spot Jack had suggested below the bluff, a mile from the Stronghold and roughly the same distance from the Army lines. On 4 April it was used for the first time, in the middle of a fierce snowstorm. Jack talked for seven hours with Canby, Meacham, Fairchild and Judge Roseborough, who had been added to the commission on a temporary basis. A further week of talking left all concerned pretty well exhausted. Canby refused a new Modoc request that they should be allowed to set up a new reservation in the lava beds but expressed his desire that a permanent settlement must include 'liberal and just treatment of the Indians'. Writing again to his wife Canby described his adversaries: 'They are the strangest mixture of insolence and arrogance, ignorance and superstition . . . They have no faith in themselves and have no confidence in anyone else. Treacherous themselves, they suspect treachery in everything.'

At a tribal council on 10 April the Riddles' worst fears were realized when the bloodlust of the militants overruled Jack's restraining authority. Despite their own misgivings about Canby's intentions, Jack and Scarface Charley bitterly opposed a scheme to murder the commissioners. Hooker Jim and others placed a bonnet on Jack's head, a shawl around his shoulders and called him a woman. They told him: 'The white man has stolen your soul. Your heart is no longer Modoc.' Shamed by the taunts, Jack threw the garments to the ground and declared: 'I am a Modoc. I am a chief. It shall be done if it costs every drop of blood in my heart. But hear me all my people – this day's work will cost the life of every Modoc brave. We will not live to see it ended.'

The decision made, Jack set about the planning of the crime with ruthless determination, as if to show his people that he was worthy to lead them to destruction. As chief he claimed the right to kill Canby himself. Schonchin John and Hooker Jim were to kill Meacham. Boston Charley and Bogus Charley were to kill the Reverend Mr Thomas. Shacknasty Jim and Barncho were to kill Dyer. But Scarface Charley vowed that he would kill any Modoc who touched his friends Frank and Tobey Riddle. Tobey, in one of her many visits to the Modoc camp as messenger, was told as she left: 'Tell old man Meacham and all the men not to come to the council tent again – they get killed.'

The following morning, Good Friday, 11 April, Jack and his co-conspirators waited at the tent, guns hidden inside their clothing. More warriors with rifles were hidden among rocks a short distance away. Canby emerged from his tent in the camp wearing full uniform but without his customary sidearms. Frank Riddle urged him and the other commissioners not to go. Most people appeared to share his disquiet. The scent of treachery was almost tangible but Canby seemed impervious to it. The Reverend Mr Thomas insisted that they at least should honour the terms of the peace conference and go unarmed. Meacham refused the offer of a pistol and wrote to his wife that she might be a widow by morning. Tobey, weeping, said: 'You no go, you no go, you get kill.' A small Derringer was dropped in Meacham's pocket where he allowed it to remain. Dyer permitted himself the same precaution. Canby meantime had ridden on ahead, unarmed, alongside Bogus Charley who carried his rifle in plain sight. The subsequent trial ensured that what followed is well recorded.

Shortly after 11 a.m. the commissioners, together with the Riddles who had come along to interpret despite their strong fears, reached the council tent. Here the smell of treachery was even stronger. The council fire around which peace terms were to be discussed had been set out of sight of the troops, there were eight Modocs instead of the agreed six, and Jack himself was clearly troubled. He told them that in his dealings with other tribes he had been given the name 'Indian's Friend'. Jack demanded the withdrawal of all US troops and when this was refused he fell into a moody silence. Schonchin John closed his speech with the words, 'I talk no more.'

There was a pause, then a war whoop which brought every man to his feet. Two youths, Barncho and Slolux, emerged from the rocks with rifles held ready. Jack took a revolver from the folds of his coat and shouted 'Ot we kau tux', the Modoc for 'All ready.' He pointed his gun at Canby's head but the first shot misfired. He turned the cylinder and fired again as the other Modocs opened up on their own targets. Jack's bullet entered Canby's head below the left eye and sliced downward, breaking his jaw. He stumbled away but Jack held him down while Ellen's Man cut his throat and shot him again in the head. They both stripped the body.

Boston Charley shot Thomas above the heart and Bogus Charley shot him in the head as he lay on the ground. The Reverend's corpse was also stripped. Commissioner Dyer and Frank Riddle turned and ran. Hooker Jim fired repeatedly at Dyer, missing each time. Then Dyer stopped and turned to face him, drawing his own Derringer. Hooker Jim dropped to the ground to avoid the shot, giving Dyer extra time to escape. Jack's half-brother Black Jim, who had been prominent at the peace talks, pursued Dyer further but turned back to help strip the bodies. Mindful of Scarface Charley's warning, no attempt was made to harm Riddle.

Meacham, who had known these Modocs personally for several years and who had done his best to both curb and aid them, refused to play the easy victim. At Jack's first signal he outdrew Schonchin John and pressed his Derringer against the Indian's chest. Twice it misfired. Schonchin John fired point-blank at Meacham's face but missed. Meacham retreated backwards uncertainly. Schonchin John emptied his revolver, missing every time. He took another gun but twice his aim was spoiled by Tobey Riddle who grappled with his arm despite several blows to her head. Shacknasty Jim took aim but Tobey turned on him and knocked the gun from his hand. Schonchin John sat on a rock and took more careful aim. He scored a direct hit in Meacham's face but by some freak combination of ballistics and bone it merely gouged out a slice of eyebrow. Meacham fired back and struck Schonchin John, who fell wounded off his rock. Other Indians fired, hitting Meacham twice more and bringing him down. He lay twitching as Shacknasty Jim began to strip him, turning away Slolux who was about to shoot him in the head, saying 'He is dead.' Tobey was left wailing beside the body but Boston Charley returned to take his scalp. The knife had begun its work before Tobey chased him off, hurling rocks and telling him that soldiers were coming. Incredibly, Meacham was still alive although the troopers found him muttering in delirium, 'I am dead, I am dead.' Brandy was forced down his throat and Surgeon Cabanis operated and saved his life.

On the far side of the Stronghold Curly-Haired Doctor tried to lure Colonel Mason into a similar trap. Mason, an experienced Indian campaigner, was suspicious and refused to talk. The Modocs attacked two officers, wounding Major Boyle in the thigh. Gillem, left in command of all the US forces, was dazed. His troops turned out in battle order but by then the damage had been done.

★ ★ ★

Newspaper reporters in the Army camp dispatched the story of Canby's murder to a shocked world. It sparked fury, shame and disgust. In Yreka and Jacksonville Secretary Delano's effigy was hanged because of his efforts at conciliation. In Washington the news was greeted with 'horror-stricken surprise'. The *Times* of London labelled it 'an outrage'. The *New York Times* reported: 'Seldom has an event created so deep a feeling of horror and indignation.' Other newspapers demanded the immediate extermination of the renegade band. One of the few dissenting voices came from the *Athens*

Northeast Georgian. Canby's Civil War successes were bitterly remembered in that part of the South and the newspaper's headlines gloated: 'Capt Jack and Warriors Revenge the South By Murdering General Canby. Three Cheers for the Gallant Modocs.' The Army was appalled and enraged by the only casualty of such high rank in the Indian wars to that date. (George Armstrong Custer, a later victim, was merely a brevet general and not entitled to the rank at the time of his death.) General Sherman telegraphed: 'Any measure of severity to the savages will be sustained.' In another message to officers he added: 'You will be fully justified in their utter extermination.'

The murders did grave damage to President Grant's peace policy, but that strategy was almost certainly dying in any case. For five years Grant, a hardened professional soldier, had counselled mercy, understanding and humanity in dealing with the Indians; that his policy had survived so long is in itself surprising.

Canby's troopers in the field took the salute over his body in a simple ceremony. His remains were taken to Yreka and from there by special train

Loa-kum-ar-nuk, a Warm Springs Indian and Army Scout, taking aim in a clearly posed photographed in the lava beds (US National Archives)

to Portland where he lay in state. The tributes paid were almost equal to those paid to Lincoln. After four services across the continent Canby was at last buried in Crown Hill Cemetery, Indianapolis.

On 14 April the War Department named Canby's successor. He was the tough Jefferson Davis, Colonel of the 23rd Infantry and a brevet Major-General, but the man on the spot was still Colonel Gillem. He was joined at his camp on the south shore of Tule Lake by Donald McKay and seventy-two Warm Springs Indian Scouts, all clad in US Army uniforms. An escaped Modoc prisoner told Jack of their arrival, of Gillem's planned attack with 1,000 men, and of Meacham's survival. Jack sent the children and the elderly to well-protected caves and placed his men behind natural and artificial barricades. The women stayed to carry water and ammunition to their men.

Reinforced by the Scouts, Gillem's assault plan was very similar to Wheaton's. This time, however, there were enough men to give it a good chance of success despite the lava maze, there was no fog to add to the confusion, and there were fewer raw recruits and over-confident Volunteers. On the other hand the Modocs were now better armed, having stripped Wheaton's fallen men of their more modern rifles and ammunition. For three days Gillem's forces advanced slowly and methodically from two sides

US soldiers engaging Modoc marksmen (US National Archives)

into the lava beds. At night howitzers and four mortars softened up the Indian positions. On the first day the Army lost five men dead and a large number wounded, the latter taken away by mule litters and by boats across the lake. The advance was temporarily halted, but Gillem and his men wore down their enemy with fatigue and force of numbers. The soldiers advanced, then rested while others took their place. The Modocs in their rifle pits and entrenchments, their nerves stretched by the night-time bombardments, enjoyed no such relief. To the immediate west of Jack's Stronghold one Lieutenant Egan tried to cross an exposed wasteland. He soon fell wounded but he and his men had dug into a crucial position within range of the Indian defenders. The young officer was tended at his post by the tireless Surgeon Cabanis. Even now the onslaught might have failed to dislodge the Modocs save for the desperate shortage of water. The band's supply, never great, had dwindled to nothing. Jack sent warriors crawling through the sagebrush to bring back water from the lake. Clashing with Army pickets, they failed to break through, but neither were they beaten back and a temporary stalemate ensued. The Army did let several old Indian women cross their lines to the shore. Among them was discovered a young warrior in disguise. He was killed and scalped by soldiers, who managed to take five scalps from his head as trophies of their daring. Hooker Jim led a raid on the Army teamsters, killing a man called Hovey. The raiders tried to encircle the baggage camp but withdrew after a few shots. This was the last action of a gruelling three-day battle that had consisted mainly of sniping and the occasional burst of individual initiative.

On the morning of the fourth day the soldiers found the Indian positions eerily deserted. Jack and his band had slipped away, leaving the bodies of two warriors and a woman, and a sick old man who was too infirm to move. The soldiers decided, incorrectly, that he was Schonchin John and shot him to pieces. Once again an Indian scalp was divided into many ugly trophies. The fusillade that killed the unknown geriatric was faintly heard by Jack's band hiding a few miles to the south. Far from being defeated they had merely retreated deeper into the lava beds where there was a little more precious water. They concealed themselves so well that the Army had little idea of their whereabouts. For several days there was an uneasy lull as the Modocs rested, creeping out from time to time to pick off the odd sentry.

Fourteen Modocs under Scarface Charley were spotted returning to the lake for more water. They beat off a company of troopers who returned to camp with three dead. The Modocs fired into the lines of Army tents. Artillery was swung around to bear on them. As each round curved through the air the Indians simply sheltered behind rocks, emerging after each shellburst to taunt the gunners. They fired bunched volleys into the camp while several hundred soldiers stood by and made no effort to stop them. All fourteen braves returned unscathed to the Modoc hide-out.

By 26 April the Warm Springs Scouts had found the Modoc camp but Gillem was determined to proceed cautiously as he did not want another tragedy. Sadly, that is exactly what he got. Captain Evan Thomas and at least sixty-four officers and men were sent ahead to reconnoitre the Modoc positions. Their chief task was to discover whether artillery could be placed to bombard the camp. Gillem expressly ordered Thomas to avoid engaging the enemy. The detachment stopped for lunch under a butte and Thomas called in his skirmishers to eat. Lieutenant Arthur Cranston and five men volunteered to explore the rugged ground and were soon out of sight of the main party. They were ambushed by twenty-four Modocs hidden in rocks on either side. Every man died in the brief slaughter. Thomas, hearing the gunshots, sent two more lieutenants, Wright and Harris, with men to dig in at the side of the butte. When they reached it the Modocs, firing from above, simply continued the massacre. Thomas's command was thrown into fatal confusion as the two dozen soldiers panicked and ran. The rest stayed for what they were sure would be a doomed last stand. Donald McKay and fourteen of his Scouts arrived on the scene to prevent their total annihilation, but not in time to save Thomas himself. All five field officers were dead, alongside twenty enlisted men. Sixteen were wounded, including the only officer to survive the engagement, Assistant-Surgeon B. Semig. Not one Modoc was reported even hurt. Indians later claimed that Scarface Charley had permitted some soldiers out of the trap, calling on his fellows to stop shooting and crying: 'My heart is sick seeing so much blood and so many men lying dead.'

Army morale plunged while its shame soared. For three hours the battle had raged within sight and sound of an Army signal station. More than twenty survivors limped back to base camp before any reinforcements were sent. A superior force had been routed and half wiped out by a small band of savages. The Army was humiliated and 'despondency pervaded the entire command'. The shock waves that this new fiasco sent through the War Department were heightened by the family connections of the dead officers: Thomas was the son of Lorenzo Thomas, a former Adjutant-General; Thomas Wright was the son of the famous Indian fighter General Wright who had drowned at sea eight years earlier; Lieutenant Albion Howe was the son of Major-General Albion P. Howe of the 4th Artillery.

On 2 May Davis arrived to take command, deeply contemptuous of much of his command. In his eyes the Thomas massacre proved that many were 'only cowardly beefeaters'. His first move was to send out McKay's Scouts to locate the enemy and protect local settlers. He waited for further reinforcements and, with the force of his personality, raised camp morale. On 6 May the bodies of Cranston and his men were found. The following day a score of Modocs attacked a supply train escort of equal numbers, sending the white men fleeing with three wounded. Davis sent two companies, under Captain Henry Hasbrouck, to sweep the region outside the lava beds. They were issued with five days' rations. On 10 May, at Dry Lake, they were attacked at dawn. Determined perhaps to atone for the shame of the previous engagements the soldiers stood their ground and coolly returned fire. Ellen's Man, who with Jack had butchered Canby, was killed in the skirmish. Jack was seen amid the fighting, wearing Canby's plundered jacket. Once again the Scouts proved invaluable. They helped push the Modocs back 3 miles towards the lava beds. It was the Army's first real, if modest, victory in the whole campaign.

The Modocs returned to their encampment with just a few casualties. But the death of Ellen's Man caused Jack more trouble. He was accused of keeping his own relatives out of danger while better men risked their lives in the forefront of battle. The band began to split in two, this time permanently. Hooker Jim, Curly-Haired Doctor and others who had been the first to urge the killing of the commissioners were losing heart. The lack of water remained a desperate problem. The setback at Dry Lake had exposed as a fraud the medicine man's supposed protection. The Modocs' winning streak was over. The band broke into two groups and both left the lava beds for the last time.

★ ★ ★

Fourteen families under Hooker Jim went west. On 18 May they blundered into a mounted squadron commanded by Hasbrouck and scattered south of Lower Klamath Lake after a running fight. Four days later most had surrendered. Hooker Jim and his fellows offered Davis their help in tracking down Jack, with or without the promise of an amnesty. It was a remarkable act of double treachery as all had earlier voted for war and several were involved in the killing of Canby and Thomas. Some had been on the brutal Lost River raid. Davis himself regarded Hooker Jim as 'an unmitigated cut-throat'. He accepted the offer.

Hooker Jim, Bogus Charley, Shacknasty Jim and Steamboat Frank were set free and pursued their task with diligence. They guessed correctly that Jack and their former comrades would head for Willow Creek, an offshoot of Lost River. They found them after three days. The four urged Jack's followers – thirty-seven warriors and their families – to surrender, saying they could not fight and run for ever. Jack's men were war-weary, tired, cold and hungry, and many were wounded. Yet the renegades were called squaws and Jack told Hooker Jim: 'You intend to buy your liberty and freedom by running me to earth . . . You realise life is sweet but you did not think so when you forced me to promise that I would kill that man Canby.' Jack sent them away to 'live like white men.'

The four men reported to Davis on 28 May that Jack intended to attack a nearby ranch. A cavalry detachment under Major John Green was the first to reach the ranch while two squadrons under Hasbrouck and Jackson followed. The following afternoon the troopers surprised Jack's band on Willow Creek, just across the Oregon state boundary. The Modocs fled to Langell Valley. The various US units now in the field vied with each other to be the first to kill or capture Captain Jack. The Modoc war ended as 'more of a chase after wild beasts'. The Indians scattered as warriors sought to save their women and children. In ones, pairs or family groups they surrendered to the soldiers.

On 3 June Jack and his family were cornered in a cave by cavalrymen under Captain David Perry. The chief was utterly dejected and only two or three braves remained with him. He agreed to give up without a struggle, explaining simply: 'My legs have given out.' He was taken in manacles to join the rest of his dispirited band at the Tule Lake Army camp. General Sherman was not best pleased with the sordid, inglorious round-up which had closed the war. He wrote: 'Davis should have killed every Modoc before taking him if possible. Then there would have been no complications.' The tribe, he said, should be dispersed throughout the reservations 'so that the name of Modoc should cease'. But Davis, not a noted humanitarian, had good reason to show restraint. He was aware of the acrimony heaped upon officers involved in the massacre of Indians elsewhere and Grant's peace policy was still not quite dead. Davis had decided that instead of taking general vengeance on the entire band, Jack and eight other supposed ringleaders should face a drumhead trial followed by swift execution. A scaffold was built. Ironically new orders from Sherman stopped it being used. The general had decided that Jack and the others involved in Canby's murder should be tried by military court while Hooker Jim and the Lost River murderers should be handed over to state courts. Six men were charged by Davis's military court. None of the four renegades joined them in the dock.

After the round-up of the last scattered Modocs Fairchild's brother James took charge of fifteen men, women and children to take them by mule wagon to the Army camp. They met a group of Oregon Volunteers who threatened the families but Fairchild persuaded them that his prisoners were unimportant Indians. A few miles on he was stopped by two horsemen who held a pistol to his head. They killed four unarmed braves in the wagon and wounded a woman before fleeing as an Army patrol approached. The murderers, although well known locally, were never pursued or charged, never mind brought to trial.

Meanwhile there was still the matter of the Lost River killers and Sherman's orders that they be handed over to civilian justice. Davis invited the families of the dead settlers to the camp to pick out the murderers. Two widows identified Hooker Jim and Steamboat Frank. The two women pulled out a knife and a pistol but were disarmed by soldiers. Neither man ever faced trial. The Modoc renegades had helped the Army restore its pride and so were rewarded. Curly-Haired Doctor, perhaps the greatest villain of the whole affair, conveniently blew out his own brains.

At Fort Klamath on 5 July the military trial opened in a bare hall dominated by a rough wooden table. Beside Jack stood his half-brother Black Jim, Schonchin John and Boston Charley. On the floor sat Barncho and Slolux, the two youths who had supplied the rifles for the *coup de grâce* on Canby and the attempt on Meacham. The Judge Advocate was Major

H.P. Curtis and the panel included Captain Hasbrouck. The Riddles were present throughout, acting as both witnesses and interpreters. An Army unit with fixed bayonets stood to one side. Among the unruly crowd of spectators, widows and reporters stood Hooker Jim, Bogus Charley, Shacknasty Jim and Steamboat Frank, who watched the proceedings with interest, occasional amusement and not the slightest sign of guilt. The defendants were charged with the murders of Canby and Thomas 'in violation of the laws of war' and the attempted slayings of Meacham and Dyer.

On the third day the Modoc renegades gave their damning evidence. That afternoon Meacham, still suffering from his terrible wounds, limped into the courtroom to give his testimony. Later he offered his services as counsel for the Modoc defendants but was persuaded by friends to withdraw the gesture. Only three witnesses were called for the defence: Scarface Charley and two Modocs whose words carried precious little weight, Dave and One-Eyed Mose. Jack's own speech was defeated and dismal. The following day all six were sentenced to death. The judge ruled that no others should be brought to trial, an instruction which greatly helped Hooker Jim and his confederates avoid the civilian courts. An Oregon sheriff later arrived with warrants for their arrest but was turned away.

On 2 October, as six nooses dangled from the scaffold, the fort chaplains explained the sentences to the condemned men. Jack said, without any obvious bitterness, that he had believed his surrender would be rewarded with a pardon. The four renegades, he claimed, had beaten both himself and the US Government. Asked who should be chief when he was gone he said that he could no longer trust any Modoc to do the job. Black Jim said he should be allowed to live to lead the tribe but Jack snorted in derision. The youngsters Barncho and Slolux simply denied that there was any blood on their hands, which was strictly true. Boston Charley confessed his involvement in the murders but declared he had believed that Canby and the commissioners were themselves plotting treachery. Schonchin John said: 'War is a terrible thing. All must suffer – the best horses, the best cattle and the best men.'

As dawn broke on 3 October 1873 the roads to Fort Klamath were packed with sightseers. There was a carnival atmosphere. At 9.30 a military detail drew up outside the guardhouse. Six figures stumbled into the morning sunshine. A wagon held just four coffins. The prisoners sat beside the boxes while a blacksmith cut their shackles. Then the wagon trundled to the scaffold where Barncho and Slolux were left on board – President Grant had commuted their sentences to life imprisonment.

Jack stood on the extreme right. Beside him, in order, were Schonchin John, Boston Charley and Black Jim. Corporal Ross put the halter around Jack's neck while fellow infantrymen did the same for the rest. One stroke of an axe cut the rope securing the trap door beneath all four men. From within a nearby stockade Modoc prisoners screamed their anguish. When the men were dead, their bodies were cut down and placed in their rude coffins. Colonel Wheaton, in charge of the arrangements, was offered £10,000 for Jack's body by a showman. He indignantly refused the offer. Instead the heads of all four were hacked off and sent to the Army Medical Museum in Washington.

Jack left two widows, Lizzie and another woman whose name was not recorded. The survivors of his band were again split in two. The larger band, 155 strong, was sent to a malarial patch of earth in the south-west corner of Indian Territory, next to the Quapaws reservation. By 1905 they had declined to just fifty-six souls. The second group rejoined their fellow Modocs on the Klamath reservation. There they held their own and thirty years later numbered 223. The Modoc name did not vanish but never again did it pose a threat to the white man.

In the 1940s the executors of a dead Army officer in Portland found three skulls in a box in a basement. One was labelled 'Captain Jack'.

CHAPTER EIGHT

The Riel Rebellion, 1885

'I am sure that my mother will not kill me'

At Fort Benton Louis Riel said farewell to a Jesuit priest. He pointed to a nearby crest and called, 'Father, I see a gallows on top of that hill, and I am swinging from it.' A year later, after leading his second uprising of Metis half-breeds in the swiftly growing nation of Canada, his hand-written message from death row said: 'I have devoted my life to my country. If it is necessary for the happiness of my country that I should now soon cease to live, I leave it to the Providence of my God.' He believed he was a Prophet. Some, friends and enemies alike, believed him mad.

The year was 1885. Canada was about to be joined from coast to coast by the last spike of the continental railway. Riel's rebellion came at the beginning of the modern age and was much more than a revolt that flickered briefly and faded after a few skirmishes. His influence was pivotal in the making of modern Canada. And the passions he inspired, among natives and Europeans, British and French, Protestant and Catholic, continue to divide Canada to this day.

★ ★ ★

The Metis were people of mixed blood who grew out of Canada's pioneer infancy. Most were the offspring of French and native Indians, although many of their cousins had English and Scots parents and grandparents. They were devout Catholics who had been trapping and settling Canada since the 1650s, the descendants of Champlain's men, the founders of Quebec. The different blood that flowed in their veins gave them a powerful sense of identity. These were no ragtag of illegitimate drifters but a proud people who had carved their own lives out of the wilderness.

They were farmers and landsmen but also hunters. By 1840 there were 5,000 of them, far outnumbering the white settlers. On one occasion more than 400 hunters, backed by 200 stockmen and 1,000 women and children, took part in a great buffalo hunt, their caravan of home-built carts stretching for miles. They left with the blessing of the Bishop of St Boniface. That evening 1,375 buffalo tongues were brought into camp and more than a million tons of meat was dried, loaded and divided democratically among all.

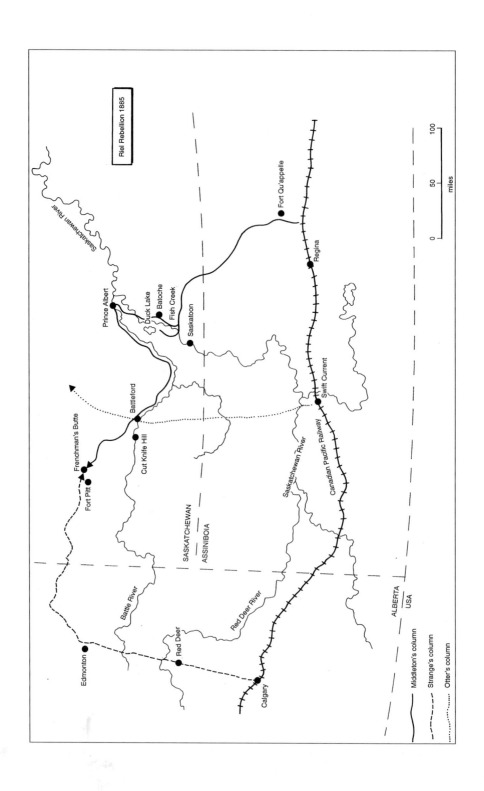

Riel Rebellion 1885

Saskatchewan River

Prince Albert
Duck Lake
Batoche
Fish Creek
Saskatoon

Fort Qu'appelle

Regina

Battleford

Cut Knife Hill

Frenchman's Butte

Fort Pitt

Swift Current

Saskatchewan River

Canadian Pacific Railway

SASKATCHEWAN
ASSINIBOIA

Battle River

Red Deer River

Red Deer

Edmonton

ALBERTA
USA

Calgary

Middleton's column
Strange's column
Otter's column

0   50   100
miles

The Metis were described by English aristocrats as 'tall, straight, well-proportioned, lightly formed and enduring'. They were dark-skinned and sometimes called 'bois brûlé', or scorched wood. They were as tough as hardwood, brave and honest, proud and independent. They wore buckskin, blue velvet, red sashes and fur, and rode horses as fierce as the plains and hills they traversed in raging sun and storm-lashed snow.

But their individualistic domination of the empty lands was not to last. In 1811 the Earl of Selkirk, a stockholder in the Hudson's Bay Company, bought 116,000 square miles of Rupert's Land, the area between Lake Superior and the Rockies, for a token ten shillings. His aim was to create a new land for Scottish Highlanders who were the victims of the Clearances. The first white settlers of the land abutting Red River quickly clashed with their Metis neighbours, with disputes over the rights to sell pemmican from buffalo hunts, and tensions over farming and hunting rights encouraged by the rival North West Company.

The first blood was shed in 1816 when a party of Metis was confronted by the colony's governor, Robert Semple, and twenty-six armed men. Insults were exchanged, and then musket balls. Only three white settlers survived. It was an act of butchery almost unique in Metis history.

The elder Louis Riel was a miller and businessman who argued incessantly with the Hudson's Bay Company over Metis rights. The Company was increasing its control over the region, quietly shutting the Selkirk colony after several failed crops, and concentrating entirely on fur. Farms fell into ruin and European colonists drifted across the American border. The Metis reclaimed lands lost earlier and asked to be left alone. The Company imposed their own definition of fair trade and in 1849 prosecuted a Metis trapper for trading across the 49th Parallel. Riel led 300 armed men to surround the courthouse. The accused man was released without violence after a new jury acceptable to both Company placemen and Metis free-traders was convened. It was an emotive victory and showed the benefit of coupling a just cause with force.

An uneasy peace held for two decades with the Red River Metis trading freely with St Paul to the south, ignoring Company edicts. But Canada was becoming a nation with the federation of four British provinces into a Dominion. The Government in Ottawa began to take notice of the settlements in Metis hands and the vast tracts controlled by the Company. There was a real threat too from the south. Thousands of American soldiers were left jobless by the end of the Civil War and many wanted a slice of the unclaimed territories north of the Parallel. Fenian sympathizers even mounted a short-lived invasion. The Government in Ottawa decided to act to expand the Dominion and extend their own ambitions as leaders of an emerging nation.

On 9 March 1869 the Government bought Rupert's Land from the Hudson's Bay Company for £300,000 although the Company would retain six million acres of the Fertile Belt, which stretched from Fort Garry to the

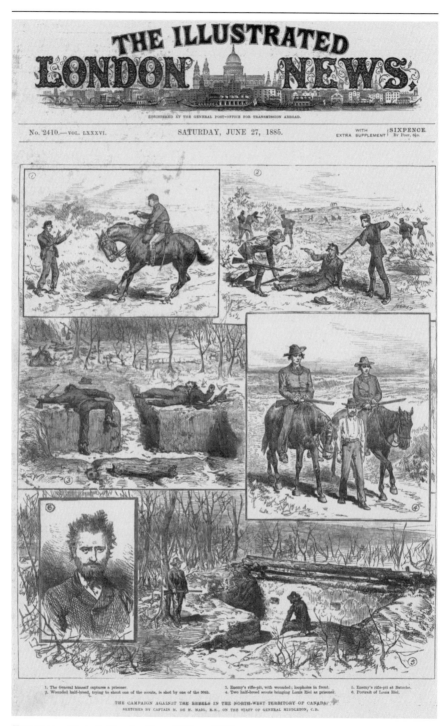

Front page, *Illustrated London News*, 27 June 1885

British Columbia border, and 50,000 acres around Company posts. The deal completely ignored the wishes of the settlers – 6,000 French-speaking Metis, 4,000 English-speaking cousins, and 1,600 whites – and, unsurprisingly, the vastly larger Indian population. The people who lived there and worked and hunted on the land felt they were being bought and sold by faceless men in the Company headquarters in Ottawa and London.

The Metis had good reason to fear the annexation of their land. Protestant Orangemen from Ontario moved steadily into the Red River region. They used whisky to buy from the Indians land to which there was no title. They regarded the Metis as contemptible half-breeds and bragged openly that this land was theirs for the taking. Their newspaper urged that the 'indolent and careless' native peoples should make way for a 'superior intelligence'. Its editor and their unelected leader, Dr John Christian Schultz, was a bigot and a bully.

The spark of conflict was provided when Prime Minister John Macdonald sent a team of surveyors to section off the Red River region into townships based on 800-acre squares. The Metis farmed their land in long strips so that everyone shared equally river bank, forests, fields and prairie. The proposed new boundaries cut through these long-established lines, leaving some with fertile fields, others with desert. In October 1869 Captain Adam Clark Webb and his team of surveyors began to lay a chain across a hayfield farmed by the Metis André Nault. The farmer knew no English, the officer no French, so an interpreter was sent for. The man who appeared, leading fifteen more Metis horsemen, was the younger Louis Riel.

Louis was born in 1845. He was only just a Metis, being one-eighth Chippewa Indian. His father, a lifelong militant and leader of the court-house revolt, encouraged a passionate belief in the Metis' right to continue their traditions. His mother taught him arithmetic, grammar, history and an equally passionate Catholic faith. Aged seven he went to study under the Grey Sisters of St Boniface and later under lay brothers in the parish library. He was still only thirteen when Bishop Tache picked him as one of the four brightest pupils sent to finish their education in Montreal. Louis won a scholarship to the seminary of St Sulpice where he gained plaudits for the sciences, Latin, Greek, French and maths. By the age of nineteen he was well briefed in the great philosophers and considered becoming a priest. But the following year he was thrown into a depression by the death of his father. 'Papa always acted with wisdom,' he tearfully wrote home. His faith was shaken and he rambled angrily about politics. Then he had a doomed love affair with a girl whose parents refused to let her marry a Metis. He walked out of the seminary in March 1865. A disturbed young man, he spent three years in Montreal, Chicago and St Paul before arriving back at his Red River homeland.

In the hayfield the would-be interpreter told Webb: 'You go no further.' The surveying party wisely withdrew. The small incident turned Riel into a leader. 'The Canadian Government had no right to make surveys in the

Louis Riel, *c.* 1880 (Public Archives of Canada)

Territory without the express permission of the people of the settlement,' he said.

Meanwhile a new Governor was en route to Red River via Minnesota. William McDougall was a well-known annexationist and no friend of the Metis. Riel, with forty armed followers, barricaded the border road and warned him not to cross the line without consent. To reinforce the point 400 more followers took over the Hudson's Bay Company's central post, Fort Garry, with no bloodshed. The Company supplies in the fort included a large amount of pemmican, enough to feed a modest army for the winter. After some bluster McDougall and his party retreated back into the United States.

Riel and his followers established themselves in Fort Garry and drew up a list of demands to be ratified by Ottawa and London. They covered eighteen points by which the Metis' rights to land and trade were guaranteed. Prime Minister Macdonald had been warned that the fearless Metis buffalo hunters were a 'very formidable enemy', and was happy to wait until things cooled down. But McDougall was seething with humiliation and ordered aides to raise a military force armed with 300 rifles.

Predictably Dr Schultz and his Canada First bigots were the first to join but McDougall could only muster sixty men. English-speaking Metis who had refused to join the rebellion also refused to play any part in crushing it. Only a few Saulteaux Indians took up the offer of free rifles – and then promptly vanished. Schultz and his force gathered at his storehouse in Winnipeg, then a nearby hamlet. Riel quickly surrounded it with 200 men and trained a small cannon on the gate. After a brief skirmish the Canadians surrendered and were taken prisoner to Fort Garry. McDougall returned to the capital.

The Comité des Métis within the fort proclaimed itself a provisional government. Macdonald was willing to conciliate because he believed that the Metis problem would eventually be solved when they were 'swamped by the influx of settlers'. A delegation of half-breeds was told, apparently with the prime minister's authority, 'Form a government for God's sake and restore peace and order in the settlement.' On 9 February 1870 a convention of all settlers, whites as well as Metis, elected the 25-year-old Riel as President.

Riel proposed to give his prisoners formal amnesties but around a dozen of them escaped beforehand, including Schultz, who had made a rope out of shredded buffalo hide, and a rough-hewn Irishman from Ontario called Thomas Scott. They began to plot their counter-revolution. They marched through snowdrifts towards Fort Garry, only to be recaptured by the renowned buffalo hunter Ambroise Lepine. Scott swore to kill Riel and may or may not have attacked the new President when Riel visited him in his cell; the evidence is unclear. Either way Scott was charged with bearing arms against the state. Lepine headed a jury of seven men which sentenced him to death. Scott was executed by firing squad on 4 March. In life he was regarded as a braggart, a bully and a drunk but in death he became a martyr. The firing squad sparked an outcry among white Canadians. Every possible prejudice against the half-breeds was whipped up by Schultz and his legions.

Riel sent a delegation to Macdonald setting out conditions for the Red River lands to join Canada as a full self-governing province, not a colony. The Prime Minister agreed to almost all the demands – except for an unconditional amnesty for all who took part in the insurrection – and the Manitoba Act was passed on 18 July. It appeared that Riel had won a stunning and almost bloodless victory and he said: 'I only wish to retain power until I can resign it to a proper Government.'

But the Manitoba Act included a clause designed to appease the vengeful Ontarians. The governor of the new province was to be accompanied by 1,200 troops to keep the peace and protect settlers from Indians. Their real task was to tame the Metis and exact punishment for Scott's death. Colonel Garnet Wolseley, the future victor of the 1873 Ashanti War, the 1879 Zulu War, the 1881 Boer War, the 1882 Egyptian War and the Sudan campaign of 1884–5, was to lead the military force. He told his wife privately: 'Hope Riel will have bolted, for although I would like to hang him to [sic] the highest tree in the place, I have such a horror of rebels and vermin of his kidney, that my treatment of him might not be approved by the civil powers.'

At thirty-seven years old, Wolseley was the Deputy Quartermaster-General of the Armed Forces in Ottawa, and the recent author of the *Soldiers' Pocket Book for Field Service*. Intelligence Officer Lieutenant W.F. Butler, later to become one of Wolseley's 'Ashanti Ring' of officers who snatched command in some of Queen Victoria's more glamorous wars, described him: 'Somewhat under middle height, of well-knit, well-proportioned figure; handsome, clean-cut features; a broad and lofty forehead over which brown chestnut hair closely curled; exceedingly sharp, penetrating blue eyes from one of which the bursting of a shell in the trenches of Sevastopol had extinguished sight without in the least lessening the fire that shot through it from what was the best and most brilliant brain in the British Army. He was possessed of a courage equal to his brain power. He could neither be daunted nor subdued. His body had been mauled and smashed many times. In Burma a gingall bullet fired within thirty yards of him had torn his thigh into shreds; in the Crimea a shell had smashed his face and blinded an eye. No one ever realised that he had only half the strength and the sight which he had been born with.'

The Red River expedition has been described as 'one of the most gruelling military movements in history'. The rebellion had touched a jingoistic nerve across the rest of Canada and volunteers flocked to join it. The expedition left Toronto on 31 May 1870. It took ninety-six days to cross the 600-mile wilderness, mainly by boat and canoe, north-west of Lake Superior. The army of 400 British Army regulars and 800 inexperienced Canadian militiamen, helped hugely by skilled Iroquois boatmen, endured forty-seven portages along the rivers – places where rapids forced them to manhandle baggage and boats over rocky trails several miles long. Sam Steele, later to become the most famous Mountie, carried a 200-lb barrel plus his own kit over one such obstacle. Redvers Buller, who became renowned as a Boer War general, was said to have managed 300 lb. And the future Duke of Somerset is alleged to have carried two barrels of pork weighing 400 lb in total. It rained for forty-five days of the journey and the men were plagued with blackflies and mosquitoes but no one signed off ill. No alcohol was allowed and there was no crime. Captain Redvers told his men of the 60th King's Royal Rifle Corps that he would not overwork them provided they overtook the other boats. They did so with a mixture of muscle power and a cunning ability to find the best routes across lake, river and rapids. On the last leg the trusting Riel sent four boatloads of experienced river Metis to guide the soldiers.

The troops arrived at Fort Garry on 24 August. Minutes before the mud-splattered army waded the Red River shallows Riel, who had intended to welcome them personally, was told by a friendly white of their real intention. He fled for his life, leaving his breakfast unfinished, and became a fugitive, saying to one supporter: 'Tell the people that he who ruled in Fort Garry only yesterday is now a homeless wanderer with nothing to eat but two dried fish.' Buller found Riel's breakfast and ate it – it was still warm. Wolseley could have pursued the rebels but he had not been given powers of civil authority and, despite the instincts he had expressed to his wife, he let them go. Riel went south to exile in the United States.

The entire military operation cost only £400,000, barely a quarter of which was paid for by London. The British Regular infantrymen were home before Christmas, not having lost a single man. The rebellion had been crushed and a Dominion Governor installed. It was an overwhelming success – but it failed to solve the real problem.

Four members of the jury that had convicted Scott were murdered. Another was savagely beaten and left for dead on American soil. Riel's own house was ransacked. One by one the promises made to the Metis in the Manitoba Act were abandoned. Security of tenure was not delivered and the Metis received only a tiny fraction of a pledged 1.4 million-acre land grant. Metis land was snatched by incoming Ontarians. The unrest led directly to the formation of the North West Mounted Police.

But the uprising had also established Manitoba as a Canadian Province, helping to ensure that Canada would eventually stretch from ocean to ocean. And Riel had given the Metis a voice and a taste for resistance.

★ ★ ★

Riel settled in the Metis town of St Joseph, now called Valhalla, on US territory. The Ontario Government offered a $5,000 reward for the capture of him or any others involved in Scott's death. Prime Minister Macdonald, however, arranged to pay Riel and Lepine £1,000 to stay quietly on the American side of the border. Despite the threat and the bribe Riel frequently slipped back into Manitoba, moving from settlement to settlement consolidating support. In 1873 he won *in absentia* the federal seat of Provencher. His arrival in the House of Commons in Ottawa to take the oath of office caused violent uproar but he was spirited safely out of the city that night.

In 1875 Macdonald granted pardons for both Riel and Lepine, provided they remained banished for a further five years. Riel began again to have mystic visions and his grip on reality weakened. He is alleged to have been a patient in several Quebec mental hospitals between 1876 and 1878. On his release he wandered the northern United States, dreaming frequently that he was divinely inspired to save his people. Although he remained in the Catholic Church he considered it soiled and corrupt, and urged that the papacy should be transferred from Rome to the Americas and a new Pope be anointed. He believed that the Metis were the chosen people destined to purify the human race. He was their 'David', picked directly by the Almighty. He described one vision: 'The same spirit who showed himself to Moses in the midst of fire and cloud appeared to me in the same manner. I was stupefied; I was confused. He said to me: "Rise up Louis David Riel. You have a mission to fulfill."' Many agreed with his opinion. One Jesuit priest said that to his followers Riel was 'a Joshua, a prophet, even a saint'. He married and became an American citizen, putting David as his Christian name on both certificates. After years of relying on hand-outs from sympathizers he settled in St Peter's, Montana, where he taught in the mission school. The flame of destiny still burned.

Meanwhile other leaders were emerging among the Metis and the Indians to the north. Gabriel Dumont, known as 'the prince of the prairies', had long led the annual buffalo hunt. Sam Steele wrote of him: 'He would kill bison by the score and give them to those who were either unable to kill or had no buffalo.' He was a renowned horseman and sharpshooter. He gradually became the leader of the Metis hunters and trappers who moved north to Saskatchewan to follow the increasingly scarce buffalo herds. The Metis set up new encampments in the St Laurent area on the South Saskatchewan, and these quickly became settled townships. Dumont built a substantial log house, with a stable, root cellar and 20 acres of cultivated land. When not leading the hunt he operated a ferry service and a small store with a billiard table. In 1875 at Batoche he and his friends organized an informal provisional government. The Metis forwarded land claims to the Canadian Government from across the north-west.

The Metis of Manitoba were overwhelmed by incomers but those who followed the buffalo to the Saskatchewan Valley were determined to beat off the white land speculators and homesteaders. They regarded the land as theirs by right, handed down to them by their Indian forefathers. The Canadian Government, having bought the wilderness from the Hudson's

Bay Company, believed that any land not held by title belonged to the Crown. A new homestead law decreed the Metis had to register their holdings like new settlers, even if the land had been held in the family for generations, and then had to wait three years for the deeds. Ottawa finally agreed that the Metis were not mere squatters but had a natural right to the land they occupied. But bureaucratic bunglings stirred up a hornets' nest of affronted Metis farmers. Worse still the Government repeated its earlier mistake in Manitoba and insisted on surveying the Metis holdings in squares rather than in the traditional strips which guaranteed access to water for all. A priest complained that Government-set boundaries would divide houses, cut off farmsteads from fields and create hardship.

Dumont and other leaders repeatedly sent petitions to Ottawa. They demanded sensible surveys, an end to delays in ownership patents, and a say in their own affairs. It was not just the Metis who felt aggrieved. White farmers and businessmen around Prince Albert, Battleford and Edmonton attacked Ottawa's incompetence and the *Edmonton Bulletin* argued that only a rebellion would force the Government to recognize their territorial rights.

But the whole issue might have remained bogged down in administrative wrangles if another factor had not come into play: the plight of the Prairies' full-blooded Indians. In the winter of 1869–70 the native Indians – Piegans, Sarcees, Bloods and Blackfeet – were massacred by smallpox caught from infected blankets handed over by white men. Stoney Indians traded pelts for whisky and guns with Americans operating on Canadian soil. In 1873 a band of drunken American wolfers slaughtered thirty Assiniboines in the Cypress Hills, in revenge for some stolen horses. The deployment of the Mounties in 1874 kept the lid on the potential powderkeg, even with the influx of Sioux following the Battle of Little Big Horn, but in 1878 a drought on the Canadian plains forced the buffalo south, and the Indians north of the Parallel faced starvation. By the following year they were eating carrion and their own dogs and horses. The Mounties did their best to distribute food but in 1883 the cash-strapped Government cut back on emergency food supplies. An agent reported that many tribes were reduced to 'mere skeletons'. Indian anger over the loss of traditional hunting lands grew in tandem with the Metis'. A band of Crees uprooted 40 miles of railroad survey stakes. Other bands refused to stay on their allotted reservations where they were supposed to learn how to plough.

Among the plains Cree, dissent over various treaties was focused by the chiefs Big Bear, Piapot and Poundmaker. They demanded their own hunting territories which they would govern themselves. In 1884 Big Bear convened the biggest assembly of plains chiefs in North American history at Battleford on Poundmaker's reserve. There one chief said they had been blind in ceding their land to the white man. During another assembly at Duck Lake the chiefs were addressed by Louis Riel. The chiefs agreed to send the Government a petition listing broken treaty promises and demanding greater autonomy. Big Bear united the plains people. His strategy was to seek a political solution rather than an armed revolt. But their growing militancy, especially among the splinter faction led by Poundmaker, heightened the Government's fears of uniting the Metis with 90,000 Indians.

Dumont realized the potential for using such fears to force Ottawa to agree to the Metis' terms. However, he spoke no English and even in his own language was no great orator. Someone else was needed to negotiate. With three companions he rode 700 miles to the Church of St Peter's mission. He told the forty-year-old Riel, now pale-skinned and gaunt, that French, English and Indian were ready to join the old cause. Louis Riel had his divine mission at last.

Riel gathered his wife Marguerite, two young children and a few possessions into a Red River cart and headed north. Outside Fort Benton he had his vision of the gallows. He ignored it and in early July the little band reached Batoche, by now the chief Metis township in the Saskatchewan Valley. At first Riel was treated as a valuable friend but not as a ruler and he failed to incorporate native soil rights in the declaration sent to Ottawa that winter. But Riel was listened to carefully by English-speaking Metis who had never followed him before, and he retained the support of the Catholic Church whose priests saw him as a hunted soul. Riel's influence grew as the Government dithered over a proposed bill of rights which demanded deeds to existing riverfront lands, a fairer deal for Indians, extra land for the Metis, reduced taxes, representation at the Dominion Parliament and a rail link to Hudson's Bay. Macdonald neither agreed nor disagreed but made secret arrangements to set up a Mounties post at Fort Carlton, 20 miles from Batoche. He also prepared to establish an investigatory commission into Metis' land claims and sent flour, bacon, tea and tobacco to the Indians. His concessions came too late.

Riel was by now convinced that a constitutional solution was impossible. He roared for armed resistance. On 5 March 1885 he declared: 'We are going to take up arms for the glory of God, the honour of religion and for the salvation of our souls.' He used an almanac to persuade his less educated followers that a partial eclipse of the sun was a sign from God. He and Dumont seized an arms cache in a Batoche store and took several white hostages. On 19 March Riel formed the Provisional Government of Saskatchewan with himself as God's Prophet. Dumont was the Adjutant-General charged with organizing 400 Metis into a cavalry squadron. Dumont's nominees were to form the council to manage the new state.

Riel demanded the surrender of Fort Carlton, manned by Major Leif Crozier and a force of Mounties. He offered them safe conduct if they surrendered, and a 'war of extermination' against those who refused. Crozier cautiously sent out a small scouting party to investigate but they were turned back by armed horsemen. Crozier then blundered, deciding on immediate action rather than waiting for reinforcements. On 26 March he led a column of 100 men – fifty-five Mounties, the remainder volunteers –

Ambush at Duck Lake (Royal Ontario Museum, Toronto)

with a small cannon and twenty horse-drawn sleighs to Duck Lake to deny the Metis arms and food held in the village store. Gabriel Dumont with Metis and Indian allies were waiting for them.

The column approached the small town in single file, struggling through deep, soft snow. Metis riflemen could be glimpsed through the trees, slowly encircling them. Crozier formed the sleds into a makeshift barricade and advanced to parley under a white flag along with his interpreter John McKay. Dumont's brother Isidore and an Indian met them but a scuffle broke out which resulted in Crozier giving the order to fire. Isidore was hit and later died of his wounds. The white men took cover behind their sleds and blazed away at caps and feathered bonnets visible above the snow, only to realize they were wasting their ammunition on headgear stuck on poles. The Metis fire grew steadily stronger as up to 150 fighters joined the fray. Crozier and his men were in a desperately exposed position. The seven-pounder was brought to bear but after three harmless shots a panicky gunner ruined it by ramming home a shell before its powder. Metis sharpshooters fired from the tree line, from a vacant log cabin, from dugouts in the snow. Riel appeared on a hill crest, riding a horse and holding aloft a large crucifix. Troopers fired at him but all missed, spurring Riel's men into more ferocious volleys.

After twenty minutes Crozier had lost a quarter of his force, 12 dead and 14 wounded, while the Metis had lost 5 men. When Crozier called the retreat Dumont, bleeding from a scalp wound, yelled for their total annihilation. Riel called a stop to that, saying: 'For the love of God kill no more of them.' The Metis collected arms and ammunition from the dead and then carried their bodies to the little cabin which had held snipers during the battle. The surviving Mounties were given safe passage to collect the corpses and Metis rebels helped them load the bodies on to wagons.

The Mounties' reputation for invincibility had been shattered. Their defeat sparked panic across Canada and encouraged Cree hotheads to launch their own attacks. Most crucially it marked the real beginning of an armed uprising. For the Metis there could be no going back.

Crozier's force staggered back to Fort Carlton, to be joined by 108 more Mounties from Regina under Commissioner A.G. Irvine. The new commander saw no point in trying to defend the flimsy fort which had been designed as a trading post, not a stronghold. Irvine decided to concentrate the entire force at Prince Albert. Over 350 Mounties, volunteers and traders were evacuated. They left a blazing fort, accidentally set aflame by a straw mattress left too close to a stove. Dumont planned to ambush the demoralized column but he was again restrained by Riel.

Irvine had a wooden palisade erected around Prince Albert's Presbyterian Church and within days 1,800 defenders, townspeople and terrified refugees from the countryside were packed within it. Corporal Donkin wrote: 'The enclosure was filled with sleighs and a restless, surging throng. The interior [of the church] was simply a vast nursery of noisy children and screaming females.' Women tended frostbitten feet and served food from two long tables. The perimeter was defended by 200 policemen and 300 volunteers. They were not attacked.

Back in Ottawa Macdonald ordered the immediate raising of a Canadian militia army. It was to be Canada's first national army. Young recruits raced to enlist, thirsty for adventure out west. Militia regiments were mustered in Winnipeg, Quebec (including the French-speaking 65th rifles), and Nova Scotia. Ontario supplied 2,000 troops. Within two months 8,000 soldiers were mobilized to subdue an estimated 1,000 fighting men among the Metis.

As exaggerated tales of slaughter spread throughout the Provinces the whites feared most that the rebellion would shift to the reservations, leading to a full-blown Indian war across Western Canada. After Duck Lake Riel did send messages to several chiefs, urging them to capture all policemen they could find. In reality few tribes saw any future in battling against the redcoats. There was no co-ordinated Cree or Blackfoot movement to reinforce the Metis in a joint revolt, as some historians have suggested. But

The battle of Duck Lake, a fanciful depiction by W. Bengough, used on a magazine cover (Public Archives of Canada)

there were some young warriors of the Cree and Assiniboine bands who saw the Duck Lake fiasco as a signal to cause some mayhem of their own.

Two days after Duck Lake Poundmaker led a breakaway band of 200 Crees on Battleford, 100 miles to the west. Over 500 people were sheltered in the NWMP barracks just outside town, alongside its garrison of just forty-three Mounties. Poundmaker's force demanded supplies and ammunition and some braves began looting Company stores and ransacking the town. Neighbouring farmsteads were burnt and one white settler who had stubbornly stayed put was killed. The Indians kept out of range of the barracks cannon and laid siege to the barracks for three weeks, but gave up and left once it became clear the defenders had plenty of food, water and ammunition.

Further north, near Fort Pitt on the North Saskatchewan, a much worse tragedy was enacted. Big Bear and his followers had wintered on a reservation at Frog Lake. On 2 April a war party of Crees from a warrior society known as the Rattlers halted a Mass at the mission church and then seized the Hudson's Bay store. They rounded up thirteen white settlers and ordered them to their camp, but the Indian agent, Thomas Trueman Quinn, refused to go. Wandering Spirit, a white-hating war chief with eagle feathers in his bonnet denoting his five previous kills, screamed at Quinn to move or die. Quinn, a burly Minnesotan, was adamant. Big Bear was too late to stop the white man taking a bullet in the chest from Wandering Spirit's rifle. The war chief started yelling 'Kill, Kill,' and other Crees took up the chant. The white captives were shoved out of the church and fell before Indian fire. Two priests were among the dead, one of them shot in the neck by Wandering Spirit. Only four of the thirteen whites survived: two widows and a young clerk were dragged off as captives and Quinn's nephew escaped to take news of the murders to Fort Pitt. Big Bear then regained control of his Crees and when the Indians surrounded the Fort he promised its defenders safe passage. The fort was handed over without a shot being fired.

So far only around 400 of an Indian population over 20,000 strong had taken up the gun and hatchet. Macdonald sent more supplies to the Blackfoot, Stoney and Saulteaux tribes to keep them loyal to the Crown. Macdonald's main priority was to get his new army into place. He reached a deal with the Canadian Pacific Railway to transport the fledging army in return for loans to meet payroll debts. The problem lay with a section of line along the north of Lake Superior which contained 86 miles of gaps where engineers were still cutting rock and building escarpments through swamp. The railroad promised to transport the troops on to the prairie in eleven days via a shuttle system of horse-drawn sleighs and wagons. For the new recruits the trip proved a nightmare as temperatures dropped to -35 degrees Fahrenheit. After one trek across the ice of the lake one trooper wrote home: 'We dared not stop an instant as we were in great danger of being frozen, although the sun was taking the skin off our faces.' He reported that one of his comrades was blinded by snow-glare and another went mad.

By mid-April the North-West Field Force had reached its dispersal point beyond Winnipeg. The first column of 800 men under Major-General Frederick Dobson Middleton was already marching north from Qu'Appelle towards Metis territory. A second column of 550 men marched out of Swift Current under Lieutenant-Colonel William Otter to relieve Battleford. And a third under the well-named Major-General Thomas Bland Strange set off from Calgary. The strategy was for Middleton to subdue the hard core of Riel's ragged army, estimated at 350 strong, of whom only 200 carried firearms. Middleton and Strange would then form a pincer to pacify the Cree Indians near Fort Pitt.

Middleton advanced slowly and cautiously. A Sandhurst graduate who had fought policing actions in New Zealand and India, the fat and be-whiskered Middleton had little faith in his green troops. He believed that a long march would teach them something of soldiering. He had absolute faith in the old-style tactics of a slow, steady advance in force and in the British square which had served so well at Waterloo. He left most of his cavalry to guard rail line and supply posts. But Canada's wild wilderness with its tough, mobile peoples was not the Waterloo plain. Dumont, who had fought the Sioux along the Missouri, believed in swift guerrilla campaigns with night raids and hit and run tactics. He was again restrained by Riel who was afraid of losing his general, but Dumont was finally allowed to plan an ambush.

On 24 April Dumont hid with 130 Metis and Indians in a coulee or small ravine on Fish Creek, a few miles ahead of Middleton's force. They dug rifle pits among the trees and thick brush, their weapons pointing uphill to catch the troopers exposed as they crossed the brow of a hill. The ambush should have been ruined when some young rebels revealed themselves by chasing stray cattle, and others fired too early. But Middleton doggedly ordered his column over the hill's crest in parade-ground ranks. They were greeted by deadly volleys from the concealed sharpshooters. Middleton's artillery men could not sufficiently depress the barrels of the two cannon and their shot shattered tree-top twigs but hit no ambushers. The Metis sang rebel songs as they blazed away; one played a flute; Dumont drank medicinal brandy from kit abandoned by a Canadian doctor. At dusk Middleton withdrew. He was so shaken that he stopped for two weeks to regroup, bury the dead, tend the wounded and call for reinforcements. He lost fifty men dead or wounded. Dumont, well dug in but still outnumbered five to one, lost four dead and two wounded.

On the same day Otter and his column received a rapturous welcome as they marched into Battleford. After a few days' rest Otter went in pursuit of Poundmaker and his braves, aiming to surprise the Indians sleeping in their camp at Cut Knife Creek. But the Cree were too wily for that and as Otter unlimbered his artillery they melted into the bush. Otter bombarded empty tepees but after a few minutes was suddenly thrown on the defensive as Indians appeared on all sides. Although Poundmaker's 300 men were armed with old muskets and bows they kept Otter's 350 well-armed men pinned down for seven hours. The Canadians eventually fought their way back to Battleford, losing 8 dead and 15 wounded. Their survival was partly due to Poundmaker who ordered his braves to let the white men return to the fort in peace.

Middleton's stalled column was now reinforced by two fresh companies and an American manufacturer with the latest war technology, a rapid-fire Gatling gun. He was also given his own navy – the flat-bottomed *Northcote* which had previously delivered mail along the territory's waterways and which the Government had rented for fifty-eight days at a cost of $14,500. Middleton armed it with the Gatling, a seven-pound cannon and thirty-five riflemen, intending to use it to bombard Batoche while his main force attacked. This plan proved to be a farce.

Dumont, now in Batoche, had been alerted by scouts who witnessed the transformation of the steamer. As the vessel approached the town it came under a furious crossfire from both banks. The skipper ordered more steam to speed through the ambush. Across the river ahead the Metis had rigged two ferry cables spaced well apart. The *Northcote* steamed under the first and its crew watched helplessly as it dropped behind them, cutting off their retreat. The second cable began to lower to catch the ship like a rat in a trap. The Metis were fractionally too slow and the steel rope scraped over the superstructure, cutting masts and rigging and severing the smokestacks which set alight the debris-strewn deck. The crew doused the flames with buckets as they dodged Metis bullets until finally their ship rounded the bend out of rebel range.

That same day, 9 May, Middleton's vanguard reached the outlying parts of Batoche. The small town appeared deserted as cannon opened fire on the houses and tepees. As Middleton ordered his first wave forward down a long grassy hillside all hell broke loose. Dumont was repeating the tactics he used at Fish Creek. His men were concealed in an intricate network of trenches and rifle pits to catch the troopers as they crossed the skyline. As troopers fell the dry brush was fired to prevent the defenders being outflanked. The soldiers fired volleys blind into dense smoke. When dusk fell Middleton ordered his men back to spend a miserable night in the shelter of a wagon stockade, their sleep broken by sporadic gunfire and a rocket which Dumont detonated at midnight.

The following day Middleton held his men back from the Metis trenches. For two more days both sides faced each other, sniping and goading, but refusing to close. Louis Riel crept back and forth along the trenches, praying with his men and urging them to trust in God. Ever more practical Dumont told them not to waste their ammunition, which was running out fast. The stalemate might have continued for much longer were it not for the frustration of Middleton's officers and men. They urged a bayonet charge, arguing that their 900 men should easily swamp barely 200 buffalo hunters. Middleton, whose nerve must have been shaken at Fish Creek, did not want to risk many more casualties.

Finally the Ontarian Colonel A.T.H. Williams took action while Middleton was eating lunch on the fourth day of the siege. Williams led his Midland Battalion pell-mell down the hillside. Their enthusiastic charge was infectious and they were joined by riflemen from Winnipeg and Grenadiers from Toronto. Middleton ordered a bugle recall but it was ignored and he was forced to move up his main body in support. Luckily for the attackers the Metis had virtually run out of bullets and were reduced to firing pebbles, buttons and scrap metal. The troopers overran the first line of trenches before they could reload. The rebels manned a second line but that too quickly fell to the roaring soldiers. One Metis who would not run was 93-year-old Joseph Quellette. Dumont urged him to retreat but the old man refused, saying he wanted to slay another Englishman.

Some Metis continued fighting right to the riverbank while others took shelter in the ruins of the town. By nightfall further resistance was useless. Men surrendered to safeguard their women and children from further bombardment. Riel and Dumont were among those who slipped away. Quellette's body was found riddled with bullet or bayonet wounds. The Metis lost 16 dead, including 75-year-old Joseph Vandal, while Middleton suffered 8 dead and 46 wounded. One in ten of all those who took part were casualties.

Riel hid and prayed in the woods for three days before giving himself up to scouts. Middleton was surprised to find him a 'mild-spoken and mild-looking man'. He appeared famished and freezing and the general gave him a greatcoat to wear over his narrow shoulders. Under heavy guard he was sent by river to Saskatoon and from there by wagon to the territorial capital, Regina, and a Mountie blockhouse. Middleton then marched to relieve Prince Albert, its inhabitants still cramped within their stockade. After being greeted as a hero he travelled on the repaired *Northcote* to receive the unconditional surrender of Poundmaker and his Crees outside Battleford.

Meanwhile General Strange and his column of 3,375 infantry, 25 Mounties and 100 volunteers completed their 250-mile march from Edmonton to Fort Pitt. The Mounties were headed by the now legendary Sam Steele in all his scarlet splendour. The force tracked Big Bear and his 200 warriors and the two sides skirmished at Frenchmen's Butte. Strange, a canny if eccentric soldier, pulled back from encircling horsemen because he knew the dangers of 'committing Custer'. Middleton with 200 more troops joined Strange's column on 6 May and took command. The fighting was almost over. Big Bear retreated into impenetrable swamps but the Indians were starving. A squad of Mounties surprised a band of Crees at Loon Lake and an inconclusive firefight ensued. Sergeant Billy Fury was wounded and several Indians killed. They were the last battle casualties of the war.

Big Bear released some white prisoners and pleaded for the shooting to stop. As his men limped in small bands to surrender at Fort Pitt, Big Bear and his twelve-year-old son walked 100 miles eastward as police, militia and soldiers turned the country upside-down looking for him. He walked

Captain French – 'since killed' – taking Indian prisoners in a sketch by Captain Haig (*Illustrated London News*)

Metis prisoners held in the NWMP prison at Regina, August 1885 (Public Archives of Canada)

unannounced into Fort Carlton and gave himself up to a Mountie sergeant. It was a brave final gesture from a chief now half-starved and ragged.

Eighteen Metis were convicted of treason at Regina and jailed for up to seven years. Eleven Crees implicated in the Frog Lake massacre were sentenced to death at Battleford. Three were reprieved but Wandering Spirit and seven others were hanged. Big Bear and Poundmaker were sentenced to three years' imprisonment, a generous gesture in white eyes but a cruel punishment to Indians. They were freed after two years but, weakened physically and spiritually, they both died within six months. Most of the seventy-three Metis prisoners were discharged and others acquitted. Riel's secretary, Jackson of Prince Albert, was found insane and sent to the Selkirk Asylum, from which he escaped and was last seen in America.

Dumont, the best general on both sides, used all his famed frontier skills to evade capture. Once convinced the war was lost he fled to Montana and plotted a daring rescue mission. He set up a secret network of relay stations along the 450 miles from Regina to Montana, each stocked with fresh horses to speed Riel to safety. But the scheme came to nothing. The guard around Riel was increased and the breakout plan abandoned. Several years later Dumont was the star of Buffalo Bill's Wild West Show.

★ ★ ★

On 28 July 1885 the trial of Louis Riel began in a hastily erected courtroom in Regina. In the opening submissions the prosecutor said it was possibly

Indian prisoners sketched by Captain H. de H. Haig (*Illustrated London News*)

the most serious trial ever to take place in Canada. Riel faced a part-time magistrate and a jury of six white settlers. Reporters from a dozen newspapers were at the Press table. Ladies, including Middleton's wife, sat in a separate section. Riel sat in a wooden box, with two Mounties on either side. His four-man defence team, hired by Quebec sympathizers and including Chief Justice Sir Charles Fitzpatrick, wore robes and wigs. The crowded room was oppressively hot.

The Government had faced severe criticism for its leniency fifteen years before, for the failure to punish Scott's murderers, and for its amnesty for Riel. Equally many French Canadians, Catholics and some white Westerners saw Riel as a patriot heading for martyrdom. Prime Minister Macdonald appears to have been genuine in his determination that there should be a fair trial under the law, rigorous justice and no more clemency if guilt were proved. There was never any real doubt about that:

Riel's indictment claimed that in committing high treason he had been 'moved and seduced by the instigation of the devil'. Standing erect and with a firm voice Riel declared himself 'Not Guilty'. The prosecution read a letter Riel had written threatening to exterminate the whites. Witnesses quoted Riel as demanding 'blood, blood . . . everybody that is against us must be driven from the country'. The facts of the uprising were not in dispute.

On his arrest Riel had claimed that captured papers would show he had never intended to make war, only to convince the Government of the need to concede a fair land deal to his people. Riel's defence team knew that such excuses would not be acceptable in court. Whatever the motives Riel had

Gabriel Dumont (Glenbow Alberta Institute)

incited revolt. They gambled on saving his life with a plea of insanity. Riel protested loudly, interrupting his own lawyers several times and saying: 'Here I have to defend myself against the accusation of high treason or I have to consent to the animal life of the asylum.' Two doctors gave evidence that Riel suffered from 'megalomania', but they could not agree on the causes of his alleged madness.

Riel defeated his own lawyers in his final statement at the end of the trial. He spoke lucidly and passionately for an hour. Everyone in the hushed courtroom listened spellbound to an electrifying defence of

The trial of Louis Riel (Public Archives of Canada)

the Metis. His less than perfect English did not detract from its eloquence. He said: 'It would be an easy matter for me today to play the role of lunatic. The excitement which my trial causes me is enough to justify me acting in the manner of a demented man. When I came here from Montana I foundthe Indians starving. The half-breeds were subsisting on the rotten pork of the Hudson's Bay Company. This was the condition, this was the pride, of responsible government! I directed my attention, to assist all classes, irrespective of creed, colour or nationality . . . No one can say the North-West was not suffering last year . . . but what I have done, and risked, and to which I have exposed myself, rested certainly on the conviction I had to do, was called upon to do, something for my country.' If anyone was mad, he argued, it was 'a monster of irresponsible, insane Government'. He added: 'The North-West is also my mother and I am sure that my mother will not kill me. She will be indulgent and will forget . . . I say humbly through the grace of God, I believe I am the prophet of the new world.' A newspaper report said that Riel spoke with terrible earnestness and the force of a trumpet blast, adding: 'That every soul in court was impressed is not untrue, and many ladies were moved to tears.'

The trial lasted five days. The jury found him guilty but his speech moved them to ask for clemency. This was denied and Riel heard Mr Justice Richardson's words: 'It is now my painful duty to pass the sentence of the court upon you, and that is . . . that on the 18th of September next you will be taken to the place appointed for your execution, and there be hanged by the neck till you are dead, and God have mercy on your soul.'

Petitions for mercy were sent to Ottawa and the political backlash from the sentence threatened to tear Quebec apart. Reprieves were granted three times to hear appeals and Macdonald ordered a new investigation into Riel's mental state. Two medical men and a North-West Mounted Police surgeon were sent to Regina. They found that Riel suffered hallucinations and held many 'eccentric and foolish' views on religion but, crucially, concluded that he was entirely capable of judging right from wrong and was therefore responsible for his actions. The police surgeon Dr Jukes said: 'I cannot escape the conviction that except on purely religious questions relating to what may be called divine mysteries he was, when entrusted to my care, and still continues to be, sane and accountable for his actions.'

During the trial and its aftermath evidence was submitted that Riel had spent nineteenth months in 1877–78 at the Beauport Asylum and other institutions in Washington and Longue Pointe. In a letter published later by the *Toronto Globe* Dr Daniel Clark of that city's Asylum for the Insane said: 'I spoke to some of the half-breeds who were in all his fights, and they said positively that Riel was apparently rational enough until the Duck Lake fight, and that after the excitement of that fight he seemed to have changed entirely and become a religious fanatic; he organised no opposition, did no fighting, but was looked upon as inspired – running about with a crucifix and calling upon the Trinity for aid.' He added: '. . . had he been an obscure man there is not an asylum in Christendom but would have committed him on the evidence, and legally so; but because he had been the indirect cause of a deplorable outbreak, his mental condition became of secondary importance, as political exigencies arose paramount.'

Appeals of mercy were swamped by others demanding that sentence be swiftly carried out. Many predictably came from Old Ontarian enemies, Protestant leaders and white businessmen. But the French-speaking and Catholic communities were also divided. Catholic missionaries in the battle area around Batoche and Duck Lake denounced Riel for the misery he had caused. And the venerable Bishop of St Albert had no pity for Riel, only for his followers. The bishop wrote to Macdonald: 'These poor halfbreeds would never have taken up arms against the Government had not a miscreant of their own nation, profiting by their discontent, excited them thereto. He gained their confidence by a false and hypocritical piety, and having drawn them from the beneficent influence of their clergy, he brought them to look upon himself as a prophet, a man inspired by God . . . and forced them to take up arms.'

Riel spent most of his time in the condemned cell praying and writing a last memoir in which he celebrated the Metis way of life. His mother and brother Alexandre visited him. His wife Marguerite did not. She suffered a breakdown when her third child died in premature childbirth while her husband was imprisoned. She was slowly starving herself to death.

Riel smuggled out several messages to friends, family and reporters. In one he scribbled: 'I have devoted my life to my country. If it is necessary for the happiness of my country that I should now cease to live, I leave it to the Providence of my God.'

On 16 November Riel walked into the crisp morning sunlight of Regina alongside a deputy sheriff and two priests, and on to the jailhouse gallows platform. He carried a crucifix and held himself with grave dignity, although onlookers detected a film of perspiration on his pale face despite the cold. One priest stumbled and Riel whispered: 'Courage, mon père.' Riel asked the crowd for forgiveness on behalf of himself and others, then knelt to pray. He stood to say the Lord's Prayer with Father McWilliams as a white hood was placed over his head. On the words 'lead us not into temptation but deliver us . . .' the trap was sprung.

★ ★ ★

The Federal Government spent over $5 million to subdue a few hundred ill-armed Metis and fewer Indian allies. The cost included $15 spent on rye whisky for Middleton's victory party. Around eighty whites and a similar number of rebels had been killed. Towns were devastated. The Government's victory helped to boost Canadian nationalism and pride at a crucial point. That sense of nationhood was further cemented nine days after Riel's death when the final spike was hammered in to complete the 2,900 miles of the Canadian Pacific Railway. The troops and Mounties stayed to further tame the wild North-West. As a direct result of the rebellion the territory finally won parliamentary representation, four seats in the Commons and two in the Senate. Land reforms were introduced. The federal grant to the territories was doubled to over $65,000. In 1888 the North-West was granted a full legislative assembly. All of these changes benefited the white population.

The Indians, especially the Cree, suffered more broken treaties and ceased to be an autonomous people. Their tragedy applied on both sides of the 49th Parallel. For the Metis the dream of a sovereign nation was over. Their townships, including Batoche, were pillaged and burnt by soldiers. Some who could prove they had played no part in the revolt received compensation. Others abandoned land claims in return for a quick cash settlement. Others struggled on even though the hostilities meant that few crops were harvested in 1886. Jobs were scarce and living was harsh until the boom years at the turn of the century. By then a great many Metis had simply uprooted their families and moved on. Metis communities sprang up in Montana and Dakota, while others spread further north and west, in places like Battle River, Green Lake and Lac La Biche.

Riel's body was cut down and given a simple burial at Regina. Three weeks later, with official approval, the corpse was sent secretly by rail in a rough pine coffin to St Boniface. He lay in his mother's house overnight and on 12 December was carried to the cathedral. The casket was placed on a platform surrounded by candles. Villagers from the region came by horse, sleigh and carriage to the requiem Mass said by Archbishop Tache, the man who had sent Riel to school in Montreal twenty-seven years earlier. Everyone was wearing black. Whole families, the tough menfolk included, shed tears. Riel lies in the cathedral yard at St Boniface, under a granite slab inscribed: 'RIEL, 16 NOVEMBRE 1885.' He was a flawed prophet who caused much suffering for a noble cause. He remains an enigma still. But his great last speech carries a resonance, a simplicity and a beauty that a century has not reduced. It included the prophecy: 'Though it may take 200 years my children's children will shake hands with the Protestants of the new world in a friendly manner.'

CHAPTER NINE

The Ashanti War of the Golden Stool, 1900

'A coffin'

In 1663 Nana Obiri Yeboa negotiated with an old lady under a Kum tree. The land he acquired became Kumasi, seat of the kings of the mighty Ashanti empire. On a Friday in 1700 within the precincts of the royal palace a golden stool, it is said, descended from the heavens to give the king a symbol of his authority. The Ashanti regalia in use until then was buried in a place marked by a sword buried to the hilt into the ground. The stool became a symbol of spiritual unity between the living and the dead, between a king and his people, between clan and state. It was sacred, political, practical and priceless.

On 25 March 1900 His Excellency Sir Frederick Mitchell Hodgson, Governor of the Gold Coast, demanded the stool for Queen Victoria. He ordered that it be brought to him, so that he might sit upon it himself. Within hours he, his wife and entourage were forced to take refuge in Kumasi's small British fort, garrisoned by a handful of British soldiers and loyal Hussans, while Ashanti snipers peppered the walls. It was the start of a strange and unnecessary small war at a time when the British Empire was preoccupied with a vastly bigger one in South Africa. A great deal of blood was shed in Britain's search for what was, for them at least, merely a political and military trophy.

★ ★ ★

The Portuguese were the first to establish trading posts and then forts on the Gold Coast, quickly followed by the Dutch and the British. They bought gold and ivory from the Fanti tribes and fought each other for domination. The Portuguese built the substantial Elmina Castle, started in 1482, but were bombarded out by the Dutch in 1637. For two centuries control of the coastal forts swung between the Dutch and the English, with encroachments by the Spanish, French, Swedes, Danes and Brandenburgers.

The source of wealth so bitterly contested switched from ivory, wood and produce, to human cargo. The plantations of the West Indies and the

American cotton states depended on slave labour. Millions of men, women and children were chained in the fetid slave dungeons before being packed into stinking ships bound west. No one knows for sure how many West Africans were enslaved, but at the slave trade's peak the British alone were shipping out 40,000 captives a year, enriching merchants in Bristol, London and Liverpool.

One of their main suppliers was the Ashanti empire which controlled the high forests 150 miles to the north. Their warriors took numerous prisoners in countless wars, sacrificed some to their fetishes and sold the surplus. It was a profitable trade for European and Ashanti slavemasters alike.

The Ashanti were a union of small states established in the early seventeenth century by Akan immigrants from the West. Before the appearance of the Golden Stool these states paid tribute to the Denkera, a more powerful regime to the south-west. The Stool was used to create spiritual unity among the states enabling them to defeat the Denkera. According to tradition the wooden stool embellished with gold was summoned from the sky by the priest Anokye before a great assembly. It descended gently on to the lap of the new king, Osei Tutu. The priest declared that the stool contained the spirits of the Ashanti ancestors and the strength of the nation depended on its preservation. From then on every Ashanti had allegiance to the Golden Stool and its guardian the King, and to his state stool and tribal chief. The Denkera were indeed defeated and the unified Ashanti nation embarked on decades of conquests, extending their empire to the northern Akim states of Sefwi, Tekyiman, Gyaman, Banda, Wassaw and Akwapim. Each conquest, each war and skirmish, brought more slaves for the ships that called to the coast. The Ashantis needed to subjugate the coastal people to control trade and profits and ensure a steady

Troops landing on the Gold Coast during the 1873–4 Ashanti War (*Illustrated London News*)

General Wolseley receiving news from Kumasi (*Illustrated London News*)

supply of Western munitions for war inland. This was what brought them into conflict with the British.

In 1807 the slave trade was banned in all British dependencies. Later that year the Ashanti crossed the sacred River Prah, attacked the Fanti federations and reached the sea. The British and Dutch commanders in their forts were forced to accept Ashanti control of the coastal region and had to pay rent for their trading establishments. With the end of the slave trade the Dutch gradually retired from the region while British merchants switched to palm oil. Cask roads were built to the ports but these were vulnerable to Ashanti raids. Tensions increased and the Ashanti refused to bear responsibility for the behaviour of their Fanti under-lords. In 1821 the British Government took over administration of the coastal forts and refused to pay any more rent to the Ashanti. The first Crown Governor, Sir Charles McCarthy, a strong abolitionist, refused to accept Ashanti authority over the Fanti chiefs. He launched a brave but doomed expedition against a new Ashanti incursion, was deserted by his native allies and ran out of ammunition. In honour of his courage the Ashanti cut off his head and took it back to Kumasi. His skull was turned into a ceremonial drinking cup for state occasions.

Almost forty years of peace followed during which the British set up a Protectorate in the coastal regions. The Ashanti were content to maintain their power in the North and the central uplands, trading in palm oil, gold, and hardwood, farm maize, manioc, plantain, bananas and yams. But their war-like nature, built out of necessity and commercial realities, erupted when King Kofi Karikari sent an army of 12,000 warriors once again across the Prah. The Protectorate tribes were reduced to 'a heap of scattered fugitives at the mercy of a pitiless and bloody foe, whose delight is to torture and who will drive them by thousands into slavery, and slaughter all the weak and sick'.

British sailors and marines garrisoning the coastal forts held back the invaders as an expedition force was dispatched from Liverpool. Its commander was Major-General Sir Garnet Wolseley, chosen out of 400 generals to lead the campaign. After fierce fighting Wolseley and his army took Kumasi at dawn on 4 February 1874.

The famous journalist and explorer Henry Stanley wrote: 'We were anxious and curious to see Kumasi, the capital of the Ashantis, with its most remarkable objects – the King's palace, the place of execution, the great market, the town square. The streets were numerous; some half a dozen of them were broad and uniform. The main avenue on which the British and local troops bivouacked during the night was about 70 yards wide; here and there were great shade trees. The houses in the principal streets were wattled structures, with alcoves and stuccoed facades, embellished with Arabic patterns. Behind each of the big buildings were groups of huts for the women, children and slaves, enclosing small courtyards. By the general order and neatness . . . I was compelled to the conclusion that they were a very clean people.'

Winwoode Reade of the London *Times* wrote: 'The King's palace consists of many courtyards, each surrounded with alcoves and verandahs having two gates or doors secured by padlocks. The rooms upstairs reminded me of Wardour Street in London.' He found books in many languages, the 17 October issue of his own newspaper, Persian rugs, Kidderminster carpets, Bohemian glass, a sword inscribed from Queen Victoria, gold-studded sandals with Arabic on the soles, caps of beaten gold covered with leopard skin, velvet umbrellas and other treasures 'too numerous to describe or even catalogue'.

The British forces looted and then dynamited the deserted King's palace. Sappers burned most of the city. The captured booty was taken by thirty porters to Cape Coast.

Wolseley, who had directed his forces from a hammock carried by four soldier-porters, puffing on a cigar while bullets whistled past in best *Boy's Own* fashion, left after two days. Karikari's envoys agreed at the Treaty of Fomena to keep the road from Kumasi to Cape Coast Castle clear and open for trade and peaceful travel. The British agreed to withdraw in return for 50,000 ounces of pure gold in reparations for the £200,000 that Wolseley had budgeted for the war. There was peace for another twenty years.

In 1895 the British asked permission to station a garrison at Kumasi because they were fearful of German and French empire-building to the north. The request was repeatedly turned down by King Prempeh I, whom British propagandists painted – probably rightly – as a bloodthirsty tyrant. A British column marched into Kumasi the following year without firing a shot. They found numerous skulls and traces of human sacrifice, adding to the Ashanti's fearsome reputation in Britain. King Prempeh and thirty of his close royal relatives and state officials were arrested and detained at Elmina Castle. Their alleged crime was failure to pay the 1874 reparations in gold. They were exiled, first to Sierra Leone and then to the Seychelles. The British stationed seven military or administration officers in Ashanti. A small British fort was built in Kumasi and garrisoned with a few British officers and Hausa troops brought over from Nigeria. A British President was installed.

The Ashanti and northern territories remained nominally independent of the British colony to the south, but resentment simmered on both sides. It was a decapitated kingdom. The British authorities believed that with Prempeh an ocean away on another continent there was nothing to stop them winning ultimate authority over a surly, mutinous and troublesome people. The key to that authority was the Golden Stool.

The symbolic important of an Ashanti stool cannot be over stressed. Since ancient times ancestor worship had been central to the Akan peoples who became the Ashanti. Clans and states were believed to be composed of both the living and the spirits of the dead. A chief was the earthly representative of his clan's most important ancestors while his own spirit was left in his ceremonial stool, which became the symbol of a clan's spiritual unity. The blackened stools of dead chiefs were kept in stool houses which on important occasions ran red with the blood of human sacrifices. The stool represented power, unity and communion with sacred ancestors at a local level. The Golden Stool represented the same, only more so, on the national stage. The British recognized that and wanted it for their own, and none more so than the Chief Commissioner of Ashanti, Captain Cecil Armitage, who was later knighted and became Governor of Gambia. He persuaded Governor Hodgson to leave the British seat of government at Christiansborg Castle at Accra and endure the 140-mile trek to the Ashanti capital.

The Governor, with Lady Hodgson and a mixed bag of British troops and local levies, reached Kumasi on 25 March 1900. Hodgson was typical of his era: bombastic, brave, loyal, cunning as far as his intellect would allow. Above all he had an unshakeable belief in his own superiority and that of the Empire he represented. He was a product of that rigid structure. Now aged forty-eight, he was a bureaucrat rather than a soldier. The son of a Wareham rector he had previously worked in the Post Office, rising to the post of Postmaster-General of British Guinea. His military experience was confined to Volunteer forces, including the Gold Coast levies he had raised in 1892. His wife Mary was the daughter of a former Gold Coast Governor.

Despite their king's absence the Ashanti were determined to honour Queen Victoria's representative. Important chiefs and their officials were summoned to welcome the Governor and his wife at a colourful grand durbar. Royal personages, state drummers, court criers, musicians, merchants and warriors in their finery packed the city's central square.

Buglers called a military fanfare as Hodgson, resplendent in full colonial uniform with medals sparkling at his chest, climbed on to a platform decorated with flags and garlands. His crass and insensitive remarks soured the mood of celebrations and sparked a war.

He boomed: 'Your King Prempeh I is in exile and will not return to Ashanti. His power and authority will be taken over by the Representative of the Queen of Britain. The terms of the 1874 Peace Treaty of Fomena which required you to pay for the cost of the 1874 war have not been forgotten. You have to pay with interest the sum of £160,000 a year. Then there is the matter of the Golden Stool of Ashanti. The Queen is entitled to the stool; she must receive it.' According to African translators he then went on: 'Where is the Golden Stool? I am the representative of the Paramount Power. Why have you relegated me to this ordinary chair? Why did you not take the opportunity of my coming to Kumasi to bring the Golden Stool for me to sit upon? However, you may be quite sure that though the Government has not yet received the Golden Stool at his [sic] hands it will rule over you with the same impartiality and with the same firmness as if you had produced it.'

Hodgson spoke with arrogance and with ignorance, having been improperly briefed by Armitage. The arrogance alone may have worked, or at least been ignored. The ignorance, to Ashanti eyes, was unforgivable. Hodgson did not initially recognize the deep offence he had caused. The Ashanti were sophisticated power-brokers and fully understood the Englishman's desire for the symbolic stool. They had expected nothing less. What they could not stomach was Hodgson's desire to sit himself upon the Golden Stool. It demonstrated that Hodgson had entirely missed the point. To try to use the stool for political purposes was reasonable and forgivable. But to demand to sit upon it as a representative of the English Queen's fat bottom was sacrilege. No Ashanti King had sat upon the Golden Stool as a matter of respect for long-gone ancestors. It was incomprehensible that a foreigner should wish to do so, no matter what power he represented. It was the 'height of sacrilege and an affront to the Ashantis'.

The Ashanti chiefs were too polite to reveal their feelings. The durbar required that their guests were treated with full kindness and they simply expressed their thanks to the Governor and their loyalty and friendship to the British Empire. They stuck to their prepared speeches which took no account of the mood of the audience. The crowd was muttering ominously and melted away in the back alleys of Kumasi to 'cook' war against the British. The Queen Mother of Edweso, Nana Yaa Asantewa – whose name is often used as the title of the subsequent war – urged her men to fight the

British. She said: 'Why should they deport the King Prempeh and then come and take the Golden Stool of Asante? We must fight them.'

Governor Hodgson was still blissfully unaware of the trouble he had caused. He sent troops and officials under Captain Armitage to search for the Golden Stool in the bush. They were quickly surrounded and outnumbered by well-armed Ashanti. Armitage decided that a display of stiff upper lip was called for. He called for afternoon tea and troopers set up their officer's field kit of folding table, chairs, stove, cups, spoons, condensed milk, tin openers and sugar. It was a bad mistake. After five minutes Ashanti snipers let rip, shattering the cosy affair. Biscuits and bone were pierced, marmalade spilt along with blood. Luckily a sudden downpour dampened the native guns, giving the British time to drag their wounded back to Kumasi.

Hodgson realized that he had insufficient troops available to back his authority. With great dignity he retreated to the fragile safety of Kumasi's small fort. With him went his wife, sixteen Europeans of whom six were missionaries, plus the mixed-race workers of the type who made the British Empire work: trading clerks, letter-writers, pastors, teachers and minor civil servants. The garrison was made up of 300 Hausas from Nigeria with 6 seven-pounders and 4 Maxim guns.

The Ashantis made one serious assault on the fort on 29 April but the Maxims spattered carnage and they were repulsed with heavy losses. Both sides settled down for a long siege. For a month the defenders remained crammed in the fort, playing and singing patriotic songs. They were hot and hungry. They were hopelessly outnumbered and the Ashanti snipers kept up a continuous bee-sting barrage, pot-shots rather than lethal attacks. The telephone wires between Kumasi and the coast had, not surprisingly, been cut. The director of Posts and Telegraphs in Accra was sent to investigate the breach in communication. He was picked up by friendly Ashanti who lashed his feet to bloody ribbons with a section of the cut wire. His life was spared and he limped to a nearby village, his shirt wrapped around his feet. The Ashanti also knew how to organize a blockade. Roads and tracks to the coast were severed. Messengers were intercepted and detained in great discomfort, but rarely killed. The Kumasi refugees were running low on food, ammunition and morale.

A relief column was sent from the coast but it was a poorly organized feeble affair. Around 250 men arrived but half were either wounded from Ashanti ambushes or ill. They brought no extra food or ammunition. They were simply more mouths to feed. Only the well-oiled machine-guns and cannon pointing from the fort's ugly and claustrophobic parapets prevented a massacre at the fort. The Ashanti generals had no intention of attacking the fort and spilling unnecessary blood. They intended to starve them out. As the weeks dragged on their strategy seemed to be working. Over 600 people, military and civilian, European, half-caste and African, were packed into an area designed to take a tenth of that number. Dozens died daily and

Sir Frederick Hodgson directing the defences in the Kumasi fort (*Illustrated London News*)

their deaths went mostly unrecorded. Two exceptions were Basel Mission School teachers Frederick Okanta and Helena Sakyiama. Their bodies, and the other victims of malnutrition and disease, were rolled or thrown outside the fort's walls. No one – for obvious reasons – was buried within. Rats and mice were consumed. The normal colonial niceties broke down. Black and white fought, cheated and stole for food. Troops on the parapets fired rockets and guns at the stars in the hope that a proper relief column was on its way.

Early in June a second column with 700 native troops under Major Morris arrived, the men already suffering from malnutrition. A council of war within the fort decided that positive action was needed to break the stalemate. It was agreed that the Governor and Lady Hodgson, together with several hundred Hausa troops and a large number of baggage handlers, should break out and make a dash for the coast. By now refugees had swelled the numbers within the fort to around 1,000. They were to be left in the charge of Captain Bishop, the medical officer Dr Hay, two clerks, 25 fit soldiers and around 90 semi-invalid troops. Their orders were to hold out with three weeks' starvation rations. If they were overrun they were told to die fighting and where possible to destroy their weapons before they perished.

At dawn on 23 June Hodgson's party moved out, treading softly as Ashanti pickets slept.

★   ★   ★

The break-out had been planned with great secrecy and caught the surrounding Ashanti off guard. An advance party under Captains Armitage and Leggett attacked an Ashanti stockade guarding the main escape route. In a short and fierce fight the Ashantis were driven off – at a cost. Leggett and another officer died of their gunshot wounds five days into the march. It took the Ashantis two days to organize an effective pursuit with a force up to 15,000 strong. Villages on the route to Accra had by then set up crude barricades while small groups of warriors harried Hodgson's rearguard. Hodgson's party included the four loyal Kings of Mampon, Juabin, Aguna and Insuta, who had shared the hardships of the siege. Sir Frederick and Lady Hodgson were carried in a hammock, although the lady later recorded several times when she had been forced by urgency to walk like everyone else.

There is no question about the bravery of such colonial figures, no matter how comic they appear almost a century later. Kumasi was, and is, carved out of Africa's densest forest among hills rising to 1,000 feet. The escape column moved down primeval tracks darkened by mammoth mahoganies and wawa trees, their lower canopies clothed in lichens and orchids, the ground a swampy tangle of bamboos and broad-leafed herbs. Their enemies, well armed and numerous, were heathens with a proven record of

Sir Frederick and Lady Hodgson crossing the Prah River (*Illustrated London News*)

mass human sacrifice if not cannibalism. Food and water was scarce. One officer had kept ground meat in a Bovril bottle which he shared with Lady Hodgson to keep up her energy and spirits. It was the rainy season and torrents battered escaper and pursuer alike. One Basel missionary died and was buried by the roadside. Others died of fatigue or eating poisonous roots.

An officer had earlier described the ordeal faced by another expedition on the same route: 'Some of them were worn to skeletons, all had drawn, haggard features; down with fever one day, staggering on the next; eating wretched food, fighting, urging, wrestling with recalcitrant carriers; streaming with perspiration all the time. They worked their way through great, gloomy forest, endless arches of colossal cotton trees under which flourished two other growths of forests. The lower a mass of twisted and tangled evergreens, the middle one hung with spiral creepers like huge serpents hundreds of feet in length. Below all there was the hot, wet earth emitting foul odours from its black mudholes, and many pools of slime-covered water.'

Reuters later reported: 'Eventually the carriers became so weakened by hunger that everything they carried was thrown away. The Governor and the whole party lived on plantains and endured great hardship. Fortunately the rains were not that heavy, otherwise Sir Frederick Hodgson thinks that all would have succumbed.' After crossing the Ofin the force was divided into two detachments to reduced the difficulty of finding food. Fever kept the Governor an extra day at the hamlet of Mampon.

They finally crossed the Prah River into the colony. During the break-out and march the column had lost 2 officers and 39 loyal Hausa troops dead and twice that number wounded or missing. The troops formed a square with Hodgson and his wife in the centre. Buglers sounded a royal salute. Hodgson responded and then fell in a dead faint. The Governor and his wife finally arrived at Cape Coast Castle and boarded the gunboat *Dwarf* for the final leg to Accra. He told reporters that he regarded his escape as 'one of the most marvellous on record'. He attributed its success to 'the secrecy maintained concerning the route chosen and the rapidity of the movements of the force during the journey from Kumasi to the coast'. The column arrived back in Accra after a march of sixteen days. The official report notes: 'The Governor and his whole party had been nearly starved on a diet of plantain. The carriers were too weak from hunger to carry the baggage and so left it behind, and in crossing a swamp near the Ofin River the party were wading shoulder high in water for two hours, finally securing a canoe and a raft by which they saved themselves.'

Hodgson reported that the Ashanti rebels had arms and ammunition 'but not in any quantity'. He said that when he left Kumasi 'the garrison was provisioned for 24 days at the end of which nothing but famine awaits them unless they are relieved'.

A full relief column under Major James Willcocks was by then approaching Kumasi. The column included 1,000 men, six pieces of

The Ashanti fire from stockades in the bush (*Illustrated London News*)

artillery and 6 Maxims. The troops included men from local forces organized along the coast: the constabulary, the West African Frontier force, the Central Africa, West Africa and Nigeria Regiments, the Sierra Leone Frontier Police and detachments of the 1st and 2nd West India Regiment. Their dashing and confident commanding officer had given a personal pledge to relieve the remaining garrison on 15 July, the day the last stocks of food were due to run out. Willcocks was a 43-year-old veteran soldier whose chest bore a glittering array of medals bravely won in Afghanistan, on the Waziri Expedition, in Sudan, Burma and Chin Lushai. Tough, honest and experienced, he had taken command of the West Africa Frontier Force two years earlier. He attacked swiftly and not always prudently. Four days before Hodgson's return he threw his men at heavily defended stockades protecting Kokofu, whose local king had joined the rebels. They were repulsed bloodily. Lieutenant Brownlie of the West African Regiment and several native soldiers were killed in action; 6 white officers and 70 native soldiers were wounded. Willcocks pressed on regardless, although with more caution.

Their advance was well organized, properly supplied and disciplined against a largely unseen enemy and the ever-present dangers of the forest. Wolseley had concluded in his previous expedition that military operations in West Africa could only be conducted with safety between December and February. Pestilence had given the Gold Coast a reputation as 'the white man's grave'. One officer asked an experienced fellow what kit he should take. 'A coffin,' was the response. Advances in military hygiene and medical resources were, however, catching up with the new century.

The enemy, while not a 'regular' army in the accepted sense, were no disorganized rabble. Under the Ashanti social system virtually the entire male population could be swiftly mobilized in tribal and clan groups. Most carried firearms, some flintlocks of dubious quality but others of British manufacture, bought in trade. Although the ammunition was poor and barrels had a tendency to explode, the Ashanti impressed the British with their understanding of marksmanship, their discipline and their musket-drill. The limited range of their weapons was no handicap in forest and bush fighting where the enemy were generally only a few yards away in dense cover. They carried swords as badges of office and knives to dispatch the fallen and to take heads as trophies or religious offerings.

Willcocks and his officers were following the path of previous expeditions whose lessons had been well learnt. An Army handbook written after the 1874 war and recently published warned: 'The topographical character of the country was such to illustrate in every engagement the difficulties and uncertainty that beset disciplined troops when fighting in woods and copses. The normal tactical formations of the Ashantis was a loose skirmishing order, which permitted them to display their aptitude for concealment and for rapid movements through thickets apparently impenetrable, to great advantage.' Wolseley's own dispatch after an early skirmish was quoted:

The relief force is ambushed at Bali (*Illustrated London News*)

'One point stands forward prominently from the experience of this day – viz., that for fighting in the African bush a very exceptionally large proportion of officers is required. Owing to the dense cover an officer can only exercise control over the men close to him, and for this kind of work there should be at least one officer to every twenty men.'

After a smart march Willcocks relieved a small British outpost and mining station at Beckwai. Bounties of up to £100 were offered to any native prepared to take a message to the besieged garrison, but no takers were found. A runner from the fort, however, reported that the garrison was almost without food 'while a final parade for the inspection of the troops has been held'.

Those remaining inside the little fort prayed for rescue and anxiously scanned the sky above the surrounding treetops for signal flares. Captain Bishop of the Gold Coast Constabulary and Mr Ralph of the Lagos police kept the native soldiers hard at drill and watch duties. According to a later tribute: 'They held their ground unflinchingly, knowing that the end must come in a short space of time if relief failed to reach them. They were assured, of course, that whatever was humanly possible would be done by Colonel Willcocks to relieve them before the last ration was eaten and the last cartridge was fired. But they could not be sure that there would not be some fatal error in the reckoning of time.'

For Willcocks the route ahead was cleared by loyal levies raised around Beckwai. They told him that many thousands of the enemy were waiting for him behind strong stockades. Sure enough he found four stockades guarding the approaches to the city on perfectly selected high land hidden by almost impenetrable bush. Mindful of his self-imposed deadline Willcocks ordered an immediate attack. Repeated bayonet charges by Yorubas of the Frontier Force 'absolutely paralysed the enemy'. After two days' fighting and sporadic sniping Willcocks entered Kumasi on 15 July to enfeebled cheers from the garrison and native soldiers 'too weak to stand upright'. British officers told him they could not have held out for more than another two or three days. Skeletal survivors were given food and medicine. Captain Bishop and Dr Hay, whose endurance and cheerfulness had saved many lives, were later awarded the Distinguished Service Order and the Companion of the Order of St Michael and St George respectively.

Two days later Mr Chamberlain announced the relief of Kumasi to loud cheers in a House of Commons otherwise preoccupied by the Boer War, the Boxer Rebellion in China and the Irish Question. A *Times* editorial said: 'In these dark days the escape of the gallant little band who were left to hold the Ashanti capital after the Governor had made his bold and successful dash to the coast is a thing of which to be proud . . . We rejoice most heartily that the gallant little band which Sir Frederick Hodgson left behind him have joined hands with the British troops under Colonel Willcock's command.' The leader writer insisted that Sir Frederick's decision to evacuate the fort and abandon wounded and civilians was justified: 'Being closely invested by vast and increasing hordes of Ashantis for several weeks he was running short of both ammunition and food. The withdrawal of the greater part of the garrison was a bold and well-managed move which, although it involved very considerable losses, averted a disaster the moral effect of which might have shaken the power of all civilised nations in West Africa.' The 'Thunderer' went on: 'But while the skilful manner in which the retreat to the coast was effected is worthy of all praise, the country should not forget the heroism of the men who remained behind to keep the Imperial flag flying in the face of savage and ruthless rebels.' It concluded: 'The honour of the British name has been upheld in West Africa and the native races will not fail to appreciate the consequences!'

After caring for the sick and wounded, and securing the Kumasi perimeter Willcocks sent out flying columns to destroy nearby stockades. He beat a large Ashanti force at Obassa on 30 September. And he had the grim satisfaction of reversing his earlier costly set-back at Kokofu. A column under Lieutenant-Colonel Morland, with 800 men and three 75-millimetre guns, swooped on the large Ashanti encampment. Willcocks sent a telegram to the Colonial Office: 'Rebel force taken entirely by surprise and, as they rushed from their war camp to occupy stockade, Major Melliss, with the F Company, Hausas, in the face of their hurried fire, charged with bayonet and dashed over the stockade, forcing rebel forces back.' The stockade was taken before the Ashanti could occupy it and those who tried were met with cruel volleys from British guns now balanced on the ramparts. The Hausas, aided by Yoruba and Nupos troops, pressed on, taking a second stockade and not stopping until they entered the town 'on the heels of the enemy'. The suddenness of the charge and the element of surprise ensured no casualties among Morland's men. The Ashanti defenders lost thirty warriors, a large quantity of guns, carbines, Sniders and powder. Their most important war camp, a rallying point for rebellious tribes, was utterly destroyed. In his telegram Willcocks praised Morland's 'able disposition' and Melliss's gallantry which in his opinion saved many lives. He added: 'There can be little doubt that Ashantis will not await arrival of bayonet charge.'

Charles John Melliss was awarded the Victoria Cross for leading the bayonet charge against the stockades. Then aged thirty-eight, he was later knighted and rose to the rank of major-general. He served in the First World War and died, aged seventy-three, in 1936.

Many other actions followed but none as dramatic. Sixty chiefs were taken prisoner before December, the rest surrendered by the end of the month, and the Ashanti warrior kingdom ended with a whimper. The Ashanti Queen, Yaa Asantewa, was captured and exiled. Total casualties, including deaths from disease among the British-led forces, were 1,007. The casualties on the Ashanti side are not known. Several Europeans allegedly saw the Golden Stool as it was taken into hiding. They described it as 'very massive, with two heavy gold chains and solid balls the size of oranges, and adorned with two symbolic figures.'

★ ★ ★

In Accra Sir Frederick Hodgson, fully recovered from an ordeal of his own making, celebrated the escape with a garden party on the well-manicured lawns of Christiansborg Castle. The guests included Gold Coast kings, Fanti chiefs, elders, European soldiers, missionaries, civil servants, African pastors, all dressed in a dazzling array of costumes from a dozen cultures. Black boys in livery passed imported drinks and small chops as an orchestra played and Lady Hodgson glowed as she described 'terrible privations'. It was her husband's swansong. He was transferred from the Gold Coast to Barbados as Governor and Commander-in-Chief. Whitehall could not openly blame him for the fiasco but was determined not to overly reward him either. He stayed in the Caribbean for four years before governing British Guinea between 1904 and 1911. He retired to his home in South Kensington, enjoying his gentlemen's clubs (Conservative, Ranleigh and West Indian) while Lady Mary published her own account *The Siege of Kumasi* to some acclaim. Frederick died in 1925, aged seventy-three.

Willcocks won immediate promotion to a brevet colonelcy on the relief of Kumasi. He was one of the last of the flamboyant Victorian adventurers and his subsequent career continued much as before. He was given the Freedom of the City of London and a sword of honour for the exploit and won a mention in King Edward VII's first speech at the state opening of Parliament. He commanded a field force in South Africa at the tail-end of the Boer War, served in India and on the 1906 Zakka Khel expedition, gaining both a knighthood and his general's pips. Although by then in his sixties, he was mentioned in dispatches twice on the Western Front in 1915 before peacefully cruising into retirement as Governor of Bermuda until 1922. He wrote several memoirs, including the splendidly titled *Romance of Soldiering and Sport*. He died in 1926.

Hodgson was succeeded as Gold Coast Governor by Sir Matthew Nathan who imported the first motor vehicle in 1903. The Ashanti kingdom was placed under martial law but there was very little more fighting. On 26 September 1901 it was formally declared a Crown Colony. Many chiefs were de-stooled and thirty more joined King Prempeh in distant exile. He was not allowed to return until 1924, after almost thirty years. He died six years later, aged fifty-nine, a sad and broken figure. Two airy, sun-swept rooms in which the king and his household spent their first period of imprisonment can now be visited on top of the seaward bastions of Elmina Castle.

Ashanti was ruled by the Gold Coast Governors through a chief commissioner in Kumasi. Tennis courts and croquet fields were created as that town was developed into one of the most modern and tranquil in West

Africa. Christian missions helped with education as roads and railways were built. The power of the chiefs was undermined. A cannon was fired in Kumasi at noon every day until 1935 to remind its people of British control. A war memorial was built outside the post office. If it was colonial tyranny it was relatively benign. The fort which had seen so much suffering from battle wounds, disease and starvation was well preserved and is now a military museum.

The Gold Coast was the first in West Africa to achieve freedom from colonization in 1957. It was called Ghana after a sixth-century Sudanese empire which had flourished a thousand miles away. The country has seen its share of turmoil, *coups* and revolutions but it has escaped the worst horrors of the continent. The Ashanti people, two million or more, continue to flourish.

The Golden Stool was hidden in a hole in the buttress of a tree outside Kumasi. Responsibility for keeping it safe and out of British hands was handed down through the generations. In 1920 a Government anthropologist, Captain R.S. Rattray of Oxford University, convinced the administration of the Stool's religious symbolism and the British gave up their search. At around the same time some tribesmen found the hiding place and stole its golden ornaments. That was sacrilege, a crime punishable only by death under tribal law. A council of Ashanti chiefs was called but the British ruled that the criminals should be deported rather than executed. The power of the Golden Stool never recovered.

Appendix

Hector 'Fighting Mac' Macdonald (1853–1903)

The fifth son of a poor Scots crofter, Hector worked as a draper's assistant before running off at the age of eighteen to enlist in the Army. He rose through the ranks to become a colour sergeant of the 92nd Gordon Highlanders by the age of twenty-one. In 1879 during the Second Afghan War a column of the Kabul Field Force was attacked by 2,000 tribesmen. General Frederick Roberts was struck by the courage and leadership shown by MacDonald in the short but vicious fight and offered him the choice between the Victoria Cross and a battlefield commission, an extremely rare promotion for an enlisted man. MacDonald chose the latter.

In 1881 Macdonald, now a 28-year-old subaltern, was among those who climbed Majuba Hill and suffered the devastating Boer attack which resulted in a bloody British retreat. MacDonald tried to hold one flank of the mountain with twenty men but within an hour he had only one private left alive and he was captured by the Boers. Three years later he was among twenty-five British officers seconded to the Egyptian Army during the failed attempt to rescue Gordon in Khartoum. He fought in battles such as Gemalzah, Toski, Tokar, Firket and Hafir, and there earned his nickname.

When in 1898 Kitchener ordered a new invasion of Sudan Macdonald was put in charge of a brigade of Egyptian and Sudanese infantry. It was Macdonald who averted disaster at the crucial battle of Omdurman. Kitchener believed that the slaughter of 10,000 Dervish infantry had concluded the battle and unwittingly ordered his army into a line of march across the front of the main Dervish army which had not yet attacked. The column was hit by a charge of 20,000 enemy. Kitchener panicked but Macdonald swung his 2,000 black troops in an arc to meet the onslaught, a technique that was later taught at Staff College. He and his men coolly held their ground and cut down the attackers. They saved Kitchener's army from destruction and ensured victory. When the battle finished Macdonald's men had on average just two rounds left per man. 'Fighting Mac' was a national hero.

Macdonald again distinguished himself in the Boer War, rising to the rank of major-general and commanding the Highland Brigade with successes at Magersfontein and Modder River. He later commanded British forces in Ceylon. In 1903 a group of schoolboys, one of them an aristocrat, alleged he had sexually assaulted them on a train. They were supported by an alleged witness, a British tea planter with a grievance against Macdonald. Charges were laid before Ceylon's Governor, Sir Joseph West Ridgeway, who became convinced that Macdonald was a practising homosexual who had used relaxed Sinhalese sexuality to take his pleasure with a large number of young men and boys. Macdonald returned to London to try to clear his name but his fall from national hero to ignominy was quickly apparent. Field-Marshall Lord Roberts told him he must prove his innocence or quit the Army.

He was ordered back to Ceylon for a court of inquiry. En route and facing public disgrace he stopped at Paris. In a room of the Hotel Regina he shot himself.

The charge against him was never substantiated and there was a widespread suspicion that he was the victim of a smear campaign motivated by class. Aristocrats and less talented officers resented the rapid promotion of a crofter's son. There was even speculation that the fat and sexually rapacious King Edward VII told him that the only honourable thing to do was commit suicide. Six commissioners appointed in Ceylon published their report in June 1903. They acquitted 'Fighting Mac' on all counts and deplored the sad circumstances which led to his suicide.

The controversy has continued ever since. In January 1995 a correspondent wrote in the *Daily Mail*: 'The disgrace of Hector Macdonald was particularly embarrassing to the British Army because almost everyone in military circles knew that General Kitchener was living with his military secretary. Court martialling Macdonald over unfounded accusations was most unfair.'

Valentine Baker (1827–89)

Valentine was the son of an Enfield merchant with rich estates in Jamaica and Mauritius. At twenty-one he went with two brothers – one of whom, Samuel, was to become a famous African explorer – to establish a farming colony in the highlands of Ceylon. He did not like hill farming and joined the Ceylon Rifles as an ensign, transferring to the 13th Lancers to fight with valour in the 1855–7 Kaffir War. In the Crimea he saw more action at the battle of Tchernaya and at the siege of Sevastopol.

By thirty-three he was in command of the 10th Hussars and reorganized the cavalry to modern efficiency. He was a distinguished author of books, pamphlets and manuals on military science and national defence. He was a spectator at the Austro-Prussian and Franco-Prussian wars, explored wild parts of Persia and Russia, and in 1874 was appointed assistant quarter-master-general at Aldershot.

The following year the 48-year-old Baker was convicted of 'indecently assaulting a young lady in a railway carriage'. He was sentenced to a year's imprisonment, fined £50 and dismissed from the Army. After his release from gaol Baker offered his services to the Turkish Army and was made a major-general. British feeling then was intensely anti-Turkish but Baker felt that the greatest threat to Europe came from Russia. The Turks were in retreat from the Russian forces but Baker commanded superb rearguard actions which averted total defeat and he was made lieutenant-general.

In 1883, after the invasion of Egypt, the British were intent on rebuilding the shattered Egyptian army along British lines. Baker was offered its command but that was withdrawn after some officers protested over his previous shameful conviction. Instead he was given command of the gendarmerie and he and his semi-military but ill-trained force were sent to the Red Sea port of Suakin in Sudan to defend it against the Mahdi's hordes. He was ordered to act with prudence and caution and to avoid any fighting. Baker took no notice.

Five weeks after landing he gathered a 3,500-strong force of gendarmerie, black Sudanese troops and a few Europeans and set out to relieve a besieged garrison 20 miles away at Tokar. At El Teb they were attacked by a much smaller force of Dervishes. Although armed with rifles, cannon and two Gatling machine-guns against Dervish clubs and spears, the Egyptian gendarmes panicked and their fighting square collapsed. They ran back and forth to avoid the slashing spears. Some knelt and begged while their throats were slit. It was total confusion and the handful of resolute Sudanese troops and British officers could do little. In total 96 officers and 2,225 men were killed. No prisoners were taken.

It was a disaster, coming shortly after the massacre of Hicks Pasha's army, and a fresh force of British regulars was dispatched to relieve Tokar. Lieutenant-General Gerald Graham routed 6,000 Dervishes at El Teb, the site of Baker's débâcle. This time disciplined fire left 2,000 Dervishes dead. Valentine Baker, seriously wounded in the face, was one of 189 British casualties.

Baker never fulfilled his hopes of reinstating himself, through battle, in the British Army. His *Times* obituary said that if it had not been for an isolated incident in a railway carriage 'his career might have been among the most brilliant in our military service'.

Bibliography and Sources

Introduction

Burroughs, Peter, 'An Unreformed Army?' included in *The Oxford History of the British Army* [general editor, David Chandler] (Oxford University Press, 1996)
Callwell, Col. C.E., *Small Wars* (London, 1906)
Farwell, Byron, *Queen Victoria's Little Wars* (Allen Lane, London, 1973)
Glover, Michael, *That Astonishing Infantry – The History of the Royal Welch Fusiliers,* (London, 1989)
Haythornthwaite, Philip J., *The Colonial Wars Source Book* (Arms and Armour Press, London, 1995)
Hibbert, Christopher, *The Great Mutiny* (London, 1978)
James, Lawrence, *The Savage Wars – British Campaigns in Africa, 1870–1920*
Judd, Denis, *Empire – The British Imperial Experience from 1765 to the Present* (HarperCollins, 1996)
Keegan, John, *The Mask of Command* (London, 1987)
Lysons, Daniel, *Early Reminiscences* (London, 1896)
Morris, James, *The Pax Britannica Trilogy* (Faber & Faber, London, 1968)
Spiers, Edward M., *The Late Victorian Army* (Manchester United Press, 1992)
Strachan, Hew, *From Waterloo to Balaclava: Tactics, Technology, and the British Army, 1815–1854* (Cambridge University Press, 1985)
Strawson, John, *Beggars in Red – The British Army 1789–1889* (Hutchinson, London, 1991)
——, *Gentlemen In Khaki – The British Army 1890–1990* (Secker and Warburg, London, 1989)

The First Kandy War, 1803–5

de Silva, Chandra Richard, *Sri Lanka, A History* (1987)
de Silva, K.M., *A History of Sri Lanka* (1981)
Knighton, William, *The History of Ceylon*
Ludowyk, Evelyn F.C., *The Modern History of Ceylon* (1966)
Miles, Lennox A., *Ceylon Under British Rule* (1964)
Pearson, Joseph, *The Throne of the Kings of Kandy* (1929)
Pieris, P.E., *Tri Sinhala, The Last Phase* (1939)
Powell, Geoffrey, *The Kandyan Wars – The British Army in Ceylon*

The Falklands, 1833

Ferns, Henry S., *Britain and Argentina in the Nineteenth Century* (Clarendon Press, Oxford, 1960)
Gough, Barry, *The Falkland Islands/Malvinas – The Contest for Empire in the South Atlantic* (Athlone Press, London, 1992)

Graham-Yooll, Andrew, *Small Wars You May Have Missed* (London, 1983)
Rock, David, *Argentina 1516–1982: From Spanish colonization to the Falklands War* (University of California Press, 1985)

The Flagstaff War, 1845–6

Barthorp, Michael, *To Face the Daring Maoris* (Hodder & Stoughton, 1979)
Buick, T. Lindsay, *New Zealand's First War* (Wellington, 1926)
Cowan, J., *The New Zealand Wars* (Wellington, 1922–3)
Gibson, Tom, *The Maori Wars* (London, 1974)
Harrop, A.J., *England and the Maori Wars* (London, 1937)
Holt, Edgar, *The Strangest War* (London, 1962)
Knox, R., *The Maori–European Wars* (Wellington, 1937)
Ryan, T., and Parham, W.T., *The Colonial New Zealand Wars* (Wellington, 1986)
Sinclair, Keith, *The British Empire – New Zealand* (Time Life/BBC Publications, 1972)
——, *A History of New Zealand* (Allen Lane, London, 1959)

The Jamaica Rebellion, 1865

Annual Registers, 1865–6
Black, Clinton V., *History of Jamaica* (Longman Caribbean, 1958)
Burns, Sir Alan, *History of the British West Indies* (George Allen & Unwin, 1954)
Jamaica Royal Commission: *Report, 1866*
Judd, Denis, *Empire* (HarperCollins, 1996)

The Arracan *Expedition, Andaman Islands, 1867*

Cipriani, Lidio, *The Andaman Islanders* (London, 1966)
Kloss, C. Boden, *In the Andamans and Nicobars* (London, 1903)
Portman, M.V., *A History of my Relations with the Andamese* (Calcutta, 1899)
Radcliffe-Brown, A.R., *The Andaman Islanders* (1948)
Regimental History: The South Wales Borderers and Monmouthshire Regiment

The Magdala Campaign, 1867–8

Acton, Roger, *The Abyssinian Expedition and the Life and Reign of King Theodore* (London, 1870)
Annual Register, 1868
Bates, Darrell, *The Abyssinian Difficulty* (Oxford, 1979)
Blanc, Dr Henry, *A Narrative of Captivity in Abyssinia* (London, 1868)
Bond, B., *Victorian Military Campaigns* (London, 1967)
Markham, Clement R., *The History of the Abyssinian Expedition* (London, 1869)
Myatt, F., *The March to Magdala* (London, 1970)
Ullendorff, Edward, *The Ethiopians* (London, 1969)

The Modoc Indian War, 1872–3

Cook, Sherbourne F., *The Conflict Between the California Indians and White Civilisation* (1976)

Dockstader, Frederick J., *Great North American Indians*
Dunn, J.P., *Massacres of the Mountains*
Glassley, Ray H., *Pacific North-West Indian Wars* (1953)
Heyman, Max L., *Prudent soldier, A Biography of Maj-Gen E.R.S. Canby* (1959)
Meacham, Alfred B., *Wigwam and Warpath* (1875)
Murray, Keith A., *The Modocs and their War* (University of Oklahoma Press, 1959)
Smith, Edward P., *Report of the Commissioner of Indian Affairs, November 1 1873* (pp. 380–2)

The Riel Rebellion, 1885

Charlebois, Dr Peter, *The Life of Louis Riel* (NC Press, 1975)
Friesen, Gerald, *The Canadian Prairies* (University of Toronto Press, 1984)
Hill, Douglas, *The Opening of the Canadian West* (Longman Press, 1967)
Maxwell, Leigh, *The Ashanti Ring – Sir Garnet Wolseley's Campaigns 1870–1882* (Leo Cooper, 1985)
Pope, Sir Joseph, *The Day of Sir John Macdonald* (Glasgow, Brook and Company, Toronto, 1915)
Ross, Alexander, *The Red River Settlement* (London, 1856)
Tanner, Ogden, *The Canadians* (Time-Life, Virginia, 1977)
Williams, Sir John, *Sir Wilfred Laurier* (Oxford University Press, 1928)

The Ashanti War of the Golden Stool, 1900

Agyermang, Fred, *Accused in the Gold Coast* (Presbyterian Press, Accra, 1972)
Allison, Philip, *Life in the White Man's Grave* (Viking, 1988)
Annual Register, 1900
Hall, Major W.M., *The Great Drama of Kumasi* (London, 1939)
Maxwell, Leigh, *The Ashanti Ring* (Leo Cooper, 1985)
McFarland, Daniel Miles, *Historical Dictionary of Ghana* (Scarecrow Press, 1985)
Myatt, Major F., *The Golden Stool: An Account of the Ashanti War of 1900* (London, 1966)
Pakenham, Thomas, *The Scramble for Africa* (Weidenfeld & Nicolson, 1991)
The Times Archives

Index